BEAline to the Is

The story of air services to offshore communities
by British European Airways,
its predecessors and successors.

Phil Lo Bao
and
Iain Hutchison

BEAline to the Islands

The story of air services to offshore communities of the British Isles
by British European Airways,
its predecessors and successors.

by
Phil Lo Bao
and
Iain Hutchison

© **Phil Lo Bao and Iain Hutchison 2002**

British Library Cataloguing in Publication data
Lo Bao, Phil
  BEAline to the Islands : the story of air services to
offshore communities of the British Isles by British
Europeans Airways, its predecessors and successors
1.   British European Airways Corporation – History
2.   Airlines – Great Britain – History
I.   Title II. Hutchison, Iain
387.7'42'06541

ISBN 0951895842

Published by
Kea Publishing
14 Flures Crescent, Erskine, Renfrewshire PA8 7DJ, Scotland

Printed by
Iain M. Crosbie Printers
Beechfield Road, Willowyard Industrial. Estate., Beith, Ayrshire KA15 1LN

Contents

Maps

Foreword

by Rod Eddington, Chief Executive, British Airways plc

No man, it is said, is an island. Nor is this country only one island. It is a collection of pieces of land as diverse and unique – perhaps even more so – than the communities that stretch the length and breadth of the mainland.

The islands around these shores – and their people – have played a crucial role in shaping not only this country, but the world as we know it. For more than 50 years British Airways, in its various forms, has been serving those communities, connecting them with the mainland and beyond and playing its part in maintaining the flow of people – and their talents and ideas – to and from these unique places.

The development of aviation in the last century has brought vital communication links between these island communities and the mainland – links that have not only acted as lifeline services but have brought major economic benefits to their people, in the shape of business and tourism.

The unique lifestyle associated with the islands round these shores is a major attraction to those living there. It is also an important element in their attraction to the tourist from the mainland and beyond.

However, it is, and always has been, vitally important to these island communities to maintain links with the mainland. From the earliest days of commercial aviation to the early days of the 21st century, British Airways and its predecessors have played a crucial role in maintaining these links.

Through our subsidiary and franchise partners, from the Channel Islands in the south to the Shetland Islands in the north, we continue to do so.

This book tells the story of those who have originated and developed those links over the last five or six decades. It chronicles the challenges, determination and commitment of the pioneers of aviation to the islands and charts the successes – and inevitable failures – that have accompanied the complexities involved in providing regular commercial air services to some of the most remote communities around these shores.

British Airways is proud of its part in that particular history.

I am delighted and honoured to have been asked to contribute to *BEAline to the Islands*.

For anyone with an interest in the history of aviation or in the social history of the islands dotted around these shores in the latter half of the 20th century, it is an essential read.

I congratulate the authors on their exhaustive research. It has produced a book containing a vast amount of informative, interesting and entertaining details.

I commend it to you.

Rod Eddington

Introduction

British European Airways Corporation was formed in August 1946 by the Labour Government, as a fully state-owned airline, to provide scheduled air services within the British Isles and across Europe. The airline faced many early difficulties as it struggled to operate inappropriate aircraft over what were often uneconomic routes and with a large number of staff. However, once its operations had been rationalised, the Corporation went on to become one of the leading airlines of the world. It was frequently at the forefront of aviation development, was the first airline to operate the turboprop Vickers Viscount, and was the first to successfully use automatic landing equipment on normal passenger services. As time progressed, its network spread throughout Europe and even slightly beyond into North Africa and the Middle East. It developed a reputation for efficient service and proudly claimed the slogan 'Number One in Europe'.

During this process, there were aspects of the Corporation's operations which rarely stimulated news headlines. These were the routes flown within the British Isles to the island communities of the Channel Islands, Isles of Scilly, Isle of Man, Hebrides, Orkney and Shetland. Some of these islands were quite popular tourist destinations, notably the Channel Islands, and the airline found its services could actually make money - at least during the summer months. But other island communities were not so popular with visitors and certainly generated no profits for the Corporation. Even the Channel Islands services were loss-making overall because the numbers of passengers carried in the winter months were so few. Despite these economic considerations BEA continued to provide services to these communities for many years. Indeed, many of the islands came to rely on the BEA service for a fast and comfortable way of reaching the mainland or other islands, and for the arrival of their daily newspapers and mail. Many folk living in these communities literally owed their lives to BEA which provided air ambulance services, particularly to the Scottish islands, enabling their transportation to mainland hospitals for routine as well as urgent treatment.

The staff who worked at the island stations were highly dedicated and loyal to the airline while the pilots who flew the routes were experienced in operating services in the most inclement weather conditions and with the minimum of navigational aids.

Although the history of BEA has been told before, this aspect of the Corporation's work has escaped comprehensive documentation. We believe that the service, which BEA provided to 'the islands' for more than a quarter of a century, was an important one. It is one which we now have pleasure in endeavouring to narrate.

Phil Lo Bao
Iain Hutchison

The Isles of Scilly

Bryher

Tresco

St Martin's

Samson

Hugh Town

St Mary's

Gugh

St Agnes

2 miles

4 km

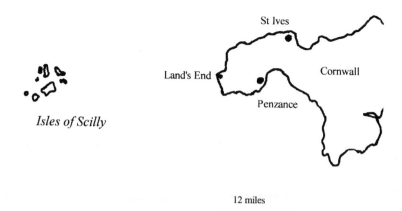

St Ives

Land's End

Cornwall

Penzance

Isles of Scilly

12 miles

20 km

Beyond Land's End - BEA and the Isles of Scilly

The Isles of Scilly lie 28 miles south-west of Land's End. There are five inhabited islands and a whole host of smaller islands and islets. The Isles of Scilly are something of a community in miniature, with schools, a hospital, banks, shops and their own local council. Altogether about 2,000 people live on the islands, but the population is greatly increased during the summer months by hordes of visitors. Indeed the Isles of Scilly have long been a favourite tourist destination, both for day-trippers from the mainland and for holidays of a longer duration.

Travel by air has, for many years, been a very convenient and smooth way of reaching these islands. The sea voyage from Penzance can be very rough even in summer, while cruising in an aircraft above the waves is much less stressful. The earliest air service to the islands seems to have commenced about 1935, but proper scheduled services did not begin until 1937. On 15 September 1937, Channel Air Ferries, which was a subsidiary of the famous pre-war airline, Olley Air Services, began services from Land's End to the main island of St Mary's using a DH84 Dragon biplane. The first flight carried a grand total of four passengers to the island and five on the return trip.

At that time there was no proper airfield on St Mary's, so the Dragon alighted on the local golf course. To warn players of an impending arrival, a bell would be rung so they could clear a fairway for the aircraft. There was no such problem on the mainland, an airfield being created at St Just, near Land's End. A hangar was built to allow the Dragon to be maintained out of the rain and protected from the south-westerly gales which often sprang up. The wisdom of the choice of site at St Just was to be questioned many times in subsequent years since the airfield was right on the cliff's edge and was prone to low cloud and fog which sometimes stopped flying for several days at a time.

Channel Air Ferries maintained the route throughout the winter of 1937/38 but, in 1938, the operation became the domain of Great Western and Southern Airlines who took over Olley Air Services and its subsidiaries. Flying soon settled into a pattern of several services a day during the summer and a more modest double return trip in the winter months. The arrival of the Second World War brought little change. The Dragons continued to cross the gap of water between Land's End and St Mary's even in the face of enemy action. Indeed, G-ACPY was shot down on 3 June 1941 by an enemy aircraft with the loss of all five passengers and the pilot. Thereafter, the service was sometimes given the protection of an RAF Hurricane, a small number of which were based at St Mary's. By the end of the war, Great Western and Southern was using three of the slightly larger DH89 Rapide aircraft on the route. The three aircraft in use in 1945 were G-ACPP, G-AGEE and G-AGUV.

In common with virtually all other internal air services, the Isles of Scilly route became the responsibility of BEA on 1 February 1947. The Great Western and Southern personnel at Land's End and St Mary's swapped their uniforms for BEA ones and the aircraft were soon repainted in BEA colours. Apart from that, little changed. The whole operation was managed by Geoffrey Waite, Station Superintendent at Land's End, and Tom Hall, Station Engineer, also based at Land's End. The Senior Pilot was Captain Hearn. Four traffic staff assisted Geoffrey Waite and there were five engineers working with Tom Hall. At St Mary's, the airline's interests were looked after by an Official-in-Charge, a job held for many years by Henry Casley, although at first the job was held by a Mr Salisbury. He had three staff assisting him. Tony Thomas and

Steve Pearce were Traffic Clerks and Charlie Trezise worked as the loader. There were no resident engineers at St Mary's, a tribute to the reliability of the Rapides. On the odd occasion when an aircraft did require maintenance, an engineer and spares would be flown out from Land's End. The whole service was very much a family affair, the staff knowing each other well and also many of the passengers. It was quite common for the pilot to greet his passengers by name as they squeezed into the Rapide's tiny cabin, having been weighed to determine where they should sit to balance the aircraft out. What the lady passengers thought about that indignity isn't recorded.

BEA was not entirely happy about its service to the Isles of Scilly. The route was totally isolated from the rest of its network and the airfield at St Just gave problems with its weather record. BEA was keen to establish a reliable service both for the islanders and the tourists, but using St Just airfield made that almost impossible. The trouble was the absence of an obvious alternative - apart from the Royal Navy air station at Culdrose. Culdrose was near Helston, which put it quite a few miles further away from the rail terminus at Penzance and it would also result in a longer flight to the Isles of Scilly. Even so, BEA decided that these disadvantages were worth coping with in order to gain a more reliable service, and the airline approached the Royal Navy and Ministry of Defence about using Culdrose as a terminal. BEA Rapides were not unknown at Culdrose, having sometimes diverted there when Land's End was fogged in. However, the Ministry was not at all keen on sharing the Naval facilities with BEA's ancient Rapides and so the Corporation had no choice but to soldier on using St Just, which it did until 1964.

Despite the military's reluctance to accommodate BEA Rapides at Culdrose, it certainly had cause to be thankful for the presence of the biplane one day in January 1952. Captain Hearn was at the controls of the morning flight when he observed an RAF Meteor jet crash into the sea. He also saw the pilot eject and land in the water. So he temporarily abandoned his route and circled the pilot in the water until he was rescued, after which the Rapide plodded on with its more normal duties.

As the tourist industry began to expand after the war, visitor numbers to the Isles of Scilly rapidly increased. BEA found that its three Rapides at Land's End were often hard pushed to cope with the demand during the summer peak. The timetable for the summer of 1956 is quite typical of the intensive service operated during the 1950s. It provided for an hourly service in each direction on a Saturday. The first flight left Land's End at 0810 and the last at 1810, with services departing from St Mary's at 35 minutes past the hour. The only variation was the absence of 1310 and 1335 flights. Even pilots need a lunch break! Turnarounds at St Mary's were achieved in five minutes, which involved a bit of smart work by Henry Casley's team. Even more remarkably, the S61 helicopter now used on the route still keeps to the five-minute turnaround. Time on the ground at Land's End was a little more generous, at 15 minutes, giving time for the aircraft to be refuelled and checked over by the duty engineer.

Passengers wishing to use the service paid £2 10s for a monthly return, or £3 for a return which was valid for 12 months. Fares, by 1956, had actually changed very little from their pre-war levels. Reservations were controlled at Land's End, although in 1961 this task was transferred to a new town office which opened in Wharf Street in Penzance. Needless to say, there was no computerised reservations system. The details of each flight were recorded on booking sheets and the passengers' names entered on these. It was a simple and almost foolproof system - provided the clerk did not forget to write the passenger's name in, or did not make the mistake of writing it on the wrong sheet. Travel Agents wanting to make bookings had to ring Penzance, as did other BEA offices, so there was always plenty of work for the two reservations staff employed there. The booking sheets were used by BEA, and its successors at Penzance, until 1979, when the station was finally connected to the British Airways computerised booking system.

Timetable information does not actually tell the full story about the number of flights. Often, two Rapides would operate on each flight, allowing the loads to be doubled. The second aircraft would depart a few moments after the first, and not infrequently they would fly in a loose formation and land, line astern, at St Mary's. BEA followed the Great Western and Southern practice of usually keeping three aircraft at Land's End. Two would normally be available for passenger services, while the third was on maintenance or standby duty. Major overhauls were not undertaken at Land's End, but in Jersey, which was the nearest large BEA maintenance base. A small section on the left-hand side of the BEA hangar in Jersey was set aside for Rapide work until 1964. Land's End airfield did not have any customs facilities so the Rapide's positioning to Jersey for overhaul had to call at Southampton, or Bournemouth, in each direction. Normally a Land's End pilot would fly as far as Southampton and a Jersey pilot would take over from there. Occasionally, however, a Land's End captain would be permitted to go all the way through to Jersey where he could enjoy a day or two in a nice hotel at the company's expense. Jersey pilots also ended up in Land's End sometimes, and also flew the occasional service to St Mary's.

There were normally three pilots based at Land's End, in addition to the senior pilot, Captain Hearn. Three of the long-serving skippers were Captains Hurcombe, Boyd and Wells. All of them knew almost every inch of the route by heart and this local knowledge was invaluable in allowing flights to operate in difficult conditions, especially ambulance flights. The hospital on St Mary's was really only a cottage hospital, so all serious cases were flown to the mainland and the BEA Rapide fleet was on permanent standby, twenty-four hours a day, seven days a week. Whenever possible, ambulance patients were carried on a scheduled service but, if they were stretcher-bound, then a special flight would be laid on and paid for by the Cornwall and Isles of Scilly Health Authority.

During the winter, life was much quieter for the staff. The number of round trips was curtailed to two or three a day and rarely was a back-up flight needed. However, there was another way of making money in the winter - the carriage of flowers. From 1957 onwards, the Rapides operated as freighters to fly the famous Isles of Scilly early daffodil blooms to the mainland. For that purpose, five of the passenger seats were removed and the flower boxes were stacked in the cabin.

Passenger figures for the route indicate just how popular it was. By 1959, the Rapides were carrying almost 30,000 passengers a year on the twenty-minute hops, quite a feat for a small aircraft. The Rapide could seat up to seven passengers, but BEA never flew them on this route with more than six and, if a heavy passenger was booked to travel, the load would be limited to five. The seventh seat was taken out to provide luggage space. BEA calculated that, by the end of 1962, its Rapides had actually flown no less than 337,527 passengers to or from the Isles of Scilly.

For the convenience of passengers, BEA arranged a bus service to connect with each flight at both ends of the route. At Penzance, a small coach conveyed passengers from the railway station to St Just, a journey of about twenty minutes. On St Mary's, a bus took passengers the short distance into the island's capital, Hugh Town. The popularity of the service is illustrated by its continued operation today.

One big problem troubled BEA's planners - what type of aircraft could be used to replace the Rapide? Even by the standards of the 1950s, they were rather old and outdated. After all, BEA was now in the forefront of aviation development with its brand new turbo-prop Vickers

A contemporary postcard showing Rapide G-AHXW, in original BEA livery, at St Mary's, c. 1952.
(Terry Faragher Collection)

BEA Rapide G-AHKU speeds along the tarmac portion of St Mary's main and very wet runway.
(Ron Rogers Collection)

Out with the old in with the new, Rapide G-AHKU and S61 G-ASNM at Land's End.
Note where the attention of the bystanders is focussed. (Ron Rogers Collection)

The two final Rapide departures from St Mary's, G-AHKU and ambulance flight aircraft G-AJCL, with the two S61s in the
background. (R. E. Gibson)

Viscounts. This was to be a problem that occupied BEA for some time to come. There was no easy solution because the airfield at St Mary's was small and quite unsuitable for any significant development. The longest of the three grass runways, Runway 10/28, at St Mary's was only 1,715 feet and was only partially paved. It wasn't only the Isles of Scilly service which utilised Rapides. They were also used on Channel Islands and Scottish services, so replacements were needed there too.

Initially, BEA considered the four-engined Miles Marathon, but while it could land at most destinations used by the Rapides, it was too large for St Mary's. In any case, BEA eventually decided that its passenger capacity was greater than that required of any on the routes currently flown by the Rapides. A more promising type was the four-engined De Havilland Heron. BEA used the prototype Heron, G-ALZL, for a few weeks during August 1951 to evaluate its suitability for some routes. Most of the Heron's time was spent on the Channel Islands flights, but the aircraft did make one visit to Land's End and St Mary's, becoming the largest ever fixed-wing aircraft in BEA colours to land at the airfields. Although BEA did later go on to buy the Heron for some of its Scottish routes, it concluded that the airfield limitations at St Mary's were just too great to allow a fully laden Heron to operate. This led the BEA planners to consider a third type, the Scottish Aviation Twin Pioneer. The 'Twin Pin', as it was nicknamed, seemed ideal. It was actually designed for short take-off and landing operations (STOL) which would make it well able to tackle the demands of St Mary's. In addition, it also seemed the most suitable type for the lower density Scottish routes. However, in one of those never to be fully understood decisions, BEA elected not to buy the aircraft.

As a result, the Isles of Scilly Rapide service appeared to have no replacement, and it soldiered on into the 1960s. By that time, BEA had progressed from the Viscount to the larger Vanguard, had entered the jet age with a fleet of Comet 4Bs, and would soon accept its first Tridents. Even the venerable DC-3 had been retired in 1962. Yet, in the south-west, the three Rapides were operating just as they had done for the last thirty or so years. They were not even deemed suitable to be painted in the new BEA black and red colour scheme, remaining in the white and silver livery overlaid with the three thin red stripes.

By 1962 BEA had just three Rapides remaining, all explicitly for the Isles of Scilly route. They were G-AGSH, G-AHKU and G-AJCL. Two of these were quite new to BEA service, G-AJCL being delivered in June 1959, and G-AGSH in January 1962. G-AJCL's arrival in the summer of 1959 was as a replacement for G-AHLL. G-AHLL had struck a hedge while landing at Land's End on 21 May, as a result of which it had been declared beyond economic repair. G-AJCL herself nearly came to grief in April 1962 after an incident at Land's End, but the damage was not serious and the local engineers were able to put the aircraft back into service fairly quickly. To cover for her short-term absence, BEA leased a Rapide from Mayflower Air Services. The delivery of G-AGSH followed an accident to G-AKZB on the grass airstrip at Land's End on 12 December 1961. G-AGSH had previously been in service with BEA between 1947 and 1956.

For all their apparent frailty the Rapides proved able to operate in the worst of weather conditions. The sea crossing from Penzance can often be very stormy during winter and boats were sometimes delayed or cancelled for days at a time. When this happened the islanders came to depend entirely on the Rapides, not only for the transport of passengers, but also the arrival of post, newspapers, medicines and any other urgently needed supplies. A typical example of this situation occurred one day in January 1954. A period of very stormy weather meant that the *Scillonian* had been unable to sail. The gale was so strong that it was claimed even the birds were walking. But the BEA Rapide, G-AHLL, maintained its service, landing in the teeth of the gale at St Mary's three times during the day and ensuring that all those who wished to get on or off the island could do so.

While the airline's hierarchy was pondering the difficult question of how to replace the Rapides, a key personnel change took place at Land's End. In March 1962, Captain Morris Hearn, or 'Skipper Hearn' as he was known locally, retired. Captain Hearn's association with the route predated BEA's responsibility for it. He began flying for Great Western and Southern in 1941 and continued with BEA until 1962. When he retired, it was discovered that he had flown a staggering 31,000-plus trips over the route. Amazingly, given the dreadful weather record at Land's End, he had been forced to make an unscheduled night stop in the Isles of Scilly on only four occasions. In recognition of his tremendous services to aviation, 'Skipper Hearn' was presented with the Queen's Commendation for Valuable Service in the Air, and, to mark his retirement, the local BEA staff presented him with a huge DIY tool set. Geoffrey Waite made the presentation.

Geoffrey Waite's association with the route went back even further. He started off as a clerk at Land's End in 1937 on the first day of regular services. He was still going strong in 1962, as Station Superintendent. Long service seemed to be a feature of the Isles of Scilly link. Geoffrey's deputy, Senior Traffic Officer Lawrence Hall, had been on the staff since 1939 and his brother, Tom, had joined the engineering team the same year.

As the days slipped by, the issue of how to replace the Rapides was becoming critical. In the end a decision was reached in 1963, and it proved to be a most imaginative and bold one - to replace the Rapide with a 26-seater S61 twin-engined helicopter. BEA had operated a Helicopter Experimental Unit since July 1947. It had undertaken trials on several passenger routes including Cardiff-Wrexham-Liverpool, London-Birmingham, London-Southampton and, more recently, Birmingham-Leicester-Nottingham. None of these services were flown for very long and they were primarily operated to give experience of helicopter flying over a scheduled passenger route. The manager of the Helicopter Experimental Unit was Captain Jock Cameron and he was extremely keen to find a route where the benefits of helicopter operations could be demonstrated.

It occurred to him that the Isles of Scilly service offered just such a possibility, so he drew up an ambitious plan to purchase two American-built Sikorsky S61 helicopters, one of which would be used for the Isles of Scilly. With some apprehension he presented his proposals to the BEA Board in 1963. Initially, the Board's attitude was one of scepticism. It did not see how a regular service could be operated with only one helicopter on station, and its members wondered what Jock intended to do with the second one. Fortunately, his answer to the latter question clinched the decision. Captain Cameron had already been approached by Shell Oil regarding the future possibility of providing helicopter support in the search for gas and oil in the North Sea. The second aircraft could be used for that. The BEA Board was now happier and sanctioned the purchase of the two S61s at a cost of about £3 million. The helicopters were due for delivery early in 1964 and it was intended they should replace the Rapides from the beginning of May. It was felt that the title, 'Helicopter Experimental Unit', would no longer be appropriate for operating a large helicopter on an established scheduled service, so a new company was set up, BEA Helicopters Limited (BEAH). BEAH was a fully-owned subsidiary of BEA and Jock Cameron became its Managing Director.

The S61s were built in the USA and then partly dismantled for dispatch to the UK by sea. The first, G-ASNL, arrived at Southampton Docks in January 1964, was assembled on the quayside, and then flown to the BEA Helicopters base at Gatwick. The second machine, G-ASNM, followed a few weeks later. Both aircraft were then used for crew training in preparation for the commencement of scheduled services on 2 May 1964.

The value of helicopters had already been proven in the Isles of Scilly. One of the BEA WS55 helicopters, G-AOCF, spent some time at Land's End in July 1963, assisting in the setting up and evaluation of the Decca Flight Log navigation system. This system was to be used by the S61s as their main navigational aid. It plotted the exact position of the aircraft on a map by means of a moving pen. On 20 July, a Rapide operated by the small company Mayflower Air Services crashed on take off from St Mary's. Its pilot, the airline's owner, Captain Peter Cleife, was badly burned in the crash. Indeed his life was only saved by the prompt action of Charlie Trezise, the BEA loader, and Paddy Daly, the senior airport fireman. Charlie sat on the Rapide roof and used a hacksaw to cut Captain Cleife out, while Paddy sprayed the pilot with water. Captain Cleife needed immediate hospital treatment. But there was a problem. Fog at Land's End prevented a BEA Rapide from operating an ambulance flight. The helicopter, however, could fly, and its pilot, Dave Eastwood, readily agreed to make the trip to St Mary's and pick up Captain Cleife. He was in hospital in Penzance little over an hour after the accident. After a lengthy period, Captain Cleife did recover from his injuries. Had the BEA WS55 not been at Land's End that day, it is very likely that Captain Cleife would not have survived.

Naturally, the introduction of the S61s was a big event, not only for the Isles of Scilly route but also for BEA. So it was decided to mark the occasion in style. A large celebration was planned for 1 May involving both S61s and a WS55, G-ANFH, which would act as a camera platform. BEA senior management from London flew down for the occasion. The small grass strips at Land's End were clearly unsuitable for a BEA Viscount to land, and so the flight from London touched down at RAF St Mawgan near Newquay. Why the much nearer Culdrose was not used is not clear. However, the two S61s picked up the passengers from Newquay and flew them west to Land's End. There, other VIPs were picked up, including the local MP, Grenville Howard; the Chairman of the Isles of Scilly Council, Tregarthen Mumford; and the Deputy Mayor of Penzance. By this time both aircraft were full. They departed from St Just at 1130 and 1135 and they carried their passengers to St Mary's for a celebration lunch in a Hugh Town restaurant. The pair then returned to Land's End and operated a second rotation, each carrying further invited guests and representatives from the press. These departed from Land's End at 1230 and 1235. A Rapide also accompanied the first helicopter, carrying additional photographers and guests.

Then things began to go wrong. The all too familiar problem of bad weather intervened. Fog and low cloud were beginning to settle over the island and the forecast was the same for Land's End. The new local BEAH Manager, Captain Doug Pritchard, was anxious not to have his helicopter in the wrong place for the first scheduled service the next day, so all the guests were hurriedly flown back to Land's End. Those who were travelling on to London found themselves making the trip back to Newquay, to join their Viscount, by bus!

As the celebrations were going on, the Rapides continued to creep in and out of St Mary's almost unnoticed. This was their last day, but the attention seemed to be concentrated on the sparkling new helicopters. No less than ten Rapide flights were scheduled for that day. The honour of flying the last scheduled Rapide service from St Mary's to Land's End fell to Ron Hurcombe who flew G-AHKU on flight BE9069 from St Mary's at 16.30. This was a truly historic occasion, since not only was this the last passenger Rapide flight by BEA from the Isles of Scilly, it was the last passenger service ever flown by a BEA Rapide and marked the end of seventeen years of unbroken service. However, G-AHKU was not actually the last Rapide out of St Mary's that afternoon. The local doctor requested an air ambulance flight and G-AJCL flew over for this purpose. Both Rapides were lined up outside the small St Mary's terminal for a few minutes. Shortly after Ron Hurcombe took off in G-AHKU, G-AJCL departed with its patient.

Once normal airline service had commenced, it was unusual to see two BEA Helicopters S61s together at St Mary's.
(R. E. Gibson)

The aircraft was flown by a visiting pilot, probably from Jersey, as the other Land's End based Captains had already left to train on the new types they were to fly. Captain Wells had gone to Scotland to fly the Highlands and Islands services on Heralds, while Paddy Boyd was transferred to the Heathrow-based Argosy fleet. Whoever flew that final Rapide flight closed a very important chapter in BEA's history. The ambulance flight cost the Local Health Board the grand sum of £13 2s. Since 1947 the Rapides had flown 384,000 passengers to or from St Mary's and operated 77,500 flights in the process. The three aircraft were sold to the west country airline, British Westpoint, who continued to fly them into St Mary's for a short period on its routes from Exeter and Plymouth.

Flying the Rapides proved very demanding to the last. Ron Rogers, who worked for BEA in its Penzance town office and until September 2001 worked for the current operator of the route, British International Helicopters, recalled how Ron Hurcombe arrived at the staff party that evening complaining how much his legs and arms ached from trying to hold the Rapide steady in the gusty conditions. Captain Hurcombe was posted to Heathrow to fly the mighty 139-seater Vickers Vanguard V953. His culture shock can hardly be imagined.

The second day of May dawned bright and clear, and so the new helicopter service commenced on schedule. The first flight was flown by Jock Cameron in G-ASNL. It left Land's End at 0900 as flight BV912. Shortly afterwards, the other aircraft departed for Gatwick leaving G-ASNL alone to maintain the vital link. This it did with incredible regularity. Indeed, since 1964 there has often only been one helicopter stationed at the Penzance base and regularity has normally been in the high ninety percent range. On one rare occasion, when a technical delay

Fuelling the S61 at Penzance.
(Ron Rogers Collection)

did occur, a lady passenger complained loudly to Donald Jarvis, the cabin attendant. His reply silenced her. 'Madam', he said, 'do you have a car?' She replied that she did. 'Well', said Donald, 'do you have a spare one in case it breaks down?' The point was well made.

For the summer of 1964, BEAH decided to operate four S61 services on weekdays, ten on Saturdays and eight on Sundays. When it is recalled that the Rapides seated only five or six passengers and the S61 could carry about twenty-six, then this represented a huge increase in capacity. But it proved more than justified. In the first full year of helicopter operations, the number of passengers carried almost doubled in comparison with the last year of the Rapides. By 1973/74, the numbers had further increased to 66,902, giving an 84% load factor. Those passengers were moved by a single aircraft. The increasing passenger numbers not only reflected the growing popularity of the Isles of Scilly as a wonderful holiday destination, but also the novelty value of flying by helicopter which encouraged quite a few passengers to embark on a day-trip. BEAH even offered a joy-rider's fare to cater for them.

The provision of Sunday services ceased at the end of the summer season in 1965 to allow a day for maintenance of the helicopter and a rest for the staff. Sunday flights only occurred if the weather on Saturdays created a backlog. But even then the airline did its best to get everyone to or from St Mary's on a Saturday, even if the fog did not lift until late in the day. This sometimes meant flying until the small hours of the morning. On one such occasion, Mike Perkiss and Jim Summerlee were the duty pilots and they continued to fly until 0200 to clear the backlog. When the aircraft finally landed at Penzance, they found a box for them had been put on board at St Mary's. It contained drinks and a 'thank you' note from the Isles of Scilly hoteliers for getting all the passengers away.

The larger S61 meant further opportunities to develop cargo traffic. The Rapide was really not designed as a cargo aircraft, but the S61 could lift much heavier loads. In 1973, the helicopter carried 248 tons of cargo. Occasionally, bulky items would be slung underneath the S61, and such cargo has included large carpets and even a cannon. Other unusual cargo carried in the helicopters with regularity included seals and birds. If an injured or an orphaned seal was found around the islands, occasionally it was airlifted to Penzance for transfer to the Seal Sanctuary at Gweek. Similarly, injured birds were often conveyed to the bird hospital at Mousehole. The flower export traffic continued to provide BEA with additional work in the traditionally slack early weeks of the year. As with the Rapides, the S61 flew only two services a day in the winter which gave plenty of time to fit in cargo flights for local growers.

Trips over the route, then and now, take the S61 about 20 minutes, with the helicopter flying at about 1,000 feet. It usually cruises at about 120 knots and can fly in wind speeds of up to 50 knots. A stronger wind makes it dangerous to start or stop the rotor blades as the wind might cause them to strike the fuselage. So long as visibility exceeds 800 metres, flights can take place. The minimum cloud base for landing at St Mary's is 200 feet.

For four months, the mainland terminal for the helicopter service continued to be Land's End. However, BEAH wanted to build a heliport closer to Penzance. Eventually, a site was found on an old rubbish tip at Eastern Green, a mile or so east of the railway station. BEA purchased the site and constructed a ten-acre heliport which continues to serve as the mainland terminal today. The heliport is fully equipped with a terminal building, hangar, fire station and a grass and concrete manoeuvring area. It is also equipped with lighting for night flying. Flights transferred from Land's End on 1 September 1964 and the terminal was officially opened by the Mayor of Penzance, Alderman Beckerleg.

Dave Davies was the General Services Officer responsible for the general running of the Heliport. He supervised the firemen, aircraft loading and unloading, and generally was in charge of keeping the place spick-and-span. He recalls one day asking Charlie, the cleaner and odd-job man, to cut back some of the undergrowth and brambles around the edge of the car park, and then to burn the foliage. Charlie was apt to muddle his words, and a little later he reported back that he had done as asked and had burnt the fuselage! Fortunately, Dave realised what he meant and the S61 was safe from Charlie's bonfire

The withdrawal of the Rapides was not quite the end of fixed-wing flying by BEA to the Isles of Scilly. Occasionally the airline found that it could not afford to keep an S61 at Penzance all winter when its schedule was so light. Demands from lucrative North Sea oil and gas exploration contracts and for crew training meant the Penzance helicopter sometimes disappeared for a few weeks or months. When it did, this was marked by fixed-wing operations and a return to Land's End. BEA had no suitable aircraft for the route, so it chartered Britten Norman Islander aircraft to fly the service. The Islander is a nine-seater aircraft with amazing STOL performance. Had it been available in 1963, BEA may well have ordered it instead of the S61. Usually, the Islander came from Aurigny Air Services in the Channel Islands. The first time this occurred was between 8 January and 1 March 1969. If passenger loads were sufficient, the Islander had to fly six trips a day to carry the same number of passengers that the S61 could transport in two trips. In early 1974, the airline used a different sort of helicopter, the smaller eight-seat S58, to cover for the absent S61. In more recent times, British Airways Helicopters and British International Helicopters have, upon occasions, used the S76 and Westland 30 helicopters, instead of the S61 and sometimes in addition to it during the summer peak.

Having the S61 at Penzance, but the main engineering facility at Gatwick, did occasionally cause problems. If an engine change was needed, a spare engine had to be taken down to Penzance. This was sometimes accomplished using the BEAH Jet Ranger helicopter, which Captain Cameron would often pilot. He would arrive at Penzance after about a two-hour flight from Gatwick and have a quick cup of tea while the engineers unloaded the engine, then take off straight away to return to his office at Gatwick. But if the Jet Ranger was away on a charter, the engine had to be transported by road. In the 1960s, the road network in the south-west was not very fast and the journey could take many hours. On one occasion Ron Rogers, from Penzance Reservations, was asked to drive the BEA van up to Gatwick with an engine. The van could just about accommodate the engine if the front passenger seat was removed. Ron recalls that it was a most uncomfortable trip since the engine was right against his left shoulder all the way. While he was happily motoring along through Devon in the middle of the night, the local police stopped him. They had noticed this strange object through the back window of the van and were keen to investigate. Ron's explanation that it was a helicopter engine was received by the two officers with some disbelief, especially as the van had BEA stickers on it, and as everyone knew BEA did not fly to Devon. In the end they let him continue his trip, but he reckons to this day those two policemen thought he was up to no good.

The Isles of Scilly are well known to sailors for their rocky coastline. Over the centuries, many ships have come to grief around the islands. Without doubt, the oil tanker, *Torrey Canyon*, was one of the most famous Isles of Scilly wrecks. The large tanker, full of crude oil, hit the Seven Sisters rocks just off the island of St Martin's in March 1967. Oil quickly began to gush into the sea and a full-scale environmental disaster threatened. The first plan of action was to try to re-float the vessel, and, for that, powerful pumps were quickly needed on board. BEAH was contacted and an S61 was chartered to fly the pumps out to the tanker from Penzance. The Isles of Scilly schedules meant that the local helicopter could not provide the necessary number of trips, so G-ASNL was flown down from Gatwick for the purpose. Many trips were made between Penzance Heliport and the *Torrey Canyon* with pumps and other equipment in a vain

Fuelling complete – lift off of the S61 at Penzance.
(Ron Rogers Collection)

The Sikorsky S61 has maintained the Isles of Scilly air service since 1964. Operated by British International,
G-BCEB hovers at Penzance. (Ron Rogers Collection)

attempt to re-float the tanker. However, oil continued to gush out and pollute the local beaches of the Isles of Scilly and Cornwall. In the end the Government ordered the Royal Navy and the RAF to bomb the tanker, which they did with Sea Vixen, Buccaneer, and Hunter jet aircraft. For the few days that the crisis lasted, Penzance was very busy with the two S61s on station and with visits by countless other helicopters for refuelling and relief of crews.

By the time that BEA became British Airways, the Isles of Scilly helicopter service was well established. BEA Helicopters was renamed British Airways Helicopters (BAH) in 1972 just prior to the merger of BEA and BOAC, and the colour schemes and company logos were changed to reflect the new identity. Apart from this, operations continued unaltered. From October 1974 onwards, BAH mainly used just one S61 on the route, G-BCEB, which was modified specifically for the service. It accommodated up to thirty-two passengers instead of the usual S61 load of twenty-six, and had a main passenger door at the front rather than in the centre. That meant passengers were not subject to a nose-full of exhaust fumes when boarding or disembarking while the engines were running. G-BCEB also had baggage lockers fitted along the left-hand side of the lower fuselage which made loading and unloading much quicker.

Passenger totals had continued to rise rapidly, with 87,289 passengers being carried in the financial year 1979/80. To cope with the demand on peak days, the aircraft would operate up to twelve trips in each direction from 0800 to 2000. In 1983, BAH began serving the second largest of the islands, Tresco. To begin with, this was a summer-only route, but it is now flown all year round.

BAH itself was privatised by the Government in September 1986. After going through several changes of ownership, the company now trades as British International Helicopters (BIH), and still flies to St Mary's and Tresco using the S61. BIH is part of the large world-wide helicopter company, the Canadian Helicopter Corporation, which is based at St John's, Newfoundland. In recent years the growth of traffic has meant that a second helicopter is stationed at Penzance during the summer. For a time, BIH used a Westland 30 but, more recently, a second S61 has been on station. The second aircraft gives the company much greater operational flexibility. It generally operates three or four scheduled flights a day and is then available for flying extra services when traffic levels require it. Pleasure flying around the Penzance area is also occasionally undertaken.

The inhabitants of the Isles of Scilly, and countless thousands of visitors, are greatly indebted to BEA for its far-sighted decision to buy the helicopter to replace the Rapides. The history of the route demonstrates yet again that a large airline, BEA, did take the needs of small isolated local communities seriously, and did so with great success.

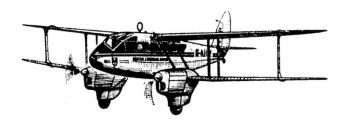

The Isle of Man

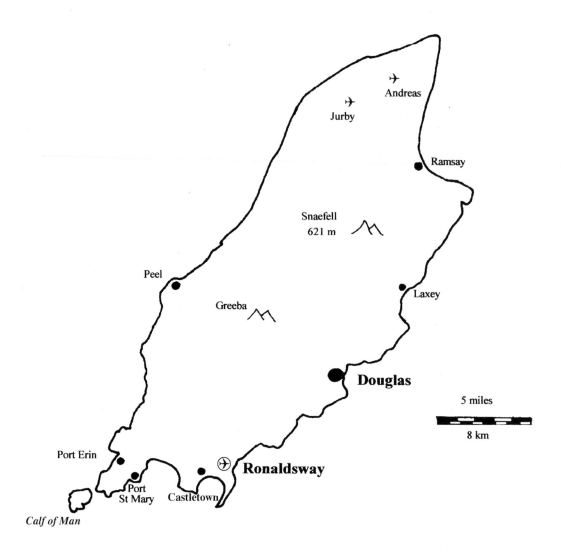

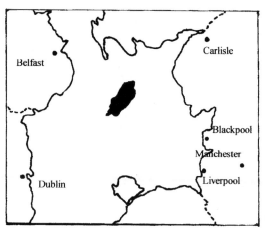

2

'Fly BEA to the Isle of Man'

'**Fly BEA to the Isle of Man**' was an advertising slogan which appeared throughout the north of England in the 1950s as BEA sought to generate passengers for its Manx services. The history of BEA's links with the Isle of Man was never as happy as those with the other island communities it sought to serve. Nevertheless, the Corporation's involvement in Manx air services began in 1947 in the same way as it did elsewhere, with the British Government's legislation giving BEA the monopoly of all scheduled services within the British Isles. Like Channel Islands Airways, Isle of Man Air Services (IoMAS), which had been providing services from the island since 1937, hoped it might be excluded from the scope of the new law since the Isle of Man was self-governing. Because of this, there was some anticipation that the Act would not apply to the Isle of Man, and Manx routes would continue to be provided by Isle of Man Air Services. Sadly, that was not to be the case, and BEA assumed responsibility for Manx routes on 1 February 1947. It inherited a network of services built up by IoMAS before World War Two.

Aviation first reached Manx shores as early as July 1911 when Claude Graham-White and George Barnes brought their aircraft to the island by steamer after competing in the London to Paris air race. Between 1911 and 1932 there were occasional visits to the Isle of Man by aircraft and there was some pleasure flying from Douglas beach. However, the first scheduled service was launched in June 1932 between Blackpool and the island using a Saro Cutty Sark amphibian. Between June and September, the aircraft carried 348 passengers and then the service was suspended for the winter. It returned in 1933 but, by then, Blackpool and West Coast Air Services had been formed and had begun by flying charter services from Blackpool to the island. Initially, Fox Moths were used but, by the summer, these were replaced by the de Havilland Dragon which operated up to three schedules a day linking the Isle of Man with Blackpool and Liverpool. Another operator, Midland & Scottish Air Ferries, began to serve the island in the summer of 1933, employing the Fox Moth and later the Dragon. Its services operated over the same routes as Blackpool and West Coast's. A final newcomer was Northern Airways, which opened a link from Newcastle and Carlisle using the Dragon. These operators used a field at Ronaldsway on the south-eastern side of the island which eventually developed into the island's main airfield.

Over the next few years, traffic began to build up considerably as passengers found the short trip by air much more comfortable than the frequently rough crossing on an Isle of Man Steam Packet Company vessel. Other carriers to serve the island during the mid-1930s included Railway Air Services and Manx Airway. All focused chiefly on the routes to Blackpool and Liverpool using Ronaldsway. A significant milestone was reached in 1937 with the formation of IoMAS by a merger of the two principal Manx carriers, Manx Airway and Blackpool and West Coast Air Services. IoMAS went on to develop a comprehensive route network linking Ronaldsway with Blackpool, Liverpool, Manchester, Carlisle, Newcastle, Glasgow, and Belfast. Some of these routes were seasonal and some were operated as multi-sector services, so most Blackpool flights continued on to either Liverpool or Manchester. Throughout the Second World War, IoMAS maintained a skeleton service linking Ronaldsway with Liverpool and Belfast. Once peace returned, it resumed a more extensive operation with all flights being operated by de Havilland Rapides. The War brought the benefit to IoMAS of a much improved airfield at Ronaldsway. Pre-war it was a simple grass airfield formed from several fields, but during the War it became a Royal Naval Air Station and was used for training gunners. The Navy laid down hard runways which provided postwar air services with a ready-made up-to-date airfield capable of handling larger aircraft when the time came to replace the Rapides.

Initially, BEA followed the same pattern of schedules and destinations as those previously operated by IoMAS. For its first summer of flying to the Isle of Man, the Corporation flew 82 flights a week to Liverpool and 27 to Manchester, mostly via Blackpool. Three daily trips linked the island with Carlisle, while there were two services a day to Belfast and one to Glasgow. As in the Scottish Islands, Channel Islands and Isles of Scilly, the personnel BEA recruited to provide these services came largely from the ranks of the previous operator. Many IoMAS staff soon found themselves kitted out in BEA uniforms. Some of them already had a long record of service and this was particularly true of BEA's Station Superintendent at Ronaldsway, Bert Wood, and his Senior Traffic Officer, Frank Gawne. Both had worked for IoMAS since its formation. Another long-time IoMAS staff member was Ronaldsway Station Engineer, Mr Acheson. The presence of these staff helped to ensure a smooth transfer of services to BEA, something which many of them found re-occurring sixteen years later when BEA passed routes over to Cambrian Airways.

BEA's operations to the island had not been under way for long before a serious accident occurred. On 15 April 1947, First Officer Alan Woodcoat was piloting Rapide G-AHKR inbound to Ronaldsway from Liverpool with five passengers and a Radio Operator on board. On arrival overhead he found the weather conditions were too poor to attempt a landing and so he decided to divert to the RAF airfield at Jurby in the north of the island where conditions were clearer. Whilst en route to Jurby, the Rapide hit high ground near Greeba in the middle of the island, and ended up upside down and badly smashed. Fortunately none of the passengers or crew was seriously injured, but the Rapide was declared a write-off. This was the only serious incident BEA experienced on its Manx network, although on 17 January 1951 a DC-3 suffered an undercarriage collapse resulting in the loss of its propellers when it taxied into some earth excavations at Ronaldsway.

There were also of course numerous incidents, some of which could have been more serious but for the professionalism of the crews involved. One potentially serious incident occurred on 14 September 1953. Captain Ian Scott was operating a Liverpool-Isle of Man-Belfast Pionair service with a full load of 32 passengers including the comedienne Tessie O'Shea. As the aircraft departed from Liverpool the crew were alerted by the fire warning light for the starboard engine coming on, and the cylinder head temperature dropping to zero. The Flight Clerk later told the Captain that flames were shooting a good twelve feet past the trailing edge of the wing. This sort of incident, in a fully loaded Pionair, at lift-off, was not desirable! The Captain kept the engine going to allow the aircraft to obtain some height. At about 200 feet, the engine was shut down and the fire extinguisher was deployed to put out the fire. Captain Scott elected to return at once to Speke and a safe landing was made. He was not amused when the ground engineer tried to tell him that the episode was his fault for not knowing how to handle the engines properly! Examination of the offending engine demonstrated that an inlet valve had broken and fallen into the cylinder. The fire was so intense that the flames had eaten through the cowling behind the engine gills. The passengers were transferred to another flight to complete their journey – all, that is, except Tessie O'Shea who chartered an aircraft.

BEA's finances were far from healthy and, as losses soared, it was recognised that decisive action would have to be taken. The timetable for the winter of 1947/48 was severely curtailed. Only four trips a day would be made to Liverpool and one each to Belfast and Manchester. The lack of activity at Ronaldsway was compensated for one day during the winter when the airline's staff handled a most unusual cargo, a prize pedigree bull which a local farmer brought over from

Ulster. It arrived in a Miles Aerovan and there was not a little trepidation amongst the staff about handling the animal. Ultimately, it proved to be rather docile.

The summer of 1948 saw operations return to a more intensive level and services were increasingly flown by the larger DC-3 aircraft. However, it appears that the Carlisle route did not resume. For the first time BEA offered a direct service from London. Until then links had been via Liverpool or Manchester, from where BEA operated a modest service to London. The DC-3s flew the London route to Northolt until 1954 when the service was transferred to Heathrow. The DC-3 took two hours to cover the distance between Northolt and Ronaldsway. Schedules show that the Northolt flight arrived at Ronaldsway at 1345 and returned at 1640. The DC-3 also took over the Blackpool route with a twice-daily service leaving the island at 1325 and 1800. The summer of 1948 proved to be a very busy time for Bert Wood and his staff on the Isle of Man. In June alone the airline carried 4,376 passengers, which was quite a feat. June was, and still is, the busiest month of the year as the island hosts the famous TT motor cycle races attracting visitors from all over the world. The busiest route from the Isle of Man was also the shortest, that to Liverpool. In the summer of 1948, BEA operated up to seven DC-3 flights a day between the two points. In addition, there were the two daily flights to Manchester and the one to London, plus the services to Blackpool and to Renfrew Airport, Glasgow. The local staff also handled the Aer Lingus DC-3 flights from Dublin. Aer Lingus flew a daily lunchtime service to the Isle of Man with an additional flight on Saturday and Sunday evenings.

By the end of the summer, the financial situation remained serious and BEA undertook a major rationalisation of its Manx routes. On 6 October 1948, the routes to Blackpool, Glasgow and Manchester were axed, while the remaining services to Liverpool and Belfast were severely curtailed. The Manx Government was very unhappy at this decision, especially as it was taken without any discussion with them. The loss of the direct service to Manchester was of particular concern to the island. This event proved to be the first of a number of unhappy episodes involving BEA and the Manx Government. The reduced frequencies meant that most of the flights were fully booked and so BEA Ronaldsway was able to report a very busy winter season.

Whilst BEA's management may have been rather unwise to make the decision to scrap these routes without any consultation, the reasons for it can be understood. The Corporation had calculated that it was making an annual loss of about £150,000 a year on its Manx services. Part of the problem lay in the highly seasonal nature of the traffic to the island. The island had been a major tourist destination for the north of England since the late nineteenth century and hordes of people flooded in during the summer. But few came in the winter. BEA found that for every twenty-five passengers it carried to the island in the summer, it was carrying only one in the winter. However BEA was a very top-heavy organisation in its early days and a lot of the problem lay in too many managers and too many staff who were not fully occupied.

Independent airlines were permitted to apply to operate some scheduled services as BEA associate airlines on routes BEA did not fly. With the withdrawal of BEA from the Carlisle route in 1947 and those to Blackpool and Glasgow in 1948, it was not long before a number of independents were licensed to fly these routes under such associate agreements. One of the first to do so was Manx Air Charters which gained permission to take over the schedule to Carlisle. Meanwhile North West Airlines Rapides and DC-3s took over services from the island to Manchester and continued to fly the route until BEA reintroduced direct services of their own in 1951. Soon, other carriers such as Mannin Airways and Air Navigation and Trading became regular visitors to Ronaldsway during the summer months of the late 1940s. Eventually, the UK Government removed BEA's monopoly and independent airlines flew even more services to the island.

BEA Rapides G-AFEZ and G-AHGH beside the Ronaldsway Control Tower, c. 1949. (Terry Faragher collection)

Pictured during TT Races week, Pionair G-ALPN fronts a sea of Rapides. (Phil Pain Collection)

BEA Helicopter Experimental Unit Bristol 171 G-AMWH departing from Ronaldsway. (Phil Pain Collection)

Pionair G-ALXL during a turnaround at Ronaldsway. (Phil Pain Collection)

Indeed, by the 1960s, there was a whole variety of companies with established routes to the Isle of Man, including such well-known names as Dan-Air and British Midland (Derby Aviation until 1964). By the mid-1960s, Dan-Air linked the island on a seasonal basis with Bristol, Exeter, Plymouth, Prestwick, Staverton and Swansea. Meanwhile, at various times, British Midland Airways operated services from Derby (later East Midlands), Birmingham and Coventry. For many years, the main competition to BEA came from Silver City Airways, which later became part of British United. It began operations to the island in 1956 following the formation of its Northern Division which developed from its takeover of Manx Airlines, Lancashire Aircraft Corporation and Dragon Air Services. Silver City and its successor companies, British United, British United Island Airways, British Island Airways and Air UK, went on to provide a comprehensive network of services to the island over the next thirty or so years with routes to Blackpool, Edinburgh, Glasgow, Leeds, Newcastle and other destinations. These carriers used the Bristol Freighter, DC-3 and Handley Page Herald as their principal operating equipment.

BEA tried to improve relations with the Manx Government and a meeting was held in January 1950 between BEA's Chief Executive, Sir Peter Masefield, and representatives of the Manx administration. At the meeting, Sir Peter sought to assure the Manx delegation that BEA was committed to providing the island with an adequate air service and took many by surprise when he mentioned that BEA would reintroduce some of the abandoned routes in due course. There was some scepticism locally, but true to his word, BEA did reinstate the Glasgow and Manchester routes in the summer of 1951. Manchester was to remain an enduring destination, although Glasgow lasted only until 1954. Furthermore, BEA promised that, by 1952, all services would be operated by DC-3 aircraft.

The promising situation did not last long. Early in 1953 the Corporation announced that it intended to raise fares on its Manx routes by 10%. The Manx Government was quick to complain, fearing BEA's price rises would damage tourism. BEA argued that it had no choice but to make such increases. However, in the course of a meeting over the situation it emerged that BEA was concentrating its efforts on its Channel Islands services rather than the Manx ones. The Manx Government had feared for some time the existence of such a strategy. BEA defended itself by pointing out that the finances of flying to the Channel Islands were better because of the longer journey lengths and the cheaper fuel available in Jersey and Guernsey. By 1953, quarterly meetings were being held between the two sides in an attempt to keep relations on an even keel. BEA did eventually accept that the Isle of Man had special needs by virtue of it being an island, and promised to try to satisfy at least some of them. Special needs or not, the finances of the Manx network did not improve. The BEA Report and Accounts for the financial year 1955/56 indicated that the losses on the routes had soared to £400,000.

One improvement promised by the Corporation was the introduction of the new four-engined turbo-prop Vickers Viscount on some Manx services. To accommodate the aircraft, a small runway extension was completed at Ronaldsway during the winter of 1953/54 at a cost of about £23,000. In July 1954, the first visit of a Viscount to the Isle of Man took place when BEA operated a proving flight from Manchester. In a rare stroke of public relations genius, BEA rostered a Manxman, Captain Tom Quirk, to fly the aircraft. It seems likely that the first BEA Viscount to land at Ronaldsway was G-AMON. A second Viscount appeared a few weeks later and treated the local press and tourist officials to a short demonstration flight. However, Viscount scheduled services did not begin until the summer of 1955 when the type made a very modest appearance on a handful of Manchester services. The summer timetable for 1955 shows a single Viscount flight from Manchester on a Friday and Saturday evening, BE626 departing from Manchester at 1940, with the return service, BE627, leaving Ronaldsway at 2055. The Friday service operated in July and August only. The Viscounts were something of a local spectacle with large numbers of people gathering at the spectators gallery to watch their arrival and departure.

The pattern of supplementing the DC-3, which BEA had now modified into the 32-passenger Pionair, with some Viscount flights from Manchester continued for several years. Viscounts also began to appear on the Heathrow route, although only once a week. The time saved by using the Viscount on the London route was most noticeable, a Viscount taking one hour and ten minutes for the trip, while the venerable Pionair took two hours. Today the sleek Manx Airlines BAe 146 jet frequently completes the sector in 45 to 50 minutes. While the Manx government was pleased to see Viscounts appearing at Ronaldsway, it still believed that the Channel Islands were getting a better deal. In the case of Jersey, this was true, many of the Jersey-London services being Viscount-operated by the late 1950s, as well as some of the services to Manchester and Glasgow. In the case of Guernsey, it was not true because the island still had a grass runway and was an all-Pionair operation.

The use of the Viscounts at the weekends indicated that there was a greater demand for travel on Saturdays and Sundays. In an attempt to even out this peak and persuade people to travel on midweek days, BEA introduced midweek fares which were up to 30% cheaper for passengers who travelled on Tuesdays, Wednesdays and Thursdays. Despite this, most people preferred to fly at the weekends, probably because many Manx hotels would only take bookings from weekend to weekend.

Apart from the handful of Viscount services to Manchester, and the once weekly service by the type from Heathrow, the Pionair remained supreme on the Manx routes. The 1959 summer timetable was typical of most years in the mid and late 1950s. It provided for twenty-one Pionair trips a week to Belfast, thirty to Liverpool, forty-one to Manchester and six to London. BEA now faced considerable competition from Silver City Airways. Silver City had become the main independent operator into Ronaldsway, its principal route being the former BEA link to Blackpool. It operated this up to fifteen times a day on peak summer Saturdays, and in the summer of 1962 it mounted a half-hourly service over the route between early morning and late evening. That was something of a contrast with 2001 when the service operated by Platinum Air 2000's 18-seater Jetstream 31 aircraft linked Blackpool with the island only twice a day. Silver City also flew to Glasgow and Newcastle. It used Herons and occasionally DC-3s, but most of the flying was carried out by the Bristol Freighters with which Silver City became synonymous. Some car ferry flights with this type were flown from the island, but on the Blackpool route the Freighter operated as a 44-seater passenger aircraft and was known as the Wayfarer. The frequency of the Wayfarer service from Blackpool presented BEA with its major concern. By the early 1960s, Silver City was carrying about half of all the air arrivals to the island. Travel by Wayfarer was certainly noisy, but the trip from Blackpool was short, usually about 25 minutes. BEA had little to offer by way of competition given that most of its services were by Pionair which was neither much faster nor quieter. The reason for the high frequency of flights from Blackpool was that it served as the coach-air terminal for many holiday companies. Passengers would be coached from all over the UK to Blackpool and flown from there to the island, a practice that continued beyond the Silver City days and into the 1970s, and a special coach park was constructed at Blackpool Airport to facilitate this arrangement.

The BEA staff at Ronaldsway were highly efficient and well able to deal with the large number of passengers descending on them during the summer peak. However, occasional hiccups did occur and these sometimes involved the temporary staff which the airline employed at the height of the season. One such staff member was John Christal who later became head teacher of the highly successful Ramsey Grammar School in the north of the island. He remembers how, one day, he caused such a blip in the smooth running of the station. It occurred during the summer of 1958 when he had been in BEA employment for only a few days. His error was to direct a passenger in transit from Belfast to Liverpool on to the wrong aircraft - to a flight going to Belfast. To the embarrassment of BEA, the presence of the passenger was not discovered until it was too late, and he ended up back where he had originally boarded. In his defence, John points out that the two Pionairs were parked side by side. The passenger had apparently got off to stretch his legs. It was a mistake anyone could make!

John also recalls that, when Ronaldsway was fogbound, flights would switch to the airfield at Jurby, near Ramsey. Passengers, firemen, airline staff, air traffic controllers and other personnel would be bused to Jurby and operations would be conducted from the old control tower and a nearby ex-military hut. Facilities were, to put it mildly, primitive, yet staff were usually more than happy to be sent to Jurby as it meant that a good bit of overtime could be earned. Diverting to Jurby, when Ronaldsway was fogbound, was a practice BEA had employed since 1947. With the unpredictable nature of the weather there were sometimes many months when Jurby did not need to be used, but sometimes sustained periods of bad weather required frequent diversions. One such incidence was in November 1948 when fog and low cloud were recurrent. Although flights were frequently delayed because of the need to use Jurby, the airline continued to fly all its services throughout the period with only one flight having to be cancelled. The use of Jurby as a diversion point continued well into the 1960s. It ended partly because the Manx Government believed the whole operation was too costly, and partly because of complaints from Cambrian Airways. One of its Viscounts had arrived over Jurby earlier than expected and could not contact the control tower. It was discovered that the controller had gone for a meal break believing the Viscount to be some way off. Cambrian was not impressed at having to keep its aircraft circling while the controller finished his tea.

When delays occurred, it was common for all the staff, including the aircrews, to pull together to try to get things back on schedule. A typical example of teamwork was demonstrated in July 1955 and was witnessed by the then editor of *BEA Magazine*, E. C. Cheesman. He was booked on the 1020 Ronaldsway-Manchester Pionair service and then on the connecting Manchester-Heathrow flight scheduled to leave Manchester at 1115. However, earlier in the morning, the Pionair operating the Manchester-Ronaldsway flights had become unserviceable and was an hour late leaving Manchester. In order to ensure that the connection was made at Manchester, the flight crew reduced their breakfast break from one hour to fifteen minutes, and the ground staff at Ronaldsway turned the aircraft round in just four minutes. As a result of these efforts, the Pionair landed at Manchester dead on schedule and Mr Cheesman was able to connect with the London flight. Such co-operation was normal and in no way a special effort simply for his benefit. Speedy turnarounds did not, however, always go to plan. Captain Bill Reid recalls an occasion in June 1953 when he was flying a Pionair on a London-Isle of Man-Belfast service, on which a 90-second transit stop at Ronaldsway turned into half an hour. The normal practice was to stop only the port engine while the Isle of Man passengers disembarked and the outbound Belfast passengers joined the aircraft. Passengers in transit from London to Belfast would remain on board during the short stop. On this particular occasion, one of the passengers travelling from London through to Belfast was the Queen of Tonga. She was keen to see what was going on and decided to disembark. It took half an hour before she was satisfied she had seen everything and re-boarded the aircraft.

The close-knit nature of the BEA team on the Isle of Man meant that social activities were common. A typical staff outing took place one Friday evening in November 1948. It was organised by Station Assistant E. Tuff and consisted of a trip to the Gaiety Theatre in Douglas, followed by visits to several local pubs with the evening topped off with fish and chip suppers. Most BEA stations, including the Isle of Man, had local staff social clubs, and inter-station competitions would be held in several sports including football, cricket and golf. BEA employed approximately thirty-five full-time staff on the island. Most worked at the airport, but there was also a town office in Douglas, situated in the Pier Arcade. From there, Mr Goodyear single-handedly supervised coach departures for the airport and made reservations. Bookings for Manx flights were controlled from Ronaldsway by a team of five staff, led for many years by John Woodworth.

Things took a tremendous step forward at the end of the summer season in 1960. BEA decided it was time to withdraw the Pionair from its Manx route network and make the operation all-Viscount. The last Pionair flight operated on 31 October and was probably BE537 to Liverpool at 1955. Making the Manx routes all-Viscount certainly gave Silver City something to think about. It too underwent some major changes shortly afterwards when it became part of British United Airways. A special Manx subsidiary called British United (Manx) was set up and the old Bristol Wayfarers were replaced by DC-3s and modern turbo-prop Dart Heralds. While becoming total committed to the Viscount may have been advantageous in some ways, it also had a drawback, namely that frequencies were reduced since the Viscount carried double the load of a Pionair.

The summer of 1962 saw BEA take its boldest step on Manx routes with the introduction of the new 132-seater Vickers Vanguard V951 on the London route. The Vanguard was scheduled to operate on Saturdays during the June to September holiday peak, arriving at Ronaldsway at 1250 as BE7024, and departing for London at 1325 as BE7027. No record can be traced as to which Vanguard first visited the island or if there was a proving flight prior to services commencing. On this occasion the Isle of Man had actually beaten Jersey since the Vanguard did not make an appearance on the London-Jersey route until 1964. In 2001, the Vanguard still holds the record for being the largest airliner to serve Ronaldsway on a regular scheduled service. Accommodating the Vanguard at Ronaldsway had been made possible by some further runway improvements. These were made over the winter of 1957 and involved widening the runway and some of the taxiways at a cost of almost £100,000. They were not undertaken with Vanguards in mind, but at BEA's request to allow Viscounts to land in crosswinds of up to 25 knots. However, the far-sighted improvements meant that the runway was suitable for the mighty Vanguard when the time came. That runway continues to serve the needs of the island and is periodically used by larger aircraft types such as Boeing 757s or Airbus 320s.

The introduction of the Vanguard could have been viewed as further evidence of BEA's commitment to Manx services. However such a conclusion would have been misplaced. The airline's financial position was again deteriorating following seven profitable years. In 1961/62, BEA recorded a loss, the outlook was not good and economies had to be made. The Manx routes were again an obvious target. Early in 1962, BEA began holding talks with Cambrian Airways about the future of the Manx routes. Cambrian was the Welsh national airline, which at that time was 30% owned by BEA. Later it became a fully-owned subsidiary of British Airways. It operated a fleet of ex-BEA Pionairs from Cardiff and Bristol to the Channel Islands, Manchester and France. In September 1962, BEA announced its talks with Cambrian had reached a conclusion and that, from 1 April 1963, all the BEA Irish Sea routes would be handed over to Cambrian. This meant the Manx routes, plus the Liverpool-Belfast direct service. To fly these, Cambrian would purchase five BEA Viscount V701s.

This decision was greeted with predictable outrage in both Liverpool and on the Isle of Man. Liverpool City Council felt snubbed by the airline and believed that Speke Airport would suffer

Pionairs G-AJIA and G-AGZB on 30 October 1960. G-AGZB RMA Robert Smith Barry had just completed the last Heathrow-Ronaldsway Pionair service. (Terry Faragher Collection)

The arrival of the first BEA Viscount, G-AMON, at Ronaldsway. (J. Young)

without BEA. The Manx Government was extremely concerned that Cambrian's services would not be sustained if profits were inadequate. Cambrian was, after all, an independent carrier which did not have the resources of the State to fall back on as did BEA. Cambrian sought to reassure the Manx Government that this would not be the case. Indeed, it argued that it would actually provide a better service than BEA had done. BEA had willingly given up these routes, so how could Cambrian be so optimistic? The answer lay in its lower salary scales, greater staff flexibility and lower depreciation costs on its aircraft.

The last day of BEA's service to the Isle of Man was Sunday 31 March 1963. There were a number of Viscount flights that day to Belfast, Liverpool and Manchester, but the last service was BE7135 to Manchester via Liverpool. It was operated by Viscount V802 G-AOJB under the command of Captain Charters. His co-pilot was Captain Baldwin. The scheduled departure time was 1820 and the aircraft actually became airborne at 1822. The aircraft was saluted, as it left the apron, by Frank Gawne. Frank had only recently become BEA Station Superintendent at Ronaldsway following the death of Bert Wood. Both men were local legends and Bert Wood had the rare ability to get on with everybody. Gordon Erridge, BEA's area manager for England and Wales, whose extended to the Isle of Man, suggested that Bert's epitaph could well be, 'See Bert, he'd do anyone a good turn.' Frank had worked alongside Bert since IoMAS days, and he was the natural successor. Yet his days as a BEA Station Superintendent were short-lived. He nonetheless accepted a similar position with Cambrian and was back on duty next day, wearing a new cap badge, ready to welcome the first Cambrian service. On the engineering front, Bill Acheson also changed insignia and became Cambrian's Station Engineer. Indeed, most of the BEA staff on the island transferred to Cambrian.

At Liverpool, a similar staff transfer took place. Harold Ayre, a BEA Duty Officer at Speke, became Cambrian's new Station Superintendent, a job which he held for many years. BEA's Station Superintendent at Speke, Tommy Adams, also joined Cambrian to become the airline's sales manager for North West England. Some of the Speke staff were able to continue their BEA service at other BEA locations, and the sales office in the city remained under BEA ownership giving the Corporation at least a token presence in Liverpool.

The transfer to Cambrian was not a simple operation. Apart from the obvious changes, such as placing Cambrian's logo over that of BEA and changing uniform badges, there were a whole host of other jobs to attend to. All of BEA's assets had to be checked and transferred, including everything from eye wash (for first aid purposes one supposes) to vehicles. During preparation of the inventory, staff at Ronaldsway discovered some ancient electric fires which BEA had inherited in 1947 from IoMAS. Bill Acheson had to undertake a complete stock check of all aircraft spares in order that Cambrian could pay the exact figure for each item. This exercise took his staff three days to complete.

The morning of 1 April brought a new colour scheme to Ronaldsway's apron. However, with so many staff continuing and the Cambrian Airways aircraft being ex-BEA, little apart from airline livery and logos actually changed. Cambrian's Viscount crews were trained by BEA and they used BEA operating procedures while Cambrian's traffic staff used documentation which was virtually identical to that of BEA. The first day, therefore, went without a hitch. Flights came and went from Liverpool, Manchester, Belfast and Heathrow. The Heathrow service carried several BEA and Cambrian senior personnel including BEA's Chief Executive, Anthony Milward, Cambrian's Operations and Traffic Director, Jim Callan, and Chief Pilot, Geoff Perrott. They were greeted on the tarmac by Cambrian's new Station Superintendent, and BEA's old Station Superintendent, Frank Gawne.

The Corporation's years of serving the Isle of Man were certainly not as happy as those experienced in Scotland, the Isles of Scilly and the Channel Islands. The Manx Government was often suspicious of BEA's commitment to the island and with good cause. However BEA had brought great progress to Manx air travel, initially with the introduction of the Pionair, and later with the Viscount and Vanguard. Politics apart, the local BEA staff under Bert Wood and Frank Gawne had always enjoyed a very high reputation on the island.

It is perhaps interesting to draw a few comparisons between 1947 and 1963. In 1947, all services were operated by five or six-seater Rapides which took 55 minutes to make the trip to Liverpool. In 1963, all services were operated by 71-passenger Viscounts which took a scheduled time of thirty-five minutes from Liverpool, and often much less. In 1947, travellers paid £1 12s 6d for a midweek ticket while in 1963 the same ticket cost £2 18s. The free baggage allowance on the Rapide was 35 lbs, but on the Viscount was only 33 lbs. Child fares were only allowed up to the age of seven in 1947 whereas, in 1963, BEA permitted children of thirteen to travel on child tickets.

Cambrian continued to provide services to the island from Belfast, Liverpool, London and Manchester into the 1970s. Its chief rival during those years was British United (later BUIA, BIA and Air UK), whose Dart Heralds maintained the old Silver City route from Blackpool. They flew a high frequency service, especially during the summer peak weekends when there were flights from early morning until 2300 hours. Other established operators, such as Dan-Air and British Midland, continued their seasonal routes to the island and they were supplemented by a variety of other carriers, such as Autair which began operating seasonal services from Teesside and Hull in 1968 although it only sustained these for two summers.

By the 1970s, Cambrian was using the larger Viscount 800 series aircraft which it had purchased from BEA. A few Liverpool services and most of the London flights were operated by the twin engined jet, the BAC 1-11. In 1973, Cambrian lost its separate identity as it became part of British Airways. British Airways continued Cambrian's Isle of Man routes until 1978 when it gave up the Liverpool and Belfast services. These were taken over by British Midland. The remaining Manchester and London services were insufficient to justify the thirty-three staff still under Frank Gawne's direction. It came as no surprise when British Airways announced that it was terminating all Manx routes on 31 March 1980 as part of a major pruning of domestic services. The London route went to British Midland and Air UK took over the Manchester link.

Neither carrier found their Manx operations financially lucrative and both were on the verge of pulling out completely by 1982. A similar problem faced the other major remaining operator to the Isle of Man, Dan-Air, which finally abandoned its Manx routes at the end of the summer of 1984. The advent of cheap foreign holidays with guaranteed sun was something with which the Isle of Man was unable to compete. However, instead of giving up their Manx routes, British Midland and Air UK elected a different strategy. The two carriers established a new company which would be dedicated to Manx routes and to be called Manx Airlines. Manx gradually developed a successful network of services from the island to Belfast, Birmingham, Dublin, Glasgow, Heathrow, Jersey, Leeds, Liverpool, Luton, Manchester and Southampton. It currently employs a single BAe 146, three BAe ATPs and a BAe Jetstream 41. Manx Airlines became a sister company to British Regional Airlines which developed into one of the UK's leading regional carriers flying an extensive network of both domestic and international routes, and using equipment similar to Manx but with the addition of a large fleet of Embraer 145 jets. In April 2001, British Regional and Manx became fully owned British Airways subsidiaries and were integrated with Brymon Airways to form British Airways CitiExpress, but permitting Manx Airlines to retain its own identity. In October 2001, it was announced that British Airways Regional would join British Airways CitiExpress which would become responsible for British

Airways' short-haul regional domestic and European network. In February 2002, a further announcement indicated that the Isle of Man route to London would be transferred from Heathrow to Gatwick with the introduction of the summer timetable, and that Manx Airlines would loose its separate identity from September 2002.

Other scheduled services to the Isle of Man are flown by British European (formerly Jersey European Airways) which links the island with Belfast, Bristol and London City. British European services are mainly operated by de Havilland Canada Dash 8 aircraft, although the BAe 146 is used on some of the London City flights. The route to London City has proved to be highly successful, permitting business travellers quick access to the heart of London and it operates up to four times a day. The other scheduled passenger carrier was Platinum Air 2000 which flew BAe Jetstream 31s to Belfast and Blackpool until its operations ceased in November 2001. In 2002, its place on the Blackpool route was taken up by Bandeirante operator, FlyKeen Airways. For the vintage airliner enthusiast, however, the main interest may well focus on the cargo operation of Emerald Airways which flies Hawker Siddeley 748s up to four times daily to the Isle of Man on cargo, mail and parcels contracts. Their Station Manager, Lance Secretan, is another long-serving employee at Ronaldsway having been Dan-Air's Station Manager for many years, and who then worked for Jersey European before transferring to Emerald. These companies have enjoyed success partly because they use aircraft ideally suited to the routes served, but chiefly because of the economic boom enjoyed by the island during the last decade of the twentieth century. The rapid growth of the finance sector on the Isle of Man has been especially stimulated by its status as a tax haven. If BEA had experienced the benefits of a similar boom, who knows what innovations the airline might have introduced to its Manx network.

21 March 1963 – Passengers board Viscount G-AOJB for the final BEA departure from the Isle of Man.
(Phil Lo Bao Collection)

The Channel Islands

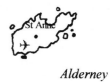

Alderney

St Anne

20 miles

32 km

Guernsey

Herm

St Peter Port

L'Erée

Sark

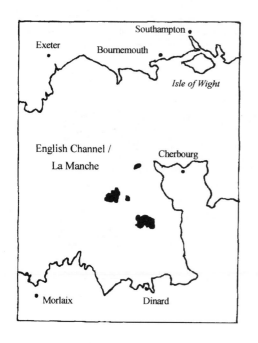

Southampton

Exeter

Bournemouth

Isle of Wight

English Channel /
La Manche

Cherbourg

Morlaix

Dinard

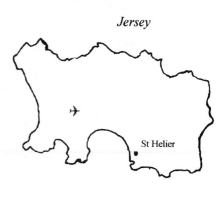

Jersey

St Helier

3

The Channel Islands - Sun, Sea and BEA

The Channel Islands consist of some of the best known and loved tourist destinations in the British Isles. There are three main islands, Jersey, Guernsey and Alderney, together with a number of smaller ones, notably Herm and Sark. Being nearly a hundred miles south of the southern coast of England and in the lee of the Cherbourg peninsula, they enjoy a mild climate and can be pleasantly warm in the summer. The Channel Islands have a distinctly continental feel, with many French street names and place names. Alderney is only ten miles from the French coast, and the other islands little more.

Given their tourist appeal, the islands were a natural target for air services and by the late 1930s the largest of the operators, Channel Islands Airways, trading as Jersey Airways and Guernsey Airways, was operating a well developed series of links to Southampton, London, Exeter and France. The company used the de Havilland Dragon biplane and then proceeded to the Rapide and the four-engined DH86. However, scheduled air services to the Channel Islands began in 1923 when British Marine Air Navigation Limited launched a weekly service between Southampton and Guernsey with Supermarine Sea Eagle flying boats. The service was taken over by Imperial Airways in 1924 and was extended to Jersey. Imperial Airways continued to fly to the Channel Islands until 1929 by which time it was using the Short Calcutta flying boat. When Imperial withdrew its service, a little known operator, Kirsten and Mace Limited, took over with a Saro Cutty Sark amphibian. This service lasted only a short time, ending in 1930. It was not until 1933 that, with the formation of Jersey Airways, scheduled services to the Channel Islands resumed.

Jersey Airways began to develop an extensive network of routes using de Havilland Dragon aircraft, which were later supplemented by the larger DH86. By 1936, the company was operating six of these aircraft while the DH89 Rapide had replaced the Dragons. It had also established a subsidiary company, Guernsey Airways, to operate connecting services to Guernsey and Alderney. At the end of 1934, Channel Islands Airways was established as the holding company for Jersey Airways and Guernsey Airways. The Channel Islands Airways name soon replaced those of the two subsidiary companies.

Jersey's airfield was built at St Peter's, about five miles from the capital St Helier, and was opened for traffic in March 1937. Until then, flights had landed on the beach at West Park which meant all schedules were determined by the state of the tide. At low tide, there would be a veritable invasion of aircraft, and as many as seven or eight could arrive at the same time. Landing on a beach used by locals and tourists for leisure was sometimes a hair-raising experience for pilots. The public seemed oblivious to the dangers of low-flying aircraft and, on a number of occasions, aircraft had to overshoot at the last minute to avoid someone in the wrong place on the beach. There were one or two accidents when aircraft hit people and there was one fatality. Guernsey's airfield, at La Villiaze, did not open until May 1939. Prior to 1939, there had been a brief service from a landing strip at L'Erée using Westland Wessex aircraft, but Guernsey Airways had used amphibians, initially the Saunders Roe Windhover, to link the island with Jersey and Alderney. Flights landed outside St Peter Port harbour and the aircraft were moored within the harbour. The service was rather erratic, as was the flying boat service from Southampton to Guernsey which had been operated by a variety of companies from the 1920s. The smallest of the main islands, Alderney, was the first to have an airfield, one being opened there in 1936.

Unlike services to the Isle of Man, the Scottish islands and the Isles of Scilly, those to the Channel Islands did not continue to operate throughout World War Two. The reason for the suspension of services was simple: the islands were occupied by German troops in June 1940 and they were not liberated until early May 1945. The Channel Islands were the only part of the British Isles to experience Nazi occupation and evidence of it is still visible, the remains of huge concrete towers and gun emplacements now serving as tourist attractions.

In the days immediately prior to the German invasion, Channel Islands Airways played its part in evacuating those islanders who wished to leave. The airline repatriated all of its aircraft except one which was undergoing overhaul. The engineers ensured that the Germans would be unable to use it. Following Germany's surrender, Channel Islands Airways was anxious to resume operations and, on 26 May 1945, Rapide, G-AGLP, arrived in Jersey. Scheduled services began again on 21 June, the first flight being from Croydon to Jersey via Guernsey. It was flown by Rapide, G-AGPH.

Channel Islands Airways was keen to build up its services as quickly as possible and by the summer of 1946, in addition to employing Rapides, it leased DC-3 and Bristol 170 aircraft to fly its routes. The DC-3 appeared for only a short time, but the company was interested in obtaining the Bristol 170 and used one of the prototypes for some weeks, mainly in August, and chiefly on the Croydon-Jersey service. The Bristol 170 flew as a passenger aircraft, in which role it was known as the Wayfarer, and could carry 44 passengers compared to the five or six accommodated by the Rapide and the 28-passenger payload of the DC-3. The writer's mother, Kathleen Lo Bao, travelled on one of the Wayfarer trips from Croydon. She was en route to Guernsey but the aircraft did not operate into Guernsey and she had to transfer to a Rapide at Jersey. She recalled the splendid views from the Wayfarer, especially when passing over Southampton where the ocean liners in the port were clearly visible. She was less enthusiastic about the noise made by the Wayfarer. In order to reduce the effect of the noise, the stewardess would supply passengers with cotton wool for their ears.

The Governments of both Jersey and Guernsey believed that plans by the UK Government to nationalise all civil air services in 1947 would not apply to the Channel Islands. As self-governing islands, they presumed that they would be free to continue to provide their own air services through Channel Islands Airways. But the UK Government had no intention of allowing the islands to be exempt. It informed both Governments that the services of Channel Islands Airways would be taken over by British European Airways. The islanders were unhappy with this high-handedness and the Governments of Jersey and Guernsey decided to resist. So, on 1 February when most UK airlines were taken over by BEA, Channel Islands Airways remained separate. A real battle of wills unfolded, with the UK Labour Government eventually informing the Channel Islands administrations that, if they did not agree to the BEA takeover, then the services of Channel Islands Airways would be prohibited from using UK airspace. This ultimatum really left the islands with little choice and Channel Islands Airways was taken over by BEA on 1 April 1947.

BEA created what can only be termed a total public relations disaster on 31 March by sending a Ju 52, which BEA called the Jupiter, to Jersey and Guernsey with BEA signs, uniforms, stickers, and other office material. The Ju 52 was an ex-German military transport, some of which BEA had inherited as war reparations. These aircraft were chiefly used on Scottish and Northern Irish routes, but the arrival of this one in the Channel Islands generated a cataclysmic response. The local populations were furious. The Ju 52 had last been seen in the islands in Luftwaffe service and now BEA dared to send one as part of its takeover of their beloved Channel Islands Airways. BEA quickly learned from its mistake and there were no more visits from the

Ju 52s. Local ex-Channel Islands Airways staff, such as Frank Ferbrache in Guernsey, W.L.G. Butt in Jersey, and Jack Keene Miller, the new BEA area manager, were quick to point out to their new masters that a certain amount of care and tact would be needed during the early days if the islanders were to accept the airline. Most of Channel Islands Airways staff transferred to BEA, and in 1971 no less than forty-four of them were still in local BEA employment. They held an anniversary dinner in Jersey in December of that year to celebrate twenty-five years of service with BEA.

BEA was keen to develop services from the islands. It inherited a network linking Jersey, Guernsey and Alderney with Southampton, as well as Jersey and Guernsey with Croydon, seasonal services from Jersey to Paris and Rennes, and inter-island services. For the summer of 1947, BEA decided to initiate some immediate improvements. From 21 April 1947, the Jersey-London service transferred from Croydon to Northolt and the airline began to use the DC-3 in place of the Rapide on the route. On the first day two DC-3s flew the route, G-AGIP and G-AHCU. Records show that there were up to seven flights a day at the weekends between Jersey and Northolt. Another innovation was the introduction of the DC-3 on the Jersey-Paris (Le Bourget) service. BEA re-opened this route on summer Saturdays, with a departure from Jersey at 1220, BE621A, and a return from Le Bourget at 1520, BE621N. The route was not very popular however, and was closed down at the end of the summer season. Although BEA did try to revive it in the summer of 1951, it lasted only a few weeks. The airline also linked Jersey with Rennes, usually twice a week, and this route was operated by the Rapides. The Rennes route lasted rather longer than the Paris one, although in June 1949 the service was re-routed to serve Dinard instead of Rennes. BEA believed that Dinard would be a more popular destination and a double daily service was provided, together with a direct Guernsey-Dinard service twice weekly.

Rennes had to wait until the early 1960s to be connected with Jersey again. Then, it was by Aer Lingus, not BEA. The Irish company flew a seasonal service from Dublin to Jersey using the turbo-prop Fokker F27 aircraft and decided to extend the weekly flight to the Breton town. BEA acted as Aer Lingus' handling agent in Jersey and Doug Lo Bao travelled on the first flight from Jersey as BEA's representative. Things did not go according to plan. Aer Lingus had evidently forgotten to verify that Rennes Airport had a ground power unit for starting the F27's engines and, when it came to departure time, the absence of suitable equipment became apparent. The Aer Lingus Captain made several attempts to start the engines using the aircraft's own batteries, succeeding just before the batteries were exhausted. Doug Lo Bao came home none too pleased; he had been hoping for an enforced night stop in a Rennes hotel at the expense of Aer Lingus!

Throughout the summer of 1947, the Rapides maintained the remainder of the Channel Islands services. They flew 42 services a week from Jersey to Southampton, 33 from Guernsey to Southampton and 21 from Guernsey to London (Croydon). Alderney was linked with Southampton twice a week, and there were 12 weekly services between Guernsey and Alderney. The busiest route of all was between Jersey and Guernsey, on which 95 weekly trips were scheduled each way for the duration of the summer. By the end of the year, BEA had operated 9,962 flights and carried 100,666 passengers on its Channel Islands routes.

If BEA was keen to develop Channel Islands services in the summer of 1947, its enthusiasm soon turned sour. As the Corporation faced huge losses, major cost cutting became necessary. The Channel Islands did not escape this, and the Corporation announced that, for the winter of 1947/48, it would suspend the direct Croydon-Guernsey service. Passengers from London to Guernsey would have to travel on one of the three daily DC-3 services from Northolt to Jersey and then connect with an inter-island Rapide. The Guernsey Government was livid, believing the loss of a direct link to London to be a serious blow to the island. It complained loudly that Channel Islands Airways would never have treated Guernsey with such contempt. The closure of the Croydon-Guernsey route also marked the end of BEA services from Croydon. The last direct service from Croydon was flown by Rapide, G-AGIF, which left Croydon at 1700 on 1 November 1947. BEA was rather taken aback by the vehemence of the Guernsey protests and a direct service was re-instated the following summer and never again suspended. When the route resumed, Northolt was used as the terminal airport for London.

BEA's staff in Guernsey, thirty-seven in total, were managed by Frank Ferbrache. Like so many of the other local staff, Frank had worked for Channel Islands Airways before the War. Unusually for a small place, BEA Guernsey initially had two town offices, the main one on the South Esplanade, and a smaller one in Smith Street which housed the reservations unit for Guernsey services. The Esplanade site contained Frank's office and was the town terminal for passengers being conveyed to the airport in BEA buses. At the airport, which is five miles from St Peter Port, Reg Brewer was in charge of passenger handling, and Ted England oversaw engineering needs. As with Frank Ferbrache, both men were veterans of pre-war Channel Islands Airways operations. Ted England went on to serve with BEA and British Airways as Guernsey Station Engineer until the airline finally withdrew from the island in 1980. If Ted England was well acquainted with the technicalities of operating aircraft, many of his passengers certainly were not. One old lady, observing the engineer plugging in a starter battery truck to a DC-3, commented in a loud voice to one of her friends, 'There you are, my dear, they are emptying the toilet'. Although Guernsey never handled as many passengers as Jersey, it was a busy station, accounting for about a third of BEA's Channel Islands passengers. Thus, in 1947 of the 100,000 or so passengers carried by BEA to and from the islands, Guernsey handled almost 30,000.

Once the financial problems of the late 1940s had been resolved, BEA gradually began to build up its Channel Islands routes. In May 1950, the airline began to link the islands with Birmingham and Manchester using the DC-3, while the following summer saw the introduction of a direct Glasgow-Jersey route, also flown by the DC-3. It was not until the summer of 1955 that Guernsey got a direct link with Glasgow. In 1956, a seasonal link between Belfast and Jersey was opened and, for the summer of 1957, an Aberdeen-Edinburgh-Jersey schedule was flown on a Sunday. This route was also DC-3 operated, although by then BEA had undertaken a modernisation programme for its DC-3s, and now called them Pionairs. The Pionair had made its debut on routes to the Channel Islands in March 1951. At Aberdeen, the departure of the Jersey-bound Pionair was a solitary affair as, at that time, no Scottish internal flights operated on a Sunday. As a result, BEA had to make a special payment for the opening of Aberdeen airfield. This was a costly exercise and the link to Aberdeen was abandoned in 1960, although the sector between Jersey and Edinburgh continued.

Another development was marked with the introduction of the Airspeed Ambassador, which BEA called the Elizabethan, to London-Jersey services in the summer of 1953. The Elizabethan flew out of Heathrow rather than Northolt, and this was the first time there had been a Heathrow-Jersey link. BEA was able to use the Elizabethan because the States of Jersey had constructed a hard runway of 4,200 feet in 1952. Jersey was always more forward-thinking in aviation matters than Guernsey and realised that a hard runway would allow modern aircraft types to use the airport. The new runway was officially opened in June 1952 and BEA sent an Elizabethan, G-ALZV, a Viking, G-AMNJ, and a Dart DC-3, G-ALXN, to participate in the celebrations. BEA Vikings occasionally appeared at Jersey after the hard runway was opened, but they were not rostered for scheduled services to the island. The visit of the Elizabethan was certainly the highlight of the day for the local BEA staff. Commanded by Captain Bill Baillie, the aircraft made a memorable low-level high-speed pass over the runway after it had taken off for its return to London. Initially, the Elizabethan operated only on Saturdays and Sundays in the summer peak, but from the summer of 1956 the type appeared on a daily basis, operating the last flight of the day from London, arriving at Jersey at 2105, and then returning on the first flight the next morning. The Elizabethan was fully pressurised, so journeys became a lot more comfortable as the aircraft flew above the weather rather than straight through it as was the practice with the Pionairs.

Achieving a hard runway in Jersey had been quite a battle. A number of local politicians believed the whole idea to be far too expensive. A public meeting was held at St Helier Town Hall to discuss the matter and several local politicians voiced their strong opposition. However the course of the meeting was altered as a result of the intervention of a BEA pilot. He spoke very forcefully in favour of building a hard runway and told the meeting that, in the view of many commercial pilots, Jersey had the worst scheduled service airfield in Europe. He observed that, in mid-winter, it had often been likened to the backyard of a pig farm. His contribution caused a great hush and certainly helped some people change their minds.

The pilot in question, Alan Voak, spoke from experience of the treacherous nature of Jersey's grass runways. He had recent memory of a very nasty incident when landing in a Pionair on which he was First Officer. It was a dark and windy night and the aircraft was directed to land on the shorter north-south runway. Towards the end of the landing, the aircraft began to slew to the left as a result of the wind, but the slippery grass made the situation worse and the Pionair swung through 180 degrees to face the way it had just come. That was not the end of the incident. The aircraft was still moving, but this time backwards. The strong wind was blowing it towards the cliffs. Eventually the Captain, Peter Loat, succeeded in stopping it just 40 yards from the cliff's edge. Alan has often wondered what the passengers thought of the incident, but he concludes that they were 'pretty hardened in those days'. In May 1952, Alan had the honour of making the first scheduled landing on the new hard runway in a Pionair commanded by Captain Bill Caldwell.

In 1952, BEA introduced a new job, that of Flight Clerk. The Flight Clerk, who worked only on Pionairs, would act as cabin crew during a flight, but on landing he (all the Flight Clerks were male) would assist local staff with the turnaround of the aircraft, including escorting passengers and completing documentation. The idea behind introducing Flight Clerks was to reduce the number of traffic staff needed at airports and they became a feature of Channel Islands, Scottish Islands and Isle of Man air journeys on BEA.

A further landmark in BEA's links with the Channel Islands occurred on 30 October 1954 when BEA transferred all its London services to Heathrow and closed down its Northolt base. All Channel Islands flights used Heathrow from the next day. The final BEA scheduled departure from Northolt was a Pionair to Jersey. BE684 departed from Northolt at 1820 and was flown by G-AHCZ commanded by Jersey-based pilot Tommy Frogatt.

The smallest of the BEA stations in the Channel Islands was Alderney. With a resident population of around 2,000, there was a limited potential for traffic, and the size of the airfield meant that only the Rapide could be used. Even so, BEA maintained scheduled services linking Alderney with Guernsey, Jersey and Southampton. In summer, this meant about 28 weekly departures, with around half of that number during the winter. The main route was to Guernsey, where newspapers, mail, medical supplies and other assorted cargo would be manipulated into the Rapide's tiny cabin. BEA opened one new, short-lived, route, from Alderney to London Gatwick. This route was flown once a week during the summer months and commenced on 28 April 1950 with G-AHXZ flying the first service. The route was quite well patronised, especially by holidaymakers, as Alderney had no direct boat service to England. Even so, it did not last very long and was abandoned at the end of the summer season of 1952. However it was notable in that it was BEA's first service into Gatwick, long before Gatwick became designated as London's second airport. BEA had no resident staff at Gatwick and an official was sent down from the London Air Terminal to oversee the Rapide's arrival and departure.

BEA maintained a small team in Alderney to handle the flights and staff the town office in St Anne. The two resident staff would usually divide their duties between the airport and town office although, at busy periods, the office in St Anne was closed, and both staff worked at the airport. In the early days the two staff were assisted at peak times by Sam Allen. Sam had been the loader and refueller at Alderney during the era of Channel Islands Airways and he was an elderly man even then. He joined the BEA team in 1947 but retired soon afterwards. He was probably the first ex-Channel Islands Airways staff member to benefit from a BEA pension. However he did come back to help out when required. Management of Alderney's staff, which was eventually increased to three, was the direct responsibility of the Station Superintendent in Guernsey, but the day-to-day running of Alderney was the job of the Official-in-Charge. The first BEA official to hold that post was Lionel Heyward, who was later promoted to Guernsey and eventually became a Duty Officer there. He was succeeded by Les Gibbins, but Freddie Farmer was the best-known BEA staff member to occupy the post.

Although his was a small station, Freddie Farmer found himself hosting not a few VIPs, including the Chairman of BEA, Lord Douglas, accompanied by the Duke of Gloucester, who visited Alderney in July 1952 aboard Rapide G-AKZB. The Governor of Guernsey also travelled to the island quite often since Alderney's affairs were under his jurisdiction and one of Freddie's duties was to stand ceremonially at the bottom of the Rapide's steps to salute him as he disembarked. Upon occasion, staff holidays or illness required BEA Alderney to borrow staff from Jersey or Guernsey. Staff were always keen for a period of duty on Alderney since it meant they were accommodated in a local guesthouse at BEA's expense. Doug Lo Bao, father of one of the authors, served his turn at managing the Alderney town office, while Dougie Garnham, from Jersey, had a spell in the traffic office at Alderney Airport. Dougie recalls that his jobs included driving the small bus to and from the airport to meet arrivals and departures, loading the baggage and tying down the freight. Whilst in Alderney he stayed at the Belle Vue Hotel which cost BEA £6 7s 6d for a week's half board.

Passengers travelling from Guernsey 'up' to Alderney (if you live in Guernsey, Alderney is always 'up') sometimes found their travelling companion to be a Guernsey policeman. In the 1950s, Alderney had no resident police, and a constable was detached from Guernsey for two weeks at a time. His duties can never have been very arduous, but the island did have one vice - sixteen pubs which all tended to ignore the laws on closing time. Most constables found it prudent to turn a blind eye to this lapse in law keeping, but one particularly zealous officer decided to enforce the 2230 closing time. As a result, several Alderney residents threw him into the harbour - or so it is alleged.

In the 1940s and early 1950s Alderney was not a well-known destination. On one occasion in 1948, a Mr Norman Davies decided he would like to visit the island. He visited his local branch of one of the UK's leading travel agents to enquire about services to the island only to be told that there was no such place and certainly no air service there. He found that quite amusing since a short while previously he had been working on the island - restoring the airfield which the Germans had destroyed at the end of the war.

Alderney was the focus of one problem for BEA. What type of aircraft could it find, suitable for the island's small airfield, that could succeed the obsolescent Rapide? One local staff member suggested that the short main runway should be fitted with arrestor wires similar to those used on aircraft carriers. Pionairs could be equipped with a hook that would enable the larger aircraft to use the airfield. Needless to say, his tongue-in-cheek suggestion was not taken up.

The obvious answer to Alderney's needs was the de Havilland Heron and, as early as August 1951, BEA had been loaned the prototype, G-ALZL, from de Havilland for a spell of duty on the Channel Islands routes. Although most of its time was spent operating from Jersey and Guernsey to Northolt and Southampton, the aircraft also visited Alderney and proved itself to be quite capable of flying fourteen passengers out of the airfield. However, it was not until 1955 that BEA finally ordered two Heron 2 aircraft to replace the Rapides on the Alderney services. Neither aircraft actually entered BEA service. In February and March 1956, BEA held talks with Jersey Airlines regarding Channel Islands routes. Jersey Airlines had begun as an air charter company in 1949 and scheduled services from both Jersey and Guernsey to Southampton had been launched on 16 June 1951. It had been able to do this through its designation as a BEA associate airline, permitted by the 1946 Civil Aviation Act and exercised with greater liberality by the newly elected Tory government. Official BEA reaction to the arrival of Jersey Airlines on these routes was one of disapproval but, in reality, the Corporation had not been greatly concerned as Jersey Airlines operated its three rotations on each route on only one day of the week. That day was Saturday when BEA was already hard pushed to cater for the demand for seats. Agreement was reached in 1956 whereby Jersey Airlines, in which BEA now had a 25% share, would give up its Southampton-Jersey service in return for BEA handing over the Guernsey-Southampton route, all services from Alderney and its services from Jersey and Guernsey to Dinard. From BEA's point of view this was an excellent arrangement since it meant it had a monopoly on the lucrative Jersey-Southampton route, and it enabled it to withdraw from Alderney, which had never been a highly profitable operation. The two Herons ordered by BEA, G-AORG and G-AORH, were delivered directly to Jersey Airlines for use on the Alderney flights.

BEA services to Alderney ceased on 20 April 1956, as did those from Guernsey to Southampton and Jersey and Guernsey to Dinard. The last day's flying from Alderney was conducted with Rapide G-AKZB, flown by Captain Stokoe. He flew two trips from Guernsey to Alderney and one from Alderney to Southampton. The last BEA departure from Alderney occurred at 1520 when G-AKZB departed as BE873 for Guernsey. A new job was found for Freddie Farmer as a Duty Officer at the Corporation's London Air Terminal. One can only imagine the shock he must have suffered at moving from the peace and tranquillity of Alderney to the hustle and bustle of central London. The other BEA station, which suffered from the route swap with Jersey Airlines, was Dinard. With the handing over to Jersey Airlines of the routes from Dinard to the islands, the BEA presence at Dinard was limited to the seasonal service from London. The airline retained a Station Superintendent there who, for many years, was Monsieur Storée. He was kept busy during the winter months looking after diversions from Jersey and Guernsey and also hosting training flights which made extensive use of Dinard's quiet airfield.

The ending of flights to Alderney and Dinard meant the need to maintain a Rapide based on Jersey had ceased. From 21 April, all BEA services to the Channel Islands were flown by Pionairs, Viscounts or Elizabethans. However, BEA's Jersey Engineering Base still overhauled the Rapides used on the Isles of Scilly service, so the aircraft continued to be a common sight in Jersey until 1964.

A great step forward occurred in 1956 with the introduction of the Viscount on some Jersey services. Initially, the type flew only from Heathrow at weekends but, as the airline's fleet of Viscounts grew, they became a more common sight on Jersey flights. From the beginning of April 1958, the Viscount began to night stop in Jersey, flying the late evening service from

Heathrow which departed at 1930, and the early morning return service the next day. During the summers of 1958 and 1959, the Viscounts also began to replace some Pionair flights on services from Jersey to Birmingham, Glasgow and Manchester. The introduction of the Viscount marked a new age in passenger comfort and speed and, generally, it was enthusiastically welcomed by the travelling public. But there are always some who prefer the old days. Tom Young, a BEA engineer, recalls travelling from Glasgow to Jersey on holiday with his wife shortly after the introduction of the Viscounts on that route. During the flight, the steward asked her if she was enjoying her flight, to which she replied 'Ach, I preferred the Dak!'

BEA was far from being able to retire its Pionairs from the Channel Islands network since Guernsey and Southampton still had grass runways making them unsuitable for Viscount operations. The Guernsey States had gradually concluded that it had to invest in a hard runway at Guernsey Airport if it was to attract the best air services, yet the cost of doing so was great and the island's government delayed for some time. Eventually a decision was taken in 1960, and a 4,800ft concrete runway was constructed together with an enlarged terminal building. During the terminal building alterations, temporary accommodation was provided in some huts behind the main hangar. These were far too small for the volume of traffic which passed through and they became saturated whenever delays occurred. The writer can remember seeing passengers sitting on the grass outside, because the huts were full, when fog had disrupted services one day in 1960. Guernsey's airport was always prone to fog and low cloud because it was on the highest part of the island.

The hard runway at Guernsey was formally opened on 1 August 1960 and BEA took part in the proceedings by sending a Viscount to the island. Viscount V701, G-AOFX, was positioned from Jersey at 0920 and remained on the ground for most of the day. It eventually departed at 1630 as BE721 to Gatwick in place of the scheduled Pionair. Initially, Viscount loads from Guernsey were restricted to 44 passengers because one end of the runway had not hardened enough to be used.

As BEA services to the islands developed, so did those of independent operators. For a time, the UK Government's restrictions meant that the independents had to operate as associate companies of BEA if they wished to operate a scheduled service. They often circumvented this restriction by flying charter services on a set timetable. Once regulations were relaxed, independent carriers rapidly expanded their operations to the islands, and to Jersey in particular. By the early 1960s, Jersey Airlines was a well-established local carrier using Heron, DC-3 and new Handley Page Dart Herald aircraft on routes primarily to the south of England and France. Jersey Airlines eventually became part of British United, and its successor airlines (BUIA, BIA and Air UK) continued to serve the islands until the late 1990s. Other companies, such as Channel Airways, Silver City, Dan-Air, Derby Airways, British Eagle, and BKS regularly flew into Jersey and some also served.Guernsey. A host of smaller, and often short-lived, carriers, such as Don Everall Aviation and Pegasus Airlines, frequently appeared at weekends. A Saturday at Jersey Airport in the early 1960s was a delight for aviation enthusiasts with comings and goings every few minutes, the more modern BEA Viscounts being contrasted with the older and more sedate Vikings and DC-3s. One of the highlights of a Saturday was the arrival of the British Eagle DC-6 from Heathrow. This service was a once-a-week event and, until the BEA Vanguard era, the DC-6 was the largest aircraft to regularly use the airport. DC-6s also visited from Sweden on Trans Air Sweden charters. Enthusiasts eagerly awaited the Trans Air Sweden movements, since sometimes the company sent a Curtiss C46 Commando instead of the DC-6.

BEA staff social activities were common in the closely-knit Channel Islands area. Inter-station matches in darts and football were popular and airline teams also participated in local

Rapide G-AGUF in BEA's initial livery at Jersey in 1947 or 1948. (British Airways Collection)

Rapide G-AHXZ is farewelled from a wet apron at Gatwick on the inaugural flight to Alderney. (British Airways Collection)

For one summer only, BEA Vanguards graced the Ronaldsway apron. G-APEM is pictured during June 1962. (Clive Dyball)

Cambrian Airways Viscount G-AOYJ awaits a load for the Isle of Man at Liverpool, November 1971. (Phil Lo Bao)

Viscounts first came to Guernsey in 1960, so visits by aircraft wearing the original Viscount colour scheme were rare. (Dave Bougourd)

Viscount V802 G-AOHJ arrives at Southampton in July 1971 operating BE3413 from Jersey. (Phil Lo Bao)

DC-3 G-AHCV on the apron at Jersey in BEA's original livery shortly after the demise of Channel Islands Airways.
(Phil Lo Bao Collection)

Pionair G-AGJV RMA John Forte *prepares to depart from Southampton Eastleigh en route for Jersey.*
(British Airways Collection)

For many years Guernsey Airport lacked a hard runway limiting BEA operations to Pionairs. Here G-AMGD is pictured about to board passengers. (Guernsey Press Co.)

Two BEA Rapides on the grass at Alderney. (Alderney Museum)

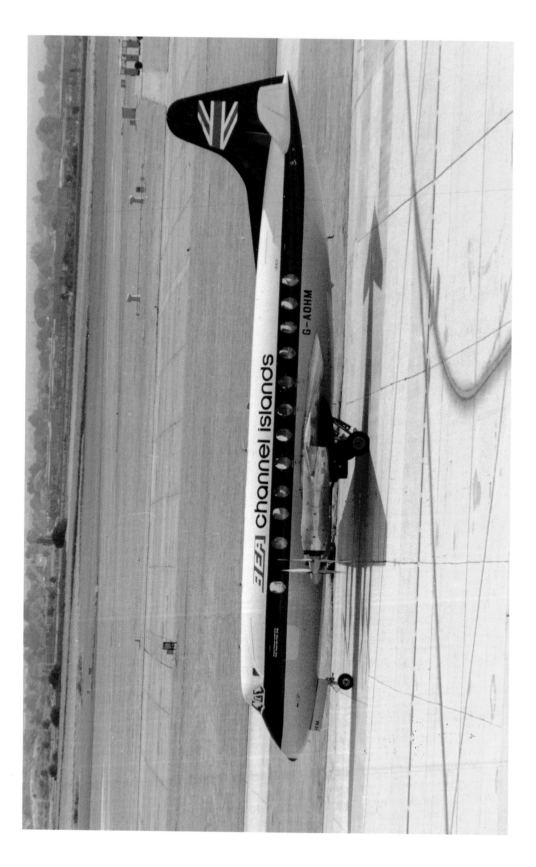

Viscount G-AOHM bears BEA Channel Islands titles.   (British Airways Collection)

Carrying BEA Scottish Airways titles, G-AOJE taxies at Eastleigh. (Phil Lo Bao)

Out with the old and in with the new, BEA Rapide G-AFRK shares the Alderney apron with its replacement, Jersey Airlines Heron G-ANSZ. (Alderney Museum)

BEA Helicopter Experimental Unit's WS55 G-AOCF displays Civil Defence titles at Southampton. (Ron Roberts)

BEA Helicopter Experimental Unit WS55 G-ANFH outside the BEA engineering hangar at Jersey. The helicopter was chartered to drop paper petals at the annual Battle of Flowers. (Phil Boots)

The first pressurised aircraft to serve Jersey in BEA service was the Elizabethan. G-ALZW is parked in front of the terminal at Jersey. (Phil Boots)

A wet winter morning in 1966 sees S61 G-ASNM arrive at Guernsey from Jersey with passengers connecting with the Viscount service to Heathrow. (Dave Bougourd)

Vanguards greatly increased the passenger capacity on the key route from Jersey to London. (Phil Lo Bao)

BEA Vikings were rare visitors to the Channel Islands but G-AMNJ RMA Lord Fisher, seen here at Prestwick, attended the official inauguration of Jersey's new runway in June 1952. (Aird Crooks)

Viscount V701 G-AMOO arriving at Guernsey. (Dave Bougourd)

Sikorsky S61 G-ASNM on the island of Sark while on an air ambulance flight in February 1966. (Guernsey Press Co.)

BEA Heralds appeared at Jersey only on peak summer Sunday afternoons. G-APWD is pictured loading baggage for its return to Glasgow. (Phil Boots)

BEA Merchantman aircraft regularly flew freight to the Channel Islands. G-APEM departs from Jersey in February 1971. (Phil Lo Bao)

56

Freshly painted in British Airways colours, Viscount V806 G-AOYR arrives at Jersey in 1974. (Phil Lo Bao)

Argosy aircraft replaced the Pionair Leopard freighters on Channel Islands freight services. G-APRN is pictured at Jersey. Note the jacks supporting the tail for loading. (Ian Law)

A very rare visitor to Southampton, Trident 2 G-AVFK on 30 September 1971. (Edward Clapham)

sports leagues. Upon occasion, this caused some difficulties. A certain Jersey-based First Officer, by the name of Hopkins, decided to form a Rugby team to play in the local league. He called it *The Windsocks*. The team members were mainly soccer players who had to be given a crash course in how to play rugby. In an early match, pilot Alan Voak was injured when he collided with an opponent. His lip was badly cut and several teeth were smashed. Alan was due on duty the next day and duly reported for work with a big plaster over his mouth. Ted Jordan, the local Flight Manager, had to let him fly due to a shortage of pilots caused by illness - and by rugby injuries. As he found it difficult to speak, it was agreed that he would leave all the radio communications and passenger announcements to his First Officer. Voak was ordered to board the aircraft well before the passengers and to stay on the flight deck during the turnaround. The Flight Manager then ordered that *The Windsocks* should not play again. Undeterred by his injury, Alan returned to playing soccer. He recalls that it was quite a common sight for the Jersey Duty Officer to come rushing down to the pitch to call him off to fly a service as a standby pilot. On more than one occasion, he flew with his football kit underneath his uniform.

On 9 June 1958, the formal opening of London Gatwick Airport took place. Gatwick was to be London's 'second airport', and BEA decided to transfer most of the London-Jersey and all of the London-Guernsey flights to Gatwick. A limited service from Jersey to Heathrow would continue to provide Channel Islands passengers with international connections. Flights to Heathrow were given the unusual flight prefix of 'BEL' to distinguish them from those bound for Gatwick. The new airport at Gatwick incorporated the latest airport design techniques and had a finger pier around which the aircraft parked. It also had its own railway station with fast electric trains linking it to London's Victoria Station. Gatwick Airport was opened by Queen Elizabeth and the first commercial flight to depart on 9 June was a BEA Pionair, G-ALXK, which operated a charter flight to Jersey. Flights from Gatwick to the Channel Islands were then maintained by a mixture of Viscounts and Pionairs and, for the first summer, there were up to seven flights a day to Guernsey and fourteen to Jersey.

BEA's hopes that Gatwick would boom as a Channel Islands terminal were soon dashed. Passengers perceived Heathrow as a better London terminal, given its international connections and good transport links, while Gatwick was seen as too far out of London and it certainly lacked international connections. BEA did try one or two international services from Gatwick - to Paris, Dinard, and Hanover via Bonn - but these were poorly supported by the travelling public. Guernsey's government was annoyed that the island was no longer linked to Heathrow, the world's premier airport, and it made its feelings known to BEA in no uncertain terms. History was to repeat itself in April 1998 when KLM uk transferred its Guernsey-Heathrow service to London Stansted, resulting in much protest from Guernsey. Given the unpopularity of Gatwick with island travellers, BEA eventually decided to return most of the Channel Islands services to Heathrow and this occurred in April 1963. A link was still kept to Gatwick, with a daily service from Guernsey, and up to twelve flights a week from Jersey. During the winter, a single daily service from Jersey via Guernsey was flown to Gatwick.

By the time the bulk of London services were returned to Heathrow they were being flown by Viscounts, Easter 1961 marking BEA's retirement of its Pionairs from the Channel Islands routes. The laying of the new runway at Guernsey meant that the Pionairs were now only needed for the Southampton route, and BEA decided that it could no longer justify keeping Pionairs in Jersey for that service only. Southampton was owned by the Ministry of Civil Aviation which had consistently refused to lay down a hard runway. So, with great reluctance, BEA decided to switch its south coast terminal to Bournemouth. Bournemouth's Hurn Airport was well equipped with a 6,000ft hard runway and an Instrument Landing System. The Corporation planned to transfer services across to Hurn on 1 April 1961, but problems with the provision of customs facilities at Southampton resulted in the transfer taking place a few days earlier, on 20 and 21 March. The final day of operations in Southampton was 20 March and, at 1720 that evening, Captain Gerry Draper taxied Pionair G-AHCX, operating BE754, from Southampton's terminal for the last time. Perhaps indicative of the passenger preference for Southampton, all 32 seats were filled. After take-off, Gerry Draper made a low pass over the airfield watched by BEA's staff.

Next day, the Pionairs began serving Hurn. However, on 1 April the Viscount replaced them and the first BEA scheduled Viscount flight from Jersey to Bournemouth landed at Hurn at 1430, G-ANHF operating flight BE8656. During the summer of 1961, twenty-three Viscount flights per week were scheduled to operate over the route. However, BEA soon found that Hurn was even less popular than Gatwick, and passenger numbers never reached predicted levels. This was partly because Hurn was too far to the west of the south coast catchment area, and partly because its ground transport links were very poor. In addition, Jersey Airlines began a Southampton-Jersey service with DC-3s and, later, Dart Heralds, which creamed off much of the traffic.

If Hurn was never very popular with Jersey-bound passengers, it did serve one useful purpose for BEA - as a diversionary airport for Heathrow. In the days before Autoland, fog could severely disrupt flights and Hurn had a good weather record. So, during the winter months, the airport was quite often used for Heathrow diversions and the small BEA team there was supplemented in the winter by additional staff from London to cope with these. On the record day for BEA diversions, Hurn handled no less than twenty-seven BEA aircraft in less than two hours. Duty Officer Peter Archer recalls that the airline only had three sets of passenger steps at Hurn, so passengers had to remain aboard their aircraft awaiting their turn to disembark which, in some instances, was a long wait - even resulting in questions being raised in the House of Commons.

The transfer from Southampton to Hurn had, as stated, removed the need for Jersey-based Pionairs and so the type was withdrawn. It appears that the last scheduled service was between Jersey and Guernsey on 31 March 1961, G-AGNK doing the honours. However, as the busy Easter season was approaching, G-AGNK remained in the Channel Islands to operate some extra flights on 3 and 4 April before finally setting off for the mainland. The type had served the Channel Islands well and had flown thousands of services to both islands since 1947, all without serious incident. There had only been two significant incidents involving Pionairs, both at Guernsey. The first occurred on 22 September 1953 when G-AGIZ undershot upon landing. The aircraft's undercarriage collapsed and it slithered to a halt on the soggiest part of the airfield. The second incident involved G-AMKE and happened on 2 August 1954. The Pionair approached the runway rather too low and hit the top of a bakery van which was travelling along the road near the threshold. The Pionair was virtually undamaged, but the bakery van was less fortunate and bread rolls were scattered across the road. The van driver, who undoubtedly had not anticipated a collision with an aircraft when he had set out that morning, received some injuries, but fortunately of a minor nature.

Overall, BEA's operations on the Channel Islands enjoyed a good safety record, there being neither fatalities nor serious injuries to either crew or passengers during the entire period of the airline's service to the islands. The only fatality involving BEA occurred at Southampton, which, like Dinard, came under the Channel Islands for BEA's management purposes. A BEA loader was killed when he walked into the tail rotor of a BEA Bristol 171 helicopter during the early 1950s. Although there were no serious accidents, a few more minor ones did occur, generally involving the collapse of part of an aircraft's undercarriage. An Elizabethan, G-ALZW, suffered the collapse of its right-hand main undercarriage when it landed at Jersey on 4 July 1956. On 17 September 1960 and on 26 November 1965, Viscounts suffered nose-wheel failures during landing at Jersey. The writer witnessed the sequence of events for the first incident. Viscount G-AOJC was landing on runway 09 and, as the nose-wheel touched the runway, there was a loud crack. The gear then gently collapsed, bringing the Viscount down on its nose. There was no fire and the passengers were quickly evacuated. G-AOJC was towed away by the engineers and temporary repairs were carried out to enable it to fly empty to Heathrow for more extensive attention. Flights in and out of Jersey were disrupted while the aircraft was cleared from the single runway. The local BKS representative did not endear himself to BEA's Senior Traffic Officer when he requested BEA pick up the bill for a meal he had been forced to provide for some of his own passengers who had been delayed because of the accident. The Senior Traffic Officer, who was well known for being forthright when required, sent him packing with the restaurant bill still in his hand.

The 1965 incident involved Viscount G-APEY. It was landing late one evening in a strong wind and suffered the same fate. On this occasion the cause of the incident was clear, the gusty wind having interfered with the Viscount's touchdown which was slightly nose first and quite hard. The First Officer on the flight was a Mr Keevey who had just returned from a period of sick leave. While the events were clearly not his fault, he was heard to mutter that he wished his doctor had signed him off for another couple of days.

As incomes increased during the 1960s, more money became available for holidays and the Channel Islands boomed. BEA was hard-pressed to meet the demand for seats at the height of the summer seasons and decided the time had come to introduce the larger Vickers Vanguard on some London-Jersey services. In preparation for this, G-APEF flew a proving flight to Jersey one miserable day in November 1963. Scheduled Vanguard services commenced in June 1964, initially with a singular Saturday service being flown by the type. As BEA's fleet of Tridents increased, there was a greater availability of Vanguards and gradually the number of Vanguard flights to Jersey grew. By the summer of 1970, many of the Heathrow services were flown by Vanguards, and the type also appeared on some of the services to Birmingham, Gatwick and Manchester. Even during the quieter winter period, the Vanguard could still be seen at Jersey on one of the daily services to London. This flight departed from Jersey at 1700, the Vanguard proving ideal for the service, not only because passenger traffic at that time of the day was high, but also it coincided with the Jersey Post Office's dispatch of mail to the UK. The Vanguard, with its huge under-floor cargo holds, could accommodate all the mail the Post Office provided.

Use of the large Vanguard did sometimes result in a few amusing incidents. On one occasion, a captain found that his aircraft appeared to lift off the Jersey runway rather sooner than he had calculated. When he arrived at Heathrow, the reason became clear. The baggage holds were empty. The cases for the flight were still on the back of a lorry at Jersey Airport. Needless to say, there were more than a few red faces as a result. Missing baggage was always a hazard of travel as one young couple found when they arrived on Jersey. Their suitcase had been mislaid and they summoned the Duty Officer to make their complaint. He was startled to hear that the young man was going to hold him personally responsible if his wife became pregnant - because her supply of contraceptive pills was in the lost suitcase. On another occasion, the departure of a Vanguard V953 flight to Heathrow was announced on the public address system and one passenger proceeded to the gate. He clearly wondered where the other passengers were and asked the clerk. He was amazed to be told that he was the only passenger on the 139-seater aircraft. He had the undivided attention of four cabin staff throughout his flight. One day, a local doctor met Duty Officer Dougie Garnham on the beach at St Ouens and, as they chatted, he told Dougie about the problems he was having in sending one of his patients to the mainland for hospital treatment. The patient required to travel on a stretcher and none of the airlines seemed to have space to accommodate it. Doug then borrowed the beach lifeguard's phone and contacted the airport where he arranged with Operations Officer, Basil Wellman, to have some seats removed from a Vanguard flight departing later that day. The stretcher was accommodated and the patient was able to reach hospital with unanticipated rapidity.

The operation of air ambulance flights was not uncommon on the Channel Island routes. Usually patients were carried on scheduled services either in a normal seat or on a stretcher, which was accommodated by removing a couple of rows of passenger seats on one side of the cabin. Occasionally, an emergency would result in the provision of an aircraft for the sole use of a patient. One such example took place on 22 January 1956, when a baby on Guernsey was diagnosed as suffering from polio. Station Superintendent Eddie West was asked by the Guernsey authorities to make an aircraft available to fly the patient to Southampton as soon as possible. BEA responded by sending a Rapide from Jersey to Guernsey, flown by the Chief Pilot for the Channel Islands, Captain Ted Jordan. Three seats were removed from the aircraft and the baby was accommodated on a stretcher with an oxygen tent. Because of the seriousness of the situation, Captain Jordan was granted permission to fly onwards from Southampton to Portsmouth Airport as the child was to be admitted to the infectious diseases unit at the hospital there. Flying onwards from Southampton to Portsmouth saved a one-hour road journey and, in probability, marked the only visit of a BEA aircraft to Portsmouth.

It was a few years before Guernsey was to witness the arrival of a Vanguard. With its shorter runway and lower load-bearing strength, it was not an ideal airport for this large aircraft. However, on 18 July 1967, Captain Maclannahan flew G-APEA to Guernsey's airport on a proving flight from London. The Vanguard then made occasional appearances, usually when bad weather had created a backlog of passengers. The Vanguard could carry the equivalent of two Viscount payloads. Only in the summer of 1971, did the aircraft operate scheduled services to Guernsey, and then only a once weekly Wednesday rotation. The Guernsey authorities actually limited the total number of Vanguard landings to 120 annually because of the runway's lower load-bearing capacity. Most of this allocation was given to the freighter version of the Vanguard, the Merchantman, which began serving Guernsey from 5 April 1970, G-APEK flying the first of these services.

One tremendous advantage which air travel had over its sea competition was that it avoided the problems of seasickness. BEA soon found that holidaymakers who arrived by steamer, and who had experienced an unpleasantly rough crossing, often decided to return by air. To cash in on this tendency, in 1953 it prudently moved its Jersey town office to Caledonia Place near the harbour. The Guernsey office was already in a similar position close to the harbour. In both offices a sign urged visitors to 'Fly BEA in exchange for your boat ticket' - and hundreds of people did so. However, sometimes it was personnel of the British Rail shipping service who had the last laugh. When fog closed the airports at Guernsey and Jersey, passengers were often transferred from air to sea. The summer of 1954 was particularly bad for fog. The two worst weekends were those of 17/18 and 24/25 July, fog shrouding both islands' airfields for much of the time and causing havoc to air services. On Saturday 17 July, no flights could land or take off at Jersey from 1700 until 2300. When the weather did improve, BEA mounted an all-out effort to move the backlog of passengers, resulting in sustained aircraft movements until 0600 the following day.

The following weekend it was the turn of Guernsey to be badly hit by fog. Several flights diverted to Jersey on the Saturday, but then Jersey too fell victim to the weather. At one point, during the early evening, there were no less than ten BEA aircraft lined up on the taxiway waiting for the fog to lift sufficiently to permit take-off. Four succeeded, but the other six had to return to the terminal. The combination of diverted Guernsey flights, departing Jersey passengers, and still more passengers checking in for flights later that evening, resulted in facilities reaching saturation point. Some passengers were taken by coach to St Helier for a meal because the airport restaurant had run out of food. Ultimately, 750 passengers had to spend that night sleeping at the airport. Next day, flying resumed, BEA making use of several Elizabethans to help clear the backlog. Guernsey continued to be affected by fog and two Pionairs again diverted to Jersey. It was the turn of these passengers to spend an uncomfortable night on the floor at Jersey Airport, as all local hotels were full. They were eventually flown to Guernsey the following day. There were indications that fog would create further problems during the next weekend, but in the end delays of only two hours occurred. Through the course of those three weekends, BEA handled in excess of 20,000 passengers on its Channel Islands services.

Whenever fog enveloped the Channel Island airfields, the staff were always willing to work as long as required in order to complete the day's flying programme even if that meant working late into the night. Pilots at mainland stations would keenly watch the half-hourly Jersey and Guernsey weather reports for signs of improvement, but UK traffic staff had their own more informal means, known as 'Freddie Miller actuals', of obtaining weather details. Freddie Miller was the Senior Operations Officer for the Channel Islands based in Jersey. He would receive telephone enquiries about the weather from the traffic staff at mainland airports, would look out of the Operations Office window across the apron, and report back with his observations. This unofficial weather information helped alert traffic staff to weather improvements so that they could have their passengers on board the delayed aircraft ready for an immediate take-off as soon as the official weather report verified Freddie's advance information, indicating that the situation had improved.

Bad weather sometimes caused a little ill feeling between the staff in Guernsey and the Operations Office in Jersey. Because Guernsey's airfield was at a higher elevation than Jersey's, it was usually first to be hit by bad weather and, quite often, flights en route to Guernsey diverted to Jersey to await an improvement. If the Jersey weather then deteriorated, preventing any flights from landing, Freddie Miller and his staff would use the aircraft diverted from Guernsey to operate outbound services from Jersey. As a result, when the Guernsey weather cleared, the passengers often had to wait in Jersey for the aircraft to return before it could take them on to Guernsey. Guernsey staff often complained about Jersey 'pinching their aircraft' but, in reality, the operations staff was simply trying to do what was most expedient to dispatch at least some passengers to their destinations.

During the early days, BEA pilots based in the Channel Islands developed their own, rather unorthodox, ways of beating the weather. One of the most experienced local pilots was Bill Caldwell who had flown for Channel Islands Airways before World War Two. His bad weather approach procedure at Jersey involved flying low over the sea towards the coast at St Ouens Bay. When he passed the El Tico beach café, he knew that the runway lay dead ahead at the top of the cliff and so he would increase his altitude. As he reached the top of the cliff he then used a tree on his right to give him his final approach line. This worked well for many years, but only until one day in 1951 when, as he employed this procedure, he found that the tree had been cut down. John Hobbs, who progressed to commands of the Vickers Viscount, Hawker Siddeley Trident, and Lockheed L1011 TriStar, was Caldwell's second officer on that occasion. He recalls that Bill Caldwell was none too pleased that 'his tree' had been cut down. As technology improved and regulations increased, such unofficial approach procedures gradually diminished out, but never entirely. The writer remembers one day, in the early 1970s, flying from Campbeltown to Islay in a BEA Viscount when such unofficial procedures were employed. The Viscount flew over the sea at a level which appeared significantly below 500 feet and, having picked up the coast of Islay, it descended further and followed the island's coast road until the airport appeared out of the gloom. A tight circuit and a perfect landing followed.

The BEA stations on Jersey and Guernsey earned extra revenue handling the services of several other airlines. Chief among these was the BEA associate company Cambrian Airways which was partly owned by BEA. Cambrian operated flights to Jersey from Cardiff, Bristol, Liverpool and, in some summers, from Swansea. Guernsey had links with Cardiff and Bristol. By the mid-1960s the airline was flying a mixture of ex-BEA Pionair and Viscount aircraft on these services and it could have as many as eight or nine departures from Jersey on peak season Saturdays. Meanwhile, the traffic unit at Bournemouth, and then Southampton, handled Cambrian Airways services which called en route from Cardiff and Bristol to Paris. Additionally, BEA Jersey handled the Aer Lingus services from Dublin which operated at a more modest frequency of once or twice a week.

At times, BEA also handled other airlines. In the early 1960s, Dan-Air contracted BEA to handle its services from Plymouth and Gatwick. BEA's Jersey staff were never too keen on handling Dan-Air since their flights always seemed to be late or not turn up at all, leaving the BEA staff to placate angry passengers. Consequently, not too many tears were shed when Dan-Air took its handling contract to Jersey Airlines. By the late 1960s, BEA was handling the flights of BKS at Jersey and Guernsey. BKS, which later became Northeast Airlines and part of British Airways, flew Viscounts from Leeds and Newcastle. The mighty Bristol Britannia aircraft occasionally operated Newcastle services.

The Corporation's staff was sometimes called upon to handle ad hoc charter flights. In the early 1960s, Pan American World Airways was an occasional visitor to Jersey with its Douglas DC-7 freighters. These aircraft appeared once or twice a year to convey Jersey cattle to the USA and flew out to New York via Shannon. The embarking of the cattle was a major task for BEA's loaders who had to construct a special ramp to reach the DC-7's cargo door. On other occasions, Air France Lockheed Super Constellation and Douglas DC-4 aircraft were handled at Jersey, while BEA Southampton handled such aircraft as a KLM Lockheed Electra and a Sabena Douglas DC-6. Southampton also handled quite a large number of Royal Flights because of the close proximity of Lord Louis Mountbatten's home at Romsey. One of the ambitions of those working there was to get a look inside a Queen's Flight Andover, but despite persistent efforts they never succeeded. The closest anyone managed was when the BEA Station Superintendent, Doug Lo Bao, was permitted to the top of the steps for a look inside, but the more lowly got no further than the bottom of the steps! Even Ernie Alvis, the BEA Station Engineer, never saw the flight deck, all technical documents being signed on the apron by one of the crew. Nat Somers, who became the owner of Southampton Airport, used to instruct his staff that Royal Flights should not be charged landing or parking fees, until he one day discovered that BEA were charging the Royal Flight for aircraft handling. From that day forth, he charged them too. The arrival of a Queen's Flight Andover always caused amusement because, as soon as the aircraft had come to a halt, an aircraftsman would run down the steps and place the propellers in a pre-ordained position and then polish the aircraft.

In 1965, the Jersey authorities decided the time had come to resurface the runway at St Peters. As this work could only be carried out during daytime, it became necessary to severely curtail operations. The winter months of November to February were chosen, as this was the time of year with the lowest aircraft activity, and the airport was to close from 0900 until 1700. BEA, and the other airlines flying from Jersey, had to reschedule their flights to fit in with these timings. However, BEA's Station Superintendent, Eddie West, believed that a midday link with

London should somehow be retained. The ideal solution seemed to be in the use of a helicopter to ferry passengers to Guernsey where they could be flown on to London in a Viscount. Passengers travelling to Jersey could then arrive via Guernsey also using the helicopter. BEA had operated helicopters for many years and in 1964 introduced the 28-passenger Sikorsky S61 to the Penzance-Isle of Scilly route. The route only required one S61, but the airline had two of the type. Consequently it was agreed with Jock Cameron, BEA Helicopters Managing Director, that the second S61 would be based in Jersey for the winter to operate the midday link. There was also talk of using the helicopter to fly the morning papers and mail from Jersey to Guernsey to save the British United newspaper plane from calling at Guernsey, however that did not materialise.

Apart from the busy Christmas period, when the runway was open all day, the helicopter made two, and sometimes three, trips between the two islands to allow the midday link with London to be maintained. During its time in the Channel Islands, the S61 flew 4,306 passengers between the two islands. Most did travel, as intended, to or from London, but the novelty of experiencing a helicopter ride also produced a fair number of day-trippers from Jersey. Sometimes the runway work at Jersey was not quite complete by 1700 and the Viscount was either delayed on the ground at Guernsey or had to hold overhead at Jersey while the various contractors' vehicles completed their day's work and were moved off the runway.

Sikorsky S61, G-ASNM, was used for the helicopter flights and, in addition to its passenger duties, it undertook crew training. On at least one of the crew training flights it made a visit to Alderney, being the first BEA aircraft to do so since the Rapides had been withdrawn in 1956. It also paid one visit to Sark. Sark does not allow motor cars, let alone aeroplanes, but the Dame of Sark gave special permission for the helicopter to land on the island one February Sunday in 1966. The objective was the evacuation of a woman who had become seriously ill and the local doctor wished to have her transferred to the Princess Elizabeth Hospital in Guernsey. The transfers were usually made by a fast ambulance launch called the *Flying Christine*. However the vessel was not available that morning, resulting in a call to the BEA Duty Officer in Guernsey to see if the S61 could be made available. He contacted Operations in Jersey who managed to track down Captain Cameron who was taking his turn as duty captain for the helicopter in Jersey. Jock Cameron was more than willing to use G-ASNM as an air ambulance and the helicopter flew to Guernsey, where it collected several BEA officials and some ambulance personnel. After a flight of just a few minutes, the helicopter alighted in one of Sark's larger fields. The patient was embarked and the helicopter lifted off for Guernsey with the Sark Volunteer Fire Brigade on standby. The fire crew probably questioned the wisdom of being in the field, however, as it had recently been used to graze cattle. When the helicopter lifted off, so did several dozen cowpats.

The maintenance needs of the S61 were catered for by one of BEA Helicopters' engineers on detachment from Gatwick. One day, this almost led to the grounding of the helicopter. The engineer was undertaking some minor work on one of the helicopter's engines prior to a service to Guernsey. He accidentally slipped off the gantry and fell to the ground knocking himself unconscious. An ambulance was summoned and, company legend has it, a very worried captain could be seen in the back of the ambulance, pen and technical log in hand, imploring the engineer to wake up and sign, since only he could authorise the helicopter as fit for service. Fortunately he revived and the helicopter departed on time.

The visit of the S61 was not the only time that a BEA helicopter came to Jersey. Each year, Jersey celebrates a *Battle of Flowers* when floral decorated floats are paraded and then torn to pieces by the crowds. Many people felt that the destruction of the floats was a great shame and the idea of dropping paper flower petals from a helicopter was suggested as an alternative. The

Battle of Flowers organisers thought this was a good idea and, for the 1965 event, a BEA WS55 helicopter was chartered to drop the paper petals. The aircraft used was G-ANFH and, in addition to its role of petal dropping, it undertook a small number of pleasure flights from Jersey Airport for £5 a time. In the summer of 1966, S61 G-ASNM visited Jersey for the same purpose, but that was the last time a BEA helicopter was used because of the high charter cost.

In April 1966, BEA resumed services from Southampton. The airfield had been bought by Nat Somers, leading to the construction of a 5,500-ft. concrete runway. This made it suitable for Viscount operations and BEA withdrew from Hurn on 31 March, re-commencing services from Southampton to Jersey the next day. The first BEA Viscount to operate to Southampton was G-AOYO. Flights to Southampton had always been popular and BEA soon found the travelling public was using the route in larger numbers than had been anticipated, resulting in many supplementary services being added that summer. All Southampton-Jersey services were flown by Viscounts, there being only two recorded visits by a BEA Vanguard to Southampton. The first occurred in January 1969 when G-APEG operated a charter for Cunard from Liverpool in connection with the inaugural sailing of the liner, *Queen Elizabeth 2*. The second visit took place one day early in January 1973 when G-APEH diverted to Southampton due to fog at Heathrow. The aircraft was on a scheduled service from Belfast at the time. Soon after landing, Southampton too was closed by fog, grounding the Vanguard there overnight. There was the possibility of using it that morning to operate a trip to Jersey to clear a backlog of passengers from the previous day, but London Operations overruled this proposal and the aircraft flew empty to Heathrow.

As the runway at Southampton was a little shorter than that at Hurn, BEA did not make extensive use of the airport for diversions from Heathrow. Normally it was only used by Viscounts from the Channel Islands. Even so, this could make it quite a busy station. In January 1971, a strike by BEA engineers at Heathrow meant that no services could operate to or from London, so BEA sent its Jersey and Guernsey-Heathrow services to Southampton, G-AOHT flying from Guernsey and G-AOHH, G-AOYN and G-AOJB from Jersey. This was the first time such an operation had taken place and it proved so successful that, on future occasions when BEA and British Airways found they could not operate services from the Channel Islands into Heathrow, Southampton was used. The airline even gave the name 'Operation Eastleigh' to these activities, Eastleigh being the name of Southampton's airport. The most intensive 'Operation Eastleigh' took place after BEA had become part of British Airways. Due to industrial action at Heathrow, all Jersey and Guernsey services were re-routed to Southampton between 31 May and 4 June 1975. During that time, the small team under Station Superintendent Doug Lo Bao handled no less than 53 diversions in addition to their regularly scheduled movements. Extra traffic, baggage loading and engineering staff were drafted in from Heathrow to help.

Generally, life at Southampton was much quieter, with two and sometimes three daily services to Jersey during the summer and thirteen flights a week during the winter. The airline also handled the flights of Cambrian Airways, which operated a daily Pionair service to Paris Le Bourget. When the Pionairs were withdrawn in 1968, Cambrian continued the route with a thrice-weekly Viscount service which, in time, was further upgraded to a BAC 1-11 jet. Southampton also played host to the occasional BAC Super 1-11 or Hawker Siddeley Trident 2. The first visit of a Trident 2 occurred on 30 September 1971 when G-AVFK under the command of Captain George Stone brought Southampton Football Club back from a European match in Bilbao. The team had travelled out in Viscount G-AOHK, but the aircraft had become unserviceable at Bilbao. Despite the efforts of the BEA engineer, Ken Cutler, who travelled with the aircrew, it could not be repaired without additional equipment from London, resulting in the dispatch of the Trident to bring the team home. BEA's London Operations decided that the Trident should land at Hurn, but representations from Doug Lo Bao resulted in a change of mind and, at approximately 2000, the aircraft landed at Southampton. It departed empty for Heathrow 45 minutes later. A local resident telephoned Air Traffic to complain about the noise the Trident made when it took off. The writer took the call while looking out of the window at the Trident which was still parked at Stand 3. The caller had actually heard an HS 125 executive jet departing and jumped to the wrong conclusion. Southampton was not the first of the Channel Islands stations to handle a Trident. In July 1967, Trident 1 G-ARPB paid a visit to Jersey, although not on a passenger service. The first Super 1-11 to arrive at Southampton was G-AVMU which arrived on 15 January 1972 operating a football charter from Manchester. It was accompanied by Viscount, G-AOHN, which was chartered by a BEA captain to bring his friends to watch Manchester United play Southampton. Who said that aircrew were underpaid?

BEA's activities in the Channel Islands were highly profitable during the summer months, but winter presented a different story. With few holidaymakers, loads were always much lower and, even although some routes were not flown in the winter and services on the remainder were trimmed to suit the lower level of demand, costs remained high. This was a problem encountered on all the island routes which had significant tourist traffic and were served by the Corporation. Consequently, whenever BEA's overall profitability suffered, it was normal to take a close look at the Channel Islands routes to consider what economies could be made. For much of the 1950s and 1960s the general profitability of BEA was high, thanks to the careful management of Lord Douglas and Anthony Milward. However things were not so rosy in 1968 and 1969. As a result, economies followed from which the Channel Islands were not exempted. What was unusual was the implementation of economies in the summer season, an indication of the seriousness of the situation. As far as the Channel Islands network was concerned, some seasonal routes, such as Belfast-Jersey, did not operate, while other routes saw a reduction of frequencies. There was talk of giving up the Southampton route and, although this did not happen, frequencies were cut to a single daily rotation. The most drastic measure taken was the abandonment of inter-island services between Jersey and Guernsey. BEA had flown this route continually since 1947. In the Rapide days, as many as 95 flights a week had operated although, in the Viscount era, services took place two or three times daily. The last scheduled inter-island BEA service operated on 31 March 1969.

The impetus to give up the route came about because of the existence of a new airline, Alderney-based Aurigny Air Services. Aurigny had taken over the Guernsey and Southampton to Alderney routes flown by the de Havilland Herons of Morton Air Services, and now wished to introduce a high frequency walk-on service between Jersey and Guernsey. The use of a 71-passenger Viscount on the short service was highly uneconomic and BEA was glad to be able to withdraw. Aurigny went on to establish itself as a major part of the Channel Islands aviation scene and now operates inter-island services between all three islands, as well as flights to Amsterdam, Dinard, London Stansted, Manchester and Southampton. Its fleet consists of the three-engined Britten-Norman Trislander as well as several Saab 340 and Short 360 aircraft.

By the mid-1960s, BEA was considering what type of aircraft it could use to replace the Viscounts on the Channel Islands routes. As far as Jersey was concerned, the BAC 1-11 500 series, which BEA called the Super 1-11, was a candidate. However the economics of operating a pure jet on the short routes were not ideal. A further problem was that Guernsey's runway was really too short for operations by fully-loaded Super 1-11s while the Guernsey States were not keen on jet aircraft because of noise levels. Even so, in November 1966 BEA placed an order for eighteen Super 1-11s, with options for a further six. It was these six which would have been used on the Channel Islands routes, but the options were not exercised and the Viscounts soldiered on until the 1980s.

The economy drive of the late 1960s reminded everyone involved how vulnerable Channel Island services were because of their seasonal nature and it was hardly surprising that, when British Airways was looking for radical economies prior to privatisation, the spotlight again fell on the islands. But more of that later.

One activity in which BEA had been engaged since 1947, and which it did not give up in the late 1960s, was the carriage of freight to and from the islands. In 1947, the Corporation operated a dedicated DC-3 freighter from Northolt to Jersey via Guernsey. It departed from Northolt at 0520 and, after a brief stop in Guernsey, arrived in Jersey at 0720. This flight was used to carry mail and newspapers to the islands although the occasional passenger was also carried. The flight continued until April 1949 when it was dropped as an economy measure. Even so, on odd occasions BEA continued to fly newspapers to the islands. This generally occurred on Christmas Day. Today, most airline services do not operate on 25 December, but for much of the 1940s and 1950s BEA did fly a single service from London to the islands carrying newspapers and any passengers who wished to travel. On 25 December 1955, Ted Jordan flew a Rapide from London to Jersey with newspapers and then continued to Alderney. As Channel Islands Flight Manager, Ted believed he should be the unfortunate pilot to do the trip rather than one of his subordinates. Once newspapers ceased publication on Christmas Day, this unusual service also ceased.

In 1961, the airline decided to re-introduce a dedicated freighter service and began to fly routes from Jersey to Heathrow and Southampton using the Pionair Leopard. The Leopard was a Pionair which retained the larger double doors of the DC-3 and without built-in airstairs. The freighter was well supported by Jersey growers who used the speedy service to deliver fresh flowers to markets on the mainland.

Following the success of this service, BEA decided to upgrade the aircraft type and, in April 1962, the Leopard was replaced by the new purpose-built, four-engined Armstrong Whitworth Argosy. By this time, the twice-weekly Southampton freighter had ceased and the Argosy therefore only operated the Heathrow-Jersey route. The Argosy had large doors at each end of its fuselage. This considerably enhanced its turnaround time by allowing freight to be simultaneously unloaded through one door and loaded through the other. The floor was fitted with a system of rollers in order that the freight could be placed on pallets and pushed along to the correct spot. This made turnarounds much easier and saved the laborious task of loading items manually as had been the case with the Leopards. For the crews, life was much improved, the aircraft being fully pressurised and having facilities for heating food – but not quite as grand as on BOAC's freighter aircraft which still carried a steward to prepare and serve the pilots' meals!

BEA Jersey was supplied with two purpose-built lorries for the loading and unloading of the Argosy with the idea that pallets could then be taken directly to the customer. This caused a few problems in Jersey given the narrowness of some of the roads. On one occasion, just after the vehicles had arrived, one of them was taking some freight to the Channel Television transmitter at the north of the island. The entrance to the lane leading to the transmitter was very narrow and the driver managed to demolish part of the entrance as he tried in vain to swing the large lorry around the tight corner. These problems were repeated on Guernsey from May 1963 when it too began to handle regular Argosy flights. The first of the type to visit Guernsey was G-AOZZ. From then until 1970 there were usually two Argosy flights a week to each island, one flight calling at both Jersey and Guernsey and the other being direct.

In 1970, BEA withdrew its Argosy fleet from service and the last scheduled cargo flight by the type took place on 30 April with a round trip between Heathrow and Jersey. Although the Argosy had been retired, freighter services, now flown by the Vickers Merchantman, continued to both islands. The Merchantman was a cargo conversion of the Vanguard and had a large freight door installed in the forward left-hand side of the fuselage, a strengthened floor and a roller system for moving pallets.

In 1971, BEA's organisational structure was radically changed. The Chairman, Henry Marking, was a keen advocate of the 'profit centre' concept and the airline was broken up into small units each responsible for its economic performance. He established several divisions, one of which was the Channel Islands Airways Division. This division was to be responsible for all BEA services from Jersey, Guernsey, Southampton and Birmingham. The inclusion of Birmingham may seem rather strange but Birmingham's route network was not yet considered large enough to warrant a division in its own right and as it too operated Viscounts it was considered compatible with the Channel Islands. Ian Scott Hill became the Director of BEA Channel Islands Airways Division and some Viscounts began to appear with *Channel Islands* painted on their upper fuselage. The Division was allocated twelve Viscounts, five of which would operate from Birmingham, four from Jersey and one from Guernsey. Of the other two, one would be on charter to Gibraltar Airways to operate the service from Gibraltar to Tangier and the other would provide the flexibility required of ongoing fleet maintenance programmes.

Alongside the Channel Islands Division, other divisions included BEA Mainline Division, which operated the airline's routes from Heathrow, the Super 1-11 Division, which flew the BAC 1-11 500 aircraft on services from Manchester and West Berlin, and BEA Scottish Airways Division which flew the Scottish internal routes. The Scottish Division mainly operated Viscounts and they had the title *Scottish Airways* painted on the upper fuselage. In order to allow operational flexibility, Viscounts from the Channel Islands Division often appeared in Scotland, and Scottish Airways' aircraft appeared in the Channel Islands. The writer, one day in August 1971, remembers seeing two Channel Islands Division Viscounts on the apron at Sumburgh, the most northerly point on the Scottish Division network. The appearance of a Scottish Airways Division Viscount could also cause some confusion at Southampton. On some days BEA had an afternoon service to Jersey which departed at about the same time as the British Caledonian flight to Glasgow. On more than one occasion, staff had to stop passengers booked on the Glasgow service from boarding the Viscount because it said *Scottish Airways* on it and Scotland was where they wanted to go. As far as can be recalled, no passenger ever actually joined the wrong aircraft. However, one afternoon a passenger turned up at the BEA Southampton check-in desk, having just arrived on the flight from Jersey, to ask what time the flight continued to Dublin. He had somehow managed to slip through the net and boarded the wrong aircraft at Jersey. He was duly sent off to Heathrow in a taxi to catch an Aer Lingus flight to his destination.

Setting up the profit centres was good for staff morale as they identified with a smaller unit more effectively than with BEA as a whole. It also gave each division more autonomy to run its own affairs. In the case of the Channel Islands Division, this was soon evident with the launching of the first new route for many years. In May 1972, BEA Channel Islands opened a Jersey to Amsterdam service, initially on a once weekly basis using a Viscount. The route was seasonal in nature but the following summer its success prompted the introduction of a further service, this time from Guernsey to Amsterdam. The Guernsey service originated in Jersey giving Jersey two flights a week to Amsterdam. It had been many years since BEA had operated a European service from the Channel Islands and one or two people pointed out that, at last, British European Airways was being true to its name since it actually now did fly to Europe.

By 1972, the process of merging BEA, BOAC and their associate companies into British

Airways was underway. A major step towards this was implemented with the combining of the Channel Islands and Scottish Divisions, together with Cambrian Airways and Northeast Airways, into British Air Services (BAS). In effect, BAS became responsible for all internal flights within the British Isles and also those international routes operated by its constituent parts. However, BAS was merely an interim arrangement. On 1 September 1973, BAS was renamed British Airways Regional and it continued to fly the BEA Channel Islands services much as before. Finally, on 31 March 1974, BEA formally ceased to exist.

BEA left behind a comprehensive network of Channel Islands routes flown by both Viscounts and Vanguards. The airline had achieved much over the twenty-seven years it had served the islands and had played an important role in the development of their tourist industries. Following the formal arrival of British Airways, little changed for some time. The Vanguards were gradually phased out and the Viscounts almost ruled supreme once again except for some flights to Jersey from Heathrow operated by Trident 1Es, inherited from Northeast Airlines, and some from Manchester using Super 1-11s. On one occasion, the staff at Jersey even handled a Lockheed TriStar which was used to clear a backlog of passengers caused by bad weather. Guernsey retained an all-Viscount service as its runway was not long enough for these other aircraft.

However things changed dramatically at the end of March 1980. With its eye towards privatisation, British Airways was seeking to put its financial house in order and embarked upon a major programme of cost cutting. Once again, the seasonal nature of the Channel Islands routes meant that they were an obvious target for the accountant's axe. The axe fell much more severely than anyone thought possible. On 31 March 1980, all British Airways services from the Channel Islands, with the exception of Jersey to Heathrow and Manchester, ceased. This meant that British Airways no longer served either Guernsey or Southampton. A gloomy final day for these stations was made even worse by dismal weather. Low cloud blotted out the airports at Guernsey and Jersey for much of the day, meaning that the final British Airways service from Guernsey did not actually take place until the next day. G-AOYJ flew the last service into Guernsey on 1 April, a round trip from Heathrow.

At Southampton, Viscount G-APEX had arrived from Jersey as flight BA5181 at 0845 and was unable to leave until 1545. It was expected that passengers for the final Jersey service in the evening would be severely delayed while G-APEX endeavoured to catch up with the backlog caused by the weather. Therefore, London Operations decided to send Viscount G-AOYG from Heathrow to Southampton to operate the evening Jersey service. It arrived as BA9035 from Heathrow at 1730. Jersey's weather again deteriorated and it was not until 1840 that the final departure became airborne as BA5185. There were still passengers on Jersey with bookings for the evening Jersey-Southampton service and they eventually arrived at Southampton at 1945 on board G-AOYN. By the time G-AOYN landed at Southampton, a large lorry from British Airways Cargo had arrived from Heathrow to collect equipment and this final flight was handled with much of the airline's stationery, furniture, and other bits and pieces already removed. The local staff of Air UK had to be co-opted to assist with the turnaround.

History, however, has a habit of repeating itself and today British Airways is again much in evidence at Jersey, Guernsey and Southampton - although often in the form of one of its subsidiary companies such as British Regional Airlines, Brymon Airways and CityFlyer Express. British Airways and its partners now operate an extensive network of services from Jersey and Southampton and a more limited programme to Guernsey, although Heathrow is again absent from the equation, London services now being operated by CityFlyer Express from Gatwick. However the extensive regional network operated by British Regional Airlines and Brymon

Airways means that the Channel Islands are linked to other parts of the UK which, in 2001, included Bristol, Cardiff, Edinburgh, Glasgow, Manchester, Newcastle, Plymouth and Southampton. Additionally, Brymon Airways operates a service from Jersey to Paris Charles de Gaulle.

Services to the Channel Islands have also been provided by a whole host of independent carriers during the last fifty years. It is not the purpose of this book to detail those, but some very famous names have been involved. Jersey Airlines (and its successors, British United Island Airways, British Island Airways, and Air UK), Silver City, British Eagle, Channel Airways, Dan-Air, and British Caledonian are just a few of the post-World War Two airlines which have been synonymous with air travel to the islands at different times. British Midland Airways, which began life as Derby Aviation, still serves the islands, as does British European, the antecedents of which are Jersey European Airways and Intra Airways - and which has no connection with the state airline which is the focus of this study. Aurigny Airways has quietly grown in stature over three decades to almost national status in the Channel Islands. Patterns have not however greatly changed during half a century for, while routes to Jersey and Guernsey have been breadwinners for many companies during summer operations, the independents have been equally vulnerable to the rapid decline in traffic which remains a feature of the winter months.

BEA's 'red square' logo was officially replaced in 1968, but repainting of an airline's fleet is not accomplished overnight. The BEA Channels Islands *titles carried by Viscount G-AOHR, which had once carried the name* Sir Richard Burton, *date it to 1971 or later. (Brian Thorne)*

The Hebrides

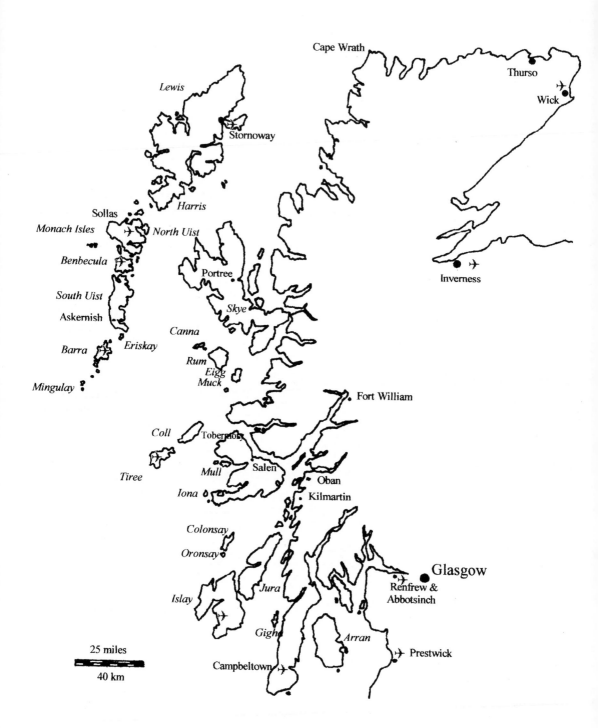

Cape Wrath

Thurso

Wick

Lewis

Stornoway

Harris

Sollas

Monach Isles

North Uist

Benbecula

Portree

Inverness

South Uist

Skye

Askernish

Canna

Barra

Eriskay

Rum

Eigg

Muck

Mingulay

Fort William

Coll

Tobermory

Tiree

Mull

Salen

Iona

Oban

Kilmartin

Colonsay

Oronsay

Glasgow

Renfrew &
Abbotsinch

Jura

Islay

Gigha

Arran

Prestwick

25 miles

40 km

Campbeltown

4

The Hebrides

In 1970 or '71, I went to the BEA office in Amsterdam to ask for a timetable of the flights to the Hebrides. They didn't have one, but they said, 'Why not try the British Tourist Authority?'

So to the British Tourist Authority, an official body, I went. The young lady at the counter assured me that, 'There are no flights to the Hebrides.'

I said, 'Yes, there are. I have been on them.' She said, 'Well, maybe there are, but they do not fly to a schedule.' I replied, 'Yes, they do. I've caught them at it!' Determined to have the final word, she replied, 'Well, perhaps they do fly to a schedule, but the schedule is not published.'

That perception of the Hebridean islands of Scotland, as experienced by Haentjens Dekker of Almen in the Netherlands when he visited the offices of British European Airways and the British Tourist Authority in Amsterdam, is perhaps not unusual. The image that these islands, which stretch like a scattered string of pearls down the western seaboard of the Scottish mainland, are remote and inaccessible is often one which still persists today. Aircraft landings on Islay and Tiree had already been recorded by the late 1920s while an airmail service to Stornoway was also being considered around this time. In 1933 a regular air route to Islay was launched and, by the outbreak of World War Two, services had been expanded to incorporate a comprehensive network of Hebridean airfields. This network included Skye, North Uist and South Uist, islands which were omitted from the points served by BEA in the postwar era.

Over the sea to Islay – and an 'island' peninsula

Scotland's first scheduled air service, operated by Midland & Scottish Air Ferries, linked Renfrew with Campbeltown. This service was a rapid evolution rather than a conscious inauguration. The first Midland & Scottish aircraft to touch down on Strath Field near Campbeltown was a de Havilland Fox Moth which arrived on 18 April 1933 to launch an experimental service that would deliver, for the first time, newspapers on the morning of their publication. Such was the interest generated that, by 26 April, 'regular service' was being publicised and the first official scheduled passenger was carried the next day. Campbeltown, of course, is not on an island, but in 1933 to all intents and purposes it might well have been. The surface journey to the town, located at the foot of the Kintyre peninsula, involved either a six-hour voyage by steamship, or a circuitous 160-mile road journey via mountain and loch, including ascent of the Rest and be Thankful, a high pass between Loch Long and Loch Fyne. These topographical considerations conspired to ensure the popularity of the air service which was timetabled as taking forty minutes. During 1933, Campbeltown developed as a veritable hub, the service being extended to Islay on 16 May, and calling on demand at Rothesay on the Isle of Bute from 24 May. A service from Renfrew to Belfast Aldergrove commenced on 30 May 1933 and some of these services also routed through Campbeltown.

In July 1934, John Sword, owner of Midland & Scottish, began to wind down the extensive air network which he had developed during the preceding fifteen months due to a conflict of interest with Scottish Motor Transport where he held the position of General Manager of its Western Division. The services to Campbeltown and Islay were the last to go, continuing operation until 29 September. George Nicholson's Northern & Scottish Airways took up the void left on these routes

James MacGeachy, BEA's man in Campbeltown, supervises the loading of a Pionair at Machrihanish, c. 1956.
(courtesy of Catherine Cameron)

'A roll of fencing wire and a flight ticket to Glasgow' – James MacGeachy's hardware shop and the BEA booking office, Union Street, Campbeltown.
(courtesy of Catherine Cameron)

on 1 December 1934. Along with Highland Airways of Inverness, Northern & Scottish Airways was acquired by the Whitehall Securities Group on 23 May 1935. With their amalgamation on 1 August 1937, they became Scottish Airways. Scottish Airways became the main provider of Scottish air services until the inauguration of British European Airways on 1 February 1947.

Throughout these events, the interests of the succession of air operators serving Campbeltown were cared for by local hardware store proprietor, James MacGeachy. MacGeachy continued this role on behalf on BEA, and his store doubled as the BEA booking office for flights to Renfrew, Islay and the BEA network throughout Europe. In 1947, his daughter, Catherine, joined him for the next seven years. Ella Logan joined MacGeachy as traffic clerk in 1956 on a temporary assignment from Islay. She was soon a permanent fixture at Campbeltown and Dudley Foy, correspondent to BEA's in-house magazine, found her still there in 1959 where she 'opens the travel side of the shop at 9.30 every morning and during the day makes bookings, issues tickets, consigns freight, makes four return journeys on the six-mile bus ride to the airport, handles the passengers and does the loadsheets – and never finishes before eight o'clock in the evening during the three months of the peak season'.

MacGeachy represented a major airline but he combined the need to present corporate image with the intimate service which typifies a small community where everybody knows everybody else. He would willingly transact bookings on a scrap of paper or in his head during casual street encounters with Campbeltonians. He was also adept at applying unorthodox ingenuity to resolve any problem which might arise, as his daughter Catherine recalls:

> The owner of a local fruit market asked Father if he could carry a large consignment of wreaths to Islay for a funeral. Father said that it would be a problem because the 32-passenger Pionair aircraft was fully booked that day. However, he told the fruiterer to bring the wreaths out to the airport and he would see what he could do. At Machrihanish, the wreaths were taken out to the aircraft during its ten-minute layover on its way from Renfrew to Islay. Father worked his way through the aircraft distributing wreaths to the passengers asking, 'Would you mind holding on to that for ten minutes?' Before the passengers had time to think about what was happening, each was caring for a wreath and the aircraft was on its way to Islay.

Islay's air passengers, when Midland & Scottish Air Ferries began services in 1933, embarked and disembarked on the shore of Tràigh Cill an Rubha at the head of Loch Indaal and opposite Bridgend. However, Midland & Scottish secured firmer ground south of Bowmore at Duich Farm which served as Islay's airfield until the opening of Glenegedale Airport in 1935 by Northern & Scottish Airways, itself only a grass field until hard runways were laid for the Royal Air Force in 1940.

Scottish Airways was flying three round trips daily except Sunday to Campbeltown, and two direct Renfrew-Islay services during the summer of 1946, when British European Airways was created following the passing of the Civil Aviation Act. Understandably, the independent Scottish airlines were opposed to their takeover through nationalisation and it is probable that BEA was lukewarm in its enthusiasm to operate Scottish domestic services. However, the 1946 Act stipulated that 'it shall not be lawful for any persons other than the three Corporations and their associates[1] to carry passengers or goods by air ... upon any scheduled journey between two places, one of which is in the UK.' The roundtrip fare from Renfrew to Islay was £3 1s 6d in

---

[1] The three Corporations were British European Airways (BEA), British Overseas Airways Corporation (BOAC), and British South American Airways (BSAA). BSAA was absorbed into BOAC in 1949. The inclusion of 'Associates' enabled the Corporations to subcontract routes to other operations and provided scope for scheduled services on some periphery routes, which did not interest the Corporations, to independent airlines which were other wise denied authority to operate scheduled services. Scottish Airlines of Prestwick operated some services for BEA under associate agreements.

The third Viscount to be built, G-AMAV Endeavour, *pictured here at Prestwick, heralded things to come during route proving trials with BEA between August 1952 and February 1953. (Aird Crooks)*

Sheep give way at Glenegedale Airport, Islay, during the layover of BEA's Viscount service from Glasgow and Campbeltown. (BEA courtesy of Janette Ridgway)

1946 – compared with the 1933 fare on Midland & Scottish Air Ferries of £4 0s 0d. Scottish Airways continued to operate its route network, serving Islay and other destinations, until 1 February 1947 when BEA formally absorbed both its flying operations and aircraft.

During the transitional period when Scottish Airways was effectively operating on behalf of BEA, Scottish Airways' de Havilland Rapide G-AFFF crashed on the Kilpatrick Hills while inbound to Renfrew from Islay. The accident was caused by confusion arising from radio messages while the aircraft was attempting to land through thick cloud at Renfrew, compounded by the erroneous intimation by another Scottish Airways Rapide approaching Renfrew that it was running short of fuel and required immediate clearance to land. In addition to the two-man crew, the five passengers aboard G-AFFF were all killed. It was a sad conclusion to a decade of Scottish Airways operations which had passed with barely a blemish.

Off the west coast of Scotland, de Havilland Rapides had proven themselves for their ruggedness and reliability since 1936 and they continued to serve Islay until their duties were taken over by Douglas Dakotas in the winter of 1952/53. Until this time, Campbeltown and Islay had been served from Renfrew by individual services, twice daily to the former and once daily to the latter but with a second service on Mondays, Wednesdays and Saturdays. The Dakota, which had undergone extensive modifications to BEA specifications at Scottish Aviation to become the 'Pionair', provided airliner comfort but a truncated service, leaving Renfrew at 1130 once daily for a sole round trip schedule serving both Campbeltown and Islay. BEA withdrew the Pionair from its fleet in 1962 and the last service operated was an inbound service to Renfrew from Islay via Campbeltown flown by Pionair Leopard G-ALTT *RMA Charles Grey* on 19 May of that year. To Islay, via Campbeltown, the Dakota's place was taken by the Handley Page Dart Herald which became the first turbo-prop aircraft to serve the island. This occurred on 15 December 1959 when Handley Page's demonstration aircraft, G-APWA, in full BEA colours, landed on the 1,344 metre runway. Handley Page's second prototype Herald, G-AODF, was also painted in BEA livery in which it undertook worldwide sales tours during 1959, clocking up 135,000 miles and making in excess of 400 landings, many of them on remote and marginal airstrips such as at Goroka in New Guinea.

The Handley Page Herald was a high-wing aircraft which was regarded as a British-built competitor to the Fokker Friendship and, in order to give the aircraft exposure to potential buyers, the Ministry of Supply purchased three, G-APWB, G-APWC and G-APWD, which it leased to BEA for operation in Scotland. BEA was already flying Vickers Viscount V701 aircraft on Highlands and Islands routes but runway lengths at some airports resulted in a payload penalty being conceded. Islay's runway at this time would have made this particularly severe and the Herald's capacity was more suited to load factors generated by the route and its operational attributes were compatible with the short landing strip. This latter capability was poignantly illustrated when the demonstrator landed on the short runway at Campbeltown's Machrihanish airport which was a challenging 973 metres.

The three Heralds had been contracted to commence their duties within Scotland during the summer of 1961. This programme fell behind schedule and the first aircraft, G-APWB, was not delivered until 10 March 1962, followed by G-APWC on 30 April and G-APWD on 18 May. Following delivery of the full complement of aircraft, they were timetabled to assume full operations on their designated routes from 21 May 1962. One aircraft was rostered to fly the Renfrew-Campbeltown-Islay service while the others were designated to the Northern Isles services to Orkney and Shetland. However, this did not immediately occur in totality because G-APWC was seconded to undertake a royal tour, carrying Princess Alexandra to Stockholm, departing from London on 24 May.

Under the command of Captain Eric Starling, BEA's Flight Manager in Scotland, and assisted by Captain Ian Montgomery, G-APWC returned on 29 May. These two senior captains were entrusted with this assignment because they represented safe and steady hands with a wealth of experience. Both men, in different circumstances, had mischievous senses of humour and could throw an aircraft about the sky when choosing to do so. Tom Young describes a test flight on a Dakota with Ian Montgomery:

> On a Friday morning, once a major overhaul was finished, if on early shift, I flew for about three hours on the aircraft. We flew down towards Derby to do the radio checks and the captain would fly outside West Kilbride to do his flying controls. Well, what he would do was cut out his engine then just drop out of the sky for a couple of thousand feet. I mean, I was left with my stomach about a thousand feet up above the plane. I said to him, 'That's terrible. What happens if it doesn't come out?' He says, 'It's alright. You're insured.' So that was that. He was a very nice individual! I went up to balance the generators on each engine. There were regulators on each side of the cockpit and I balanced them from there.

Tom also recalls taking his wife on one of her first flights, a trip on the Heron from Renfrew to Inverness. 'Captain Starling was flying and he couldn't get one of the engines to start. So he took off on three engines, started the fourth engine when he was airborne, and came back down again to pick up the passengers. My wife wasn't fussy about it at all!'

In practical terms, the Herald was ideally suited to island operations, its low fuselage and large freight door enabling baggage and cargo to be handled with a minimum of equipment. However, BEA found that the aircraft required a consistent and unrealistically high load factor of eighty percent to cover operating costs and, when the agreement with the Ministry of Supply expired in October 1966, it was not renewed by the airline and the last Herald service, under the command of Captain W. H. Burnett, was concluded with the inbound service to Renfrew from Islay via Campbeltown on 31 October. The Vickers Viscount which replaced the Herald to Islay, now with a longer runway, had a considerably larger capacity. On a one-for-one comparison with the Herald, it hardly represented an improvement in economics but BEA did feel that the change was justified because it offered type compatibility with much of the rest of the European turbo-prop fleet.

The Viscount continued to serve the Glasgow-Campbeltown-Islay route until 1977, by which time BEA had been absorbed into British Airways and these four-engine aircraft, which had latterly revived the name of George Nicholson's Scottish Airways by sporting *BEA Scottish Airways* titles, flew in the standard British Airways livery of the 1970s which had replaced the distinctive appearance of not just BEA and BOAC but the colourful liveries of Northeast Airlines and Cambrian Airways. After thirty years of scheduled air service by the state airline, Islay and Campbeltown again had an independent airline to serve their needs, but one which was already highly familiar with many Highland and Island communities. Loganair, under the leadership of Captain Duncan McIntosh, had begun air taxi and charter operations in 1962 but soon began third level services on routes not served by BEA. Loganair's arrival at Islay and Campbeltown in 1977 came at a time when it had graduated from the Piper Aztec, its workhorse during the 1960s, to the Britten-Norman Trislander. Having been spoiled for many years by the Viscount with its roomy cabin and large oval windows, some travellers needed to be persuaded that the Trislander was a beneficial move. Many island communities required such persuasion when a familiar aircraft departed for the last time and a stranger arrived in its wake. However, the Trislander brought a vastly improved schedule with two direct services daily to each destination, avoiding the triangular route through Campbeltown for Islay passengers and making day return trips to and from Glasgow possible for the first time since the withdrawal of BEA's Rapides to these destinations in 1952. From 26 October 1981, the Trislander was replaced on these routes by the de Havilland Canada DHC-6 Twin Otter and, while this was occasionally supplemented by the

Britten-Norman Islander between Glasgow and Campbeltown, and by the Embraer Bandeirante between Glasgow and Islay, the Twin Otter remained the mainstay of both routes until 1986 when the Shorts 360 appeared on some Campbeltown services, and likewise on Islay routes from 1988. In 1989, the Shorts 360 was responsible for all of the Glasgow-Islay schedules and in the year 2000 was operating two daily round-trip schedules for Loganair offering almost a three-fold increase in capacity from that initially offered by the Trislander. A short intermission occurred during 1997 when the service was operated by British Regional Airlines following the management buy-out of Loganair.

During the pre-war years of air services to Islay, from the very first incursions by Midland & Scottish Air Ferries, the airlines' local agent on the island was Tom Caskie. Caskie had been recruited when Midland & Scottish had made its first exploratory extension from Campbeltown in 1933 and he had interrupted his deliveries of meat to offer the crew of the landing aircraft any assistance which they might need. On board was James MacGeachy who recruited Caskie on the spot as the airline's agent on Islay. Caskie immediately embarked on his first flight, accompanying the party back to Campbeltown - and left his customers without their meat that day! BEA's interests during the 1950s were cared for by Andy Morrison. Island air fares have always been a sensitive issue and remain so. During his incumbency, Morrison noted that, 'As a holiday centre there has been a steady build up of traffic in the postwar years. 1956 was the best year, (but) there has been a noticeable decline since the slight increase in domestic fares. Nevertheless, over 10,000 will have been handled by the year end (1958) – and the population is only 4,000'. Andy Morrison left BEA during the mid-1960s to go into business in Bowmore and, in the year 2000, in his seventieth year, he was still in business, supplying outdoor sports equipment from his shop in Falkirk. Jack Ridgway, who began his career with BEA as a traffic clerk at Edinburgh Turnhouse at a salary of £7 0s 6d a week, succeeded Morrison. Until his transfer to Kirkwall in 1973, he tended BEA's interests on Islay including the airline's operations on behalf of the Scottish Air Ambulance Service, the importance of which should not be underestimated:

> Like my colleagues in the Highlands and Islands, I am on permanent 24-hour call to alert and handle
> the ambulance service, day or night, without extra pay. The girls at the telephone exchange must
> always know where I am so they can warn me that the ambulance is needed.

Jack made this statement in 1972, which is hardly in the dark ages, yet seems light years away from the era of pagers and mobile telephones.

Islay had special associations with the Scottish Air Ambulance Service. The service was inaugurated here by Midland & Scottish Air Ferries when, in 1933, its de Havilland Dragon G-ACCZ, piloted by Jimmy Orrell, evacuated fisherman John McDermid from Tràigh Cill an Rubha. McDermid had been on hand forty years later when a BEA Viscount delivered Ann Heads with her newly born baby to Islay. Mrs Heads, on her outward air ambulance flight from the island a few days earlier, had become the Service's ten thousandth passenger. In between these events, Islay had also been the scene of the singular air ambulance tragedy to occur during BEA's 26-year operation of the Service. On the night of 28 September 1957, de Havilland Heron G-AOFY *Sir Charles Bell* crashed on high ground while trying to land in appalling weather conditions in order to evacuate a seriously ill patient. All on board, Captain Paddy Calderwood, Radio Officer Hugh McGinlay and Sister Jean Kennedy, the volunteer nurse, were killed. Captain Calderwood was cremated while Hugh McGinlay was buried in Dalnottar Cemetery, Clydebank, where a memorial recalls the tragedy. Sister Kennedy was buried on the Isle of Coll and her sacrifice was marked by BEA which renamed G-ANXA, one of its two remaining Herons, in her honour.

Airline histories are full of 'might have beens' and BEA in Scotland is no exception. One example was the proposed Heron service between Edinburgh and Bergen which was contemplated following the discovery of oil in the Scottish and Norwegian sectors of the North Sea, but did not materialise. Another concerns a lost opportunity on Islay which might have resulted in a similar service to that enjoyed by the Isle of Scilly. Jack Ridgway drew Glasgow's attention to the availability of the Machrie Hotel along with a considerable area of land with golf course, fishing loch – and suitable space for a helicopter operation. The asking price was around £30,000 and Tony Naylor, BEA Operations Manager, was confident that Jack could manage the hotel as well as the air service. Tony undertook a survey and then made a recommendation to London that BEA purchase the property. London agreed that the scheme had merits, but this was six months later by which time the hotel proprietors' accountant had snapped it up. It was one of many frustrations of limited autonomy experienced by Tony and of what Eric Starling had referred to as 'the palsied hand of London' – and Eric was himself a Londoner by birth! The Machrie Hotel's association with air travel goes back to the very first arrival. This was on 16 July 1928 when a Captain Stirling made the first landing on the island in an Avro two-seater. His passenger was Glasgow businessman, Robert Paul, and they had lunch with Duncan McIntyre, the proprietor of the Machrie estate and hotel during their one hour stay on Islay.

Tropical Tiree

To the north-west of Islay lies the almost tropical Isle of Tiree. Its silver beaches are a long way from Bondi, but they regularly sparkle below a window of blue sky through which the sun smiles while evading the rest of Scotland and leaving it under its all too familiar blanket of cloud. Tiree is also an unlikely haven for aficionados of the surfboard.

On Tiree there are memories of an aircraft landing at Gott Bay in 1928. And on 19 July 1929, an open-cockpit de Havilland DH60X Cirrus II Moth of Manchester-based Northern Air Lines under the command of Captain A. N. Kingwill alighted on The Reef, future location of the island's airfield. Captain Jimmy Orrell of Midland & Scottish Air Ferries made a survey flight to Tiree on 27 May 1933, setting out from Renfrew in Airspeed Ferry G-ACBT but having to abandon this aircraft at North Connel airfield, near Oban, due to engine trouble. The survey was completed using DH84 Dragon G-ACCZ but scheduled services did not result. Captain David Barclay, who began his airline pilot career with Midland & Scottish on 3 August 1934, made an exploratory landing, as chief pilot of Northern & Scottish Airways, in DH84 Dragon G-ACJS on the sands of Gott Bay at 6.00am on 4 October 1935. Barclay's flying logs show that he made further visits to Tiree in DH84 Dragon and Spartan Cruiser II aircraft during 1936, but it was not until 1938 that Tiree gained a regularly sustained scheduled air service. By this time Northern & Scottish Airways had joined with Highland Airways to form Scottish Airways; and its Western Isles scheduled network was already extensive, encapsulating Islay, Skye, Barra, South Uist, Benbecula, North Uist, and Harris - all served from Renfrew. David Barclay developed great skill in finding his way around Scotland in all conditions. The reason for his success was perhaps explained when he revealed to Bill Reid that, when he began flying, he received 'trip pay'. This meant that, if the weather was bad and he battled his way over the mountains to Inverness in a Rapide, did a couple of unsuccessful QDL/QDM let-downs, and then, short of fuel, braved the elements to divert back to Glasgow – he didn't get any pay!

On 25 May 1938, Barclay carried a party, which included Scottish Airways' Managing Director George Nicholson and Air Superintendent Bill Gairdner in Spartan Cruiser III G-ADEL, to undertake an inspection of the aerodrome. A thrice-weekly scheduled service from Renfrew followed a few days later with Spartan Cruisers being the favoured aircraft type. Scottish

Steps are positioned against a Rapide at Stornoway, March 1948. (Alex G. W. Miller)

Tiree's Station Superintendent, Colin MacPhail, and Mary Munn, his assistant, 1948. (Alex G. W. Miller)

Airways generally operated to Tiree on a simple round-trip rotation from Renfrew. However, passenger demand to all of the airline's island destinations both enabled and made expedient a high degree of flexibility. As a result, services to Tiree often continued onwards to one or more of the Outer Hebridean airfields, or also called at Islay. By the summer of 1939, Tiree was timetabled as being served daily except Sunday as part of a Western Isles routing which officially varied on alternate days and unofficially varied as required by prevailing traffic demand. Indeed, the Tiree stop appeared in the Scottish Airways schedule as being 'on request and subject to 12 hours' notice being given'. The alternating routes operated were, on Mondays, Wednesdays and Fridays, Renfrew-Tiree-Benbecula-North Uist-Benbecula-Barra-Renfrew; and on Tuesdays, Thursdays and Saturdays, Renfrew-Tiree-Barra-Benbecula-North Uist-Tiree-Renfrew.

The grass aerodrome established on Tiree was requisitioned by the Royal Air Force with the declaration of World War Two and became an RAF Coastal Command station in 1942 by which time three hard runways had been laid. Reef Airport at Tiree, more than fifty years after the end of World War Two, retains many reminders of the period when it was a hive of Coastal Command activity. Scottish Airways' fleet of Spartan Cruiser II and Spartan Cruiser III aircraft was also subjected to war-time requisition following which Tiree was served by de Havilland Rapides. By late 1940, the Western Isles circle from Renfrew through Tiree continued from North Uist onwards to Stornoway while Barra entailed a slight deviation when demand required. From this, a pattern developed where Tiree, Benbecula and North Uist all became regular stops on the Renfrew-Stornoway service. When, in 1947, BEA took over the Hebrides services from Scottish Airways, Tiree remained an integral part of this wider Hebridean network. However, by 1950, BEA was operating service S214A from Renfrew to Tiree with a continuation to Barra 'on request and subject to tide and weather', and onwards to Benbecula also 'on request'. These were still flown with the de Havilland Rapide which BEA referred to as its Islander Class. A separate service, S212A, operated Renfrew-Benbecula-Stornoway. From the winter of 1952/53, the Douglas Dakota, or Pionair, operated a four times weekly schedule from Renfrew as BE948, leaving at 0825 and reaching Tiree at 0925, Benbecula at 1020 and Stornoway at 1110. Upon three of these days it continued to Inverness, arriving at 1220 where there were fifty minutes for aircraft servicing and crew refreshment, Kenneth McLean maintaining that Mrs McBey's lunches were the highlight of the Hebrides service for pilots. The aircraft, as BE949, then retraced the whole route from Inverness to land back at Renfrew at 1700.

However, the level of Tiree's population made it unlikely that it would ever generate a high volume of traffic. As a result, Tiree and Barra tended to become paired in the provision of air services, not because of any great affinity or links between the two islands, but simply because their geographical proximity and traffic levels made similar demand on BEA's obligation to serve island communities, a role which was enhanced for both communities with the replacement, in 1955, of the de Havilland Rapide by the four-engined de Havilland DH114 Heron 1B. Herons served Tiree well for eighteen years, but in 1973 two Short SC7 Skyliners succeeded them. BEA was by this time in the turmoil of transition to British Airways which, along with the Skyliners, had a short tenure on the Tiree and Barra routes. Indeed, Scottish Division had been formed on 1 November 1967 with great optimism of operational autonomy resulting in a truly Scottish airline which would establish its own unique identity and would forge direct links to Europe. One innovation, which occurred on 28 April 1969 when Isla Roelfina Smith took to the air, was the introduction of female flight attendants to the Scottish routes. With her appointment came the announcement that it was now Scottish Division's policy to employ Flight Clerkesses instead of Flight Clerks 'with the ultimate aim of having a 50/50 contingent'. BEA Scottish Division became BEA Scottish Airways Division on 1 April 1971, but its reign as an autonomous entity was short-lived and, on 1 September 1971, control was passed to British Air Services (BAS), a BEA subsidiary which already controlled Cambrian Airways and Northeast Airlines. British Air Services simultaneously became a separate organisation from BEA, and both came under the management of the British Airways Board, a body created by an Act of Parliament which was to oversee the creation of British Airways in 1974. It was BAS which decided upon acquisition of the Skyliners. Tony Naylor observes that BAS ignored the Scottish Office's financing of one of the Herons for the Scottish Air Ambulance Service and its failure to consult it influenced its decision to pass the contract to Loganair.

Just as James MacGeachy was the face of BEA in Campbeltown, that of Colin MacPhail was indelibly stamped on the airline's operation at Tiree. BEA's traffic here might have been light and its aircraft diminutive but this was MacPhail's domain. The Tiree booking office was listed in BEA timetables quite simply as 'Colin MacPhail, Crossapol House. Telephone No. Scarinish 9'. This was MacPhail's home where he conducted his duties for BEA outwith the time of the arrival and departure of the aircraft. MacPhail had become the representative for Northern & Scottish Airways in 1936, well before Tiree received regular visits by the airline and its successor, Scottish Airways. He therefore, undoubtedly, was able to adopt a nonchalant approach to his duties from this undemanding start. The story of the arrival on the island of Lord Douglas of Kirtleside, Chairman of BEA, became part of Hebridean aviation folklore. Some moments after the aircraft carrying Lord Douglas taxied to a halt, MacPhail appeared on the tarmac to open the Rapide door. The Chairman, unused to being kept waiting, demanded to know if MacPhail was expecting him to which MacPhail replied, 'If you are Lord Douglas, I was. If not, I wasn't.' MacPhail was assisted by Mary Munn who began her airline career in 1943.

Colin MacPhail was succeeded by Archie MacArthur, and Archie continued his duties when Loganair took over from British Airways in 1975. Ten years after the transfer, Scott Grier, Managing Director of Loganair, was quite put out when he discovered that islanders still referred to their air service as being run by BEA – until it was explained that, to people on Tiree, whoever the operator, while Archie still ran the station, it would always be BEA, 'Big Erchie's Airline'. Loganair, which began its incumbency on the Glasgow-Tiree route with Britten-Norman Trislanders, but for two decades has primarily used DHC-6 Twin Otter aircraft to the island, now has its interests at Reef Airport tended by Ishbel MacKinnon, Archie's daughter.

Until the end of 1947 BEA had a maintenance base at Tiree's Reef Airport. Gordon Maddiss, an airman of the Royal Canadian Air Force who married an Oban girl, became BEA's Mechanic on Tiree where he was licensed to taxi, and provide maintenance on, Rapide and Dakota aircraft. Visiting air-crew occasionally had time to linger on Tiree on those occasions when no passengers were booked on the Barra sectors. On one such occasion Kenneth McLean, along with David Barclay, took his 'brand new' wife along for the ride. During the two hours at their disposal before they had to pick up the return schedule, the threesome took their packed lunches to a beach at the edge of the airfield. Recalling that it had been quite an effort to return to duty, the Heron, and Renfrew, Kenneth McLean and his wife had left behind a souvenir, their entwined initials drawn in the sand. Recalling those pleasant times, Kenneth McLean reflects, 'Over a week later, when I next flew into Tiree, they were still there to be seen.'

Barra – airport with a sea view

Most of Scotland's island airports are within 'spitting distance' of the sea, but none of them can compete with Barra. Here operations are planned around the submergence of the island's Tràigh Mhòr airfield below the twice-daily advance of the tide across its silver sands. Jimmy Orrell of Midland & Scottish Air Ferries first landed on them on 14 June 1933 in DH84 Dragon G-ACCZ

The World's link with Barra – BEA's Rapide. (courtesy of Eva Edmiston)

A Heron makes a winter approach to Barra. (BEA via Cyril Horn)

'The Hut' at Barra provided all essential facilities. (Bill Dunn)

while Glyn Roberts of West of Scotland Air Services trundled across the rippled 'runway' two years later in his Short Scion, G-ADDP. David Barclay failed in his efforts to find a site for a conventional airfield prior to the launch of scheduled services between Renfrew and Barra by Northern & Scottish Airways in 1936. Attempts during the 1990s to take Barra's airport on to dry land have also been frustrated.

Front man on the island in the pre-war days of Barra air services was John MacPherson, local entrepreneur and larger-than-life personality, who was also known as The Coddy. It was The Coddy who casually punctured David Barclay's frustration at being unable to locate a suitable square of grass on the island which would accommodate an airfield with his nonchalant suggestion of, 'Why don't you just use the beach?' The MacPherson dynasty ruled the sands of the Tràigh Mhòr for longer than the 28-year tenure of BEA. Although John MacPherson took already overdue retirement at the end of World War Two, his son, Angus, succeeded him until 1950. Angus, was followed by his sister, Catherine (variously known as Katie and Kitty), who guided mini-airliners on to the beach and islanders on board until 1980, by which time the confused identity of the two Short Skyliner aircraft serving Barra indicating the demise of BEA and the arrival of British Airways had faded and their successor, Loganair, was firmly established.

Despite lack of economic viability, BEA had clung jealously to its right to operate its traditional Scottish island routes, a vice-like grip which was only loosened with the creation of British Airways. This was conceded with the greatest of caution and it was the third-level routes from Glasgow to Tiree and Barra which were the first to be relinquished. This move had been preceded by a proposal for BEA to take over Loganair and equip it with three Trislanders for use on routes to Campbeltown, Islay, Tiree and Barra, and for the Scottish Air Ambulance Service. Loganair had nonetheless remained independent. Barra services and the MacPherson connection continued yet further when, upon Katie's retiral, her niece, Una MacPherson, became Loganair's 'woman on Barra' for a time. Katie was a shy, modest person loved by generations of air-crew and travellers who, in the early days, remember her slim figure on the beach, armed with walkie-talkie, giving the pilots of inbound aircraft the latest conditions in order that they could exercise their best discretion in selecting their landing approach.

BEA's arrival at Barra was not without event, two de Havilland Rapides being damaged beyond repair. The first of these was G-AGJF which was written off on 6 August 1947. This was followed by G-AGPH *Sir Henry Havelock* when it met its demise on 6 December 1951. On a non-urgent ambulance flight at the time, the fate of G-AGPH demonstrated the unseen traps which could lurk under the pools of surface water left on the landing run by the receding tide. The aircraft's wheels were caught in the grip of soft sand, causing it to flip over on its back. The two elderly patients on board, returning to their homes on North Uist following hospital confinements, were shaken and bruised but otherwise apparently unhurt. One lady, 81-year-old Mrs MacKillop of Lochportain, did however die upon her return home a day later, although it is unclear whether this might have been attributed to shock resulting from the incident on the beach, the effects of her medical condition (both of her legs had been amputated), or a combination of both of these traumas. The Rapide had routed through Barra on its way to North Uist in order to collect a patient there who was inbound to Glasgow. Nurse Whelan, on board with the two ladies, was having her first taste of travel as an ambulance escort to the Hebrides. On the ground and quick to render assistance were Catherine Macdougall, the district nurse from Castlebay, and workmen from the Hebridean Shell Grit Company. A first-hand account is contained in a letter from Nurse Macdougall to Mrs MacKillop's daughter written on 8 February 1952:

I received your letter several days ago and indeed know how you must feel about having your mother involved in a 'plane crash at the evening of her day. Although I am in the district in Castlebay, which is the south side of Barra, I was down at the 'plane the day the accident happened. I am afraid that I cannot give you a very clear account of what happened as after I saw the 'plane crash I moved so quickly that I cannot recapture it very well.

I do know, however, that when I got out to the 'plane I found a hole at the front and tore it wide open. The men and nurse in the 'plane had lifted your mother by this time and passed her out, through the hole, to me. (She was first out.) With the help of the men who were working nearby, we lifted her into my van which I had drawn up nearby for readiness and I drove her to the nearest house, took off all her clothes, and rolled her in blankets and packed her with hot water bottles. She then took some hot tea and kept telling me how grateful she was and kept saying 'Mo ghradh orsa'[2]. However, when I went to see her later on in the day she didn't seem to recognise me, but then she would have seen many new faces. The woman in the house where we took her was very kind indeed and did not waste any time collecting loads of blankets and hot water bottles. I did not see your mother again as the house is not in my district as I have already said. Nurse Peterhannah from Northbay saw them off in the morning. So now you can rest assured that your mother got every possible attention and was in a cosy warm bed within minutes of the accident.

While other aircraft have been 'caught' on the beach at Barra, for the most part, with careful scheduling to avoid high tide, aircraft have come and gone as consistently and as uneventfully as the rhythms of the sea with which they co-exist. At the beginning of the BEA phase, services from Glasgow to Barra were scheduled to operate six days a week, as a continuation of the Tiree service, and with further extension to Benbecula on two of those days. However, the extension to Barra, and to Benbecula, was operated 'on request' or 'subject to demand', indicating a somewhat ad hoc schedule. However, by 1950, Barra was quite definitely in the schedule as an extension of the Tiree service six days a week with the usual get-out clause linked to tides and weather. A year later, the call at Barra was 'promised' only three days each week. And from 1952 the words 'on request' were reappearing in timetables, sometimes with the offer of only two flights a week, on a Monday and Friday. That the service, still operated by the de Havilland Rapide, was flown non-stop from Renfrew must have been little consolation for the low frequency. BEA withdrew the Rapide from service in Scotland at the end May 1955 by which time its replacement, the de Havilland DH114 Heron 1B, which the Corporation called the *Hebrides* Class, had already made its first appearances on Barra - on 20 March to give crews route experience, then on 28 April for an ambulance flight, and on 2 May via Tiree for a service flight, all under the command of Captain David Barclay. The Herons flew to many parts of Scotland during their eighteen years of service, but it is Barra and its beach airstrip with which they shall always be associated and for which their fixed undercarriage was ideally suited.

Kenneth McLean found that the beach at Barra could be deceptive. 'With an onshore wind the sand remained shining wet and very reflective, especially on a bright or sunny day. Even flying over the beach for a visual inspection before landing could not entirely confirm that the wet surface was only wet sand and not residual standing water.' One Heron captain was caught and landed in several inches of water resulting in flaps damaged to such a degree that the aircraft could not return to Renfrew until replacement flaps were fitted.

The Herons could also get stuck in the sand – and did. G-ANXA was rescued from the advancing tide on 30 March 1968 but the airport fire tender, which had gone to the aid of the aircraft, was not. Tony Naylor, BEA Operations Manager, observing that the sunken fire tender had required a four-man crew while Barra had only 'a man and a boy', arranged for a four-wheel drive Land Rover to replace the lost machine. The Land Rover was fitted with the mandatory

---

[2] In this context, 'Mo ghradh orsa' literally means 'My everlasting gratitude to you'.

fire extinguishing equipment – and a winch for hauling aircraft out of trouble. Captain Harry McDowell recalls that Barra's first postwar terminal, 'the Hut', originally had a wooden shed alongside to house fire fighting equipment mounted on a medium-sized trolley:

> Some years after it was installed, it was decided that a couple of blokes from Renfrew Airport should go out to Barra to check the functioning of the equipment. On arrival, they decided to take the apparatus out of its shed to inspect it in good light. However, on opening the doors, they found that the only way they could get it out was by letting the air out of the tyres in order to reduce the height – the doors being too low – then to re-inflate them after it was outside. Just as well the equipment had never been needed in anger.

In the late 1960s, Barra was connected to the National Grid and this enabled installation of instruments, heating and refreshment facilities to the wooden terminal. It still remained in the eyes of Willa Stewart, a regular traveller to Barra at that time, 'a glorified garden shed'. Before 'the Hut', there had been indeed a single-roomed shed used by The Coddy and which Radio Officer Tom More describes as being anchored to the ground by telegraph poles.

The Short Skyliners, which replaced the Herons during the final hours of BEA before it was subsumed into the new British Airways, had but a brief tenure. Indeed, they were not BEA's first choice as a Heron replacement. BEA had intended to acquire the Britten-Norman Trislander, but a financial crisis within Britten-Norman at that time persuaded it to seek an alternative. Ironically, Loganair introduced the Trislander when it began operating the Glasgow-Barra service under contract to British Airways in October 1974 and Loganair took over the route in its own right in 1975. That year, Loganair also launched a Barra-Benbecula-Stornoway service. This followed the re-organisation of local government in Scotland and the creation of Comhairle nan Eilean, the Western Isles Islands Council, which brought the islands of the Outer Hebrides under the one administrative structure for local services. Loganair introduced the de Havilland Canada DHC-6 Twin Otter to the Glasgow-Barra route in 1981 and, after an attempt to introduce the Shorts 360 in 1994 was abandoned, the Twin Otter continued to provide Barra's air link to the mainland, a service which it has now been performing for longer than the much-loved Heron. On the Barra-Benbecula-Stornoway service, the Islander was displaced by the larger Trislander in 1981 and the DHC-6 Twin Otter from January 1983. Following its 1997 demerger from Airlines of Britain Holdings (ABH), which included British Midland Airways, British Regional Airlines, Manx Airlines and Business Air, Loganair's services from Glasgow to Barra and Tiree briefly became its trunk services until it gradually began to rebuild what had been a comprehensive network until ABH had introduced major restructuring in 1994 and again in 1995. During the 1990s, the possibility of building a conventional airstrip on Barra, or neighbouring Vatersay, became a subject of controversy and while some commentators took the view that, 'if something isn't broken, don't try to fix it', others argued that construction of a hard runway was inevitable and was merely a decision postponed. However, upgrading of shipping services has seen a decline in passenger numbers while increasing ease of vehicle access by ferry and then causeway to Benbecula is forecast to further diminish air traffic. Barra is no longer as remote as in the days of the Rapides of BEA and its predecessors, and of the four-engined Herons.

Benbecula – air hub of the Uists

Regular air services to the Isle of Benbecula were preceded by those launched by Northern & Scottish Airways to Askernish, on the Isle of South Uist, and to Sollas, on the Isle of North Uist, in February 1936. This operation was integrated with Northern & Scottish services to Barra and to Skye so that a day's flying would incorporate each island, subject to demand and operating with a high degree of flexibility in the order served. Benbecula appears to have followed in July

1936 when the island was timetabled as 'on demand'. It first appears in the flight logs of David Barclay, who as chief pilot would normally have the privilege of inaugurating new services, on 2 July 1936 when he flew a schedule in Spartan Cruiser II G-ACSM over a circuit which operated Renfrew-North Uist-Benbecula-South Uist-Skye-Renfrew, accumulating a total flying time of four hours and twenty minutes. The beach landing site at Northton on the Isle of Harris had similarly been added as an 'on demand' call during the previous month. The island pivot for this operation was the grass strip at Sollas, North Uist, where a hangar was erected, fuel supply installed, and resident pilot appointed. In 1936, the North Uist pilot was New Zealander, John Hankins. There are recollections of early flights to Benbecula alighting on the sand at Sulamul until a day arrived when the tide was too high for this to be accomplished. Instead, Hankins landed on grass at Balivanich, where Benbecula's airport would later be built.

South Uist and Benbecula were not linked by road until 1943. However, air services to Askernish on South Uist were suspended in 1939 prior to declaration of war and not resumed. The timetable for that summer stated that 'Passengers to and from South Uist will be set down or picked up at Benbecula'. By this time, the grass field at Benbecula had become established and had a modest wooden terminal building with a large sign proclaiming that this was 'Balivanich Airport'. North Uist continued to be the northern terminus of 'Air Line 333' to the Outer Hebrides, with Harris remaining as an optional extra, subject to pre-arrangement. The outbreak of World War Two that September saw unprecedented activity in the islands and the arrival of many unfamiliar accents as military personnel were positioned at locations throughout the Hebrides which were considered of strategic importance because they faced the Atlantic and the convoy routes. After an initial shutdown of civilian flights to the Hebrides upon the outbreak of the War, services were resumed, but aircraft had their windows masked and passengers required a permit issued under Defence Regulations by the Military Permit Office. Control of airfields was often lost by the civilian operators and Balivanich was taken over by RAF Coastal Command in 1941 which set about laying runways on the site of the grass airfield. World War Two was therefore responsible for elevating Benbecula's status in the Uists in the postwar years. Of the wartime hangars erected at Benbecula, two found their way, in 1949, to Amsterdam where they were joined together and mounted on concrete blocks to give them additional height to form one large building. As 'Hangar Seven' at Schiphol Oost, it was used to accommodate the Douglas DC-6s of KLM Royal Dutch Airlines. It was demolished in the mid-1980s.

Sollas continued to be used for scheduled services until October 1945 when Scottish Airways dropped it from its schedule and focused services on Benbecula which could be reached by cart from North Uist at low tide. A causeway now links North Uist with Benbecula via the Isle of Grimsay. Sollas airfield did however continue to be served for air ambulance flights during the 1950s until deterioration set in, and then a nearby beach was used. BEA pilots used conventional navigational aids to fly to Balivanich and then switched to visual flying for the final approach over the hills of North Uist to Sollas.

While Herons succeeded the Rapides for ambulance duties to Sollas, Benbecula's hard runway attracted Dakota operations and became linked into the circle route which, for example in 1949, left Renfrew at 0810 for the 75-minute flight to Balivanich, then continued onwards to Stornoway and Inverness. The return service left Inverness at 1225, via Stornoway to call at Benbecula at 1425 and, following a twenty minute stop, touched down at Renfrew at 1625. However, Rapides were still the order of the day when, in 1947, BEA took over from Scottish Airways and this brought a benefit to air-crew. As Radio Officer Alex Miller recalls, 'In 1947, eggs were still rationed and the egg lady at Benbecula did quite a business with Rapide crews. More than once a passenger was denied a seat because of the weight of eggs in the freight compartment.' The authors are grateful to Dr John Macleod for his assistance in tracking down the identity of 'the egg lady' as Flora Macmillan. The Rapide continued to serve Benbecula on scheduled services until 1952, operating as an extension of the Renfrew-Tiree-Barra service and supplementing the Dakota service.

Coll Macdonald joined the staff at Benbecula as a traffic clerk in November 1950:

> Working at a small station like Benbecula provided excellent experience for a young man just joining the airline and it served me well for the next thirty-nine years. I did everything from reservations, ticket issue, check-in, manifesting, load sheets, baggage handling and sales returns to donning overalls to help the engineer change wheels, mag. drop, etc. There was very little excitement at Benbecula although once an Icelandair DC-4 made an emergency landing with a runaway propeller. The noise before he managed to shut down the engine was horrendous. I am convinced the ground was shaking. We had no suitable steps for a DC-4 and passengers had to disembark by ladder. There was no Customs either until an officer arrived from Stornoway the following day. BEA provided two aircraft to take the passengers to Glasgow the same day. Otherwise, overnight accommodation would have been an acute problem. Our engineer managed to feather the propeller and we all watched apprehensively as the aircraft took off for Prestwick three days later on three engines.

Coll was one of three BEA personnel at Benbecula, the others being Donald Macdonald, the station superintendent, and Mike Vivian, the engineer. Coll was made redundant in 1953 when the Renfrew management decided that there was insufficient work for the engineer. If the engineer could do the traffic clerk's duties as well, the traffic clerk could be dispensed with. No engineers volunteered for this dual role, but Coll took up the offer of a new post at Manchester's Ringway Airport.

During the brief period when Tiree was a calling point on BEA's Western Isles route, Harry McDowell recalls one day taking advantage of perfect flying conditions:

> The weather was very sunny with excellent visibility and I was flying the scheduled service on a Dakota aircraft. On passing Lochboisdale, I decided to give the passengers a treat by going down low so that they could enjoy the scenery close up. We flew up the west coast of South Uist just above the beach and everyone seemed to enjoy it immensely. My First Officer on that flight was Bill Innes whose home for many years had been in that part of the world. A month or two later he spoke to me and said, 'You remember that low level flight we had up South Uist? Well, my brother was on the beach that day and he saw us coming very clearly but, as soon as we passed over him, we vanished immediately because we were lost to sight in the cloud of sand we had raised!' Perhaps that time we were just a little on the low side, but we had no complaints.

In 1962, the Dakota was replaced on the Renfrew-Benbecula-Stornoway-Inverness route by the Vickers Viscount. With its panoramic passenger windows and four powerful turbine engines, the Viscount was the ultimate in domestic air travel in Scotland during the BEA era. The Viscount remained in service to Benbecula with British Airways for a further decade until, in an effort to make Highlands and Islands services self-financing, they were replaced by Hawker Siddeley 748 aircraft in 1982. Glasgow-Benbecula became a stand-alone service with Loganair's Western Isles inter-island service maintaining an air link between Benbecula and Stornoway. In October 1991, Loganair introduced a Glasgow-Benbecula service, using the Shorts 360 but with a BAe ATP seeing occasional Saturday use, in direct competition with British Airways' service. This service was sustained for one year only. British Airways had introduced the ATP to Benbecula in 1989. In 1996, the ATP continued to serve Benbecula in British Airways colours but, from October, the operating airline was Manx Airlines Europe under a franchising arrangement. Manx Airlines Europe was simultaneously rebranded as British Regional Airlines and included incorporation of Loganair. Loganair re-emerged as an independent airline six months later following a management buy-out.

BEA FLIGHT BULLETIN

From Captain _G. BEAL_ to all passengers

RMA _G-AGJW "Wilfred Parke"_

TIME

Local time is _4.57 pm_ { the same as / one hour ahead of / one hour behind } Local time in _U.K._

POSITION

Iona.

HEIGHT	SPEED	
	AIR SPEED	CORRECTED FOR WIND (SPEED OVER GROUND)
_5500_ Feet	_150_ m.p.h.	_185_ m.p.h.
Metres	k.p.h.	k.p.h.

INFORMATION

We are now _22_ miles from _Tiree_ At _5.10 pm_ hours we pass _Lochgilphead,_ _5_ miles to our right/left. We call next at _Glasgow_ arriving there at approximately _5.25 pm_ LOCAL ~~GREENWICH~~ time.

NOTES

_____

_____

The traffic officer who will meet you on landing will be glad to assist you in any way he can.

The name of your ~~Steward/Stewardess~~ _Flight clerk._ is _MR. FULTON._

PLEASE
PASS ON
QUICKLY

F.144 (4th)   B R I T I S H   E U R O P E A N   A I R W A Y S

'We are now above Iona'. (courtesy of John S. Groome)

Lewis – link between west and north

Stornoway, the Hebridean metropolis on the Isle of Lewis, should have been an early objective for the introduction of air services. Lewis is the biggest and most populous island in the Outer Hebrides and Stornoway is the only town which can truly claim this description without having to attempt to stifle a blush. Air operators did indeed have aspirations of serving Stornoway. As early as 1928, Aerial Taxis Ltd of Glasgow submitted a proposal to the government suggesting that it take over the West Highland mail contract from the steamers of David MacBrayne Ltd in a role which would also carry passengers and goods. The company was reported to favour the use of seaplanes but it admitted that the route had not been surveyed and that no decision had been reached on the type of aircraft it might use.

There remained no serious contenders for several years. A possible clash of interest between Northern & Scottish Airways, whose network by the mid-1930s dominated the north-west, and Highland Airways which was bound to look westward for expansion from its Inverness base having consolidated its position to the north, was averted when the two airlines were combined to form Scottish Airways. While George Nicholson of the former and Edmund Fresson of the latter could therefore decide upon a mutually acceptable strategy for serving Stornoway, there were other players holding an interest. One of these was Captain Glyn Roberts of West of Scotland Air Services (WoSAS) who proposed a seaplane service, while the other party consisted of the officials and representatives of Stornoway itself. Stornoway Town Council could undoubtedly see the benefits of an air link with the mainland, but they were reticent about authorising the expenditure for providing a landing ground, which Fresson required, while there remained hope that this might be avoided through WoSAS's intended use of the waters of Stornoway Harbour.

Fresson made several visits to Stornoway, beginning with a pre-arranged landing on the golf links at Melbost on 8 March 1934 in de Havilland Dragon G-ACIT, an aircraft which was to become part of the BEA fleet in 1947. A year later, arriving on 15 March 1935 and touching down on the beach at Melbost, Fresson was back in Stornoway and now making a concerted effort to persuade the town council to provide an airstrip on the golf links. However, the council could not be impelled to commit capital expenditure to the idea and already had notions of the town's air services being provided by flying boats. Saunders-Roe A.17 Cutty Sark flying boats of British Amphibious Airlines had appeared in Scotland in 1932 and 1933, and there had been periodic visits of British Flying Boats' Saro A.19 *Cloud of Iona*. The value of air access for Stornowegians was emphasised on 9 March 1937 when Fresson landed on the sands at Melbost on his first air ambulance flight to Lewis, conveying a convalescing islander home. He used the trip to urge the town council again of the need for an airfield. However, it was in 1937 that Glyn Roberts also began pursuing the realisation of his long-standing plans for a Hebridean flying boat service, to be operated by a float-equipped Short Scion Senior. Materialisation of Roberts' plans seemed to recede with the passing of the months, but a glimmer of hope remained until the end of 1938. However, by that time Fresson had begun having grass strips prepared on the golf links at Melbost. The airport was completed in August 1939 and, as a member of the wartime Associated Airways Joint Committee (AAJC), the Southern Division of Scottish Airways extended the Renfrew-originating Hebrides route northwards to Stornoway in May 1940. The Northern Division of Scottish Airways launched scheduled services between Stornoway and Inverness on 24 May 1944. A four-and-a-half year delay had been imposed by the intervention of World War Two, during which time RAF Coastal Command had taken over the airport and laid hard runways.

Upon declaration of World War Two, Western Isles air services, in common with other civilian air services, had been prohibited. However, Scottish Airways' Southern Division was granted permission to resume its Hebridean services in 1940 and they were relaunched on 14 May. The route from Renfrew to North Uist was extended to Stornoway on 20 May 1940 and inaugurated by Captain Bill Baillie. Services over the following three weeks were erratic as AAJC aircraft were, on more than one occasion, put on standby for employment in the impending evacuation of Dunkirk. Scottish Airways' 1941 timetable shows a service leaving Renfrew at 0900 six days a week, calling at Tiree, Benbecula and North Uist, and arriving at Stornoway Airport at 1325. On three days of the week, a second service left Renfrew forty-five minutes later but this aircraft remained overnight in Stornoway, returning to Renfrew on the following morning. Immediately following World War Two, three flights a week followed this route; three called only at Tiree during the flight from Renfrew to Stornoway, and three were non-stop. All of these services were operated by de Havilland Rapide aircraft.

With the arrival of BEA in 1947, Stornoway was served by Junkers Ju 52 aircraft, which the Corporation called its *Jupiter* class. Ten of these aircraft, which came from Germany as part of war reparations, joined the BEA fleet. Five had initially gone to Railway Air Services, and two to Scottish Airways. One of the Scottish Airways Ju 52s was damaged at Glasgow only days before being due to transfer to the service of BEA, while the second Scottish Airways Ju 52 was not flown by BEA in regular service but was used as a spare parts source for other aircraft in the fleet. The Jupiters proved to be uneconomic on the Scottish internal routes, were problematic to operate because they required ground equipment to start the engines, a facility not available at island airports, and were dangerous to crews because of fumes accumulating in the cockpit. John Corrigan, who was stationed at the engineering base at Renfrew Airport, does not however condemn them totally out of hand:

> Initially they were based at Speke Airport, near Liverpool, and were converted into passenger aircraft by Scottish Aviation Ltd at Prestwick. They fitted them out with beautiful blue upholstered seats and they were very comfy and reliable for the Scottish routes. Spares, however, were a major problem with a great deal of cannibalisation required to keep the fleet flying. The engines had about as much compression as a burst balloon – fortunately there were three! The oil level indicator was a cork on the end of a wire, sticking straight up from the tank in each nacelle encased in a glass tube – usually broken, with the cork waving in the breeze! The cockpit was like a plumber's shop with massive radiator-type valves and controls, and I think an outside mirror to let you see if Number Two engine in front of you had an exhaust fire, a common occurrence on all three when starting up. The air wheel-brakes were supplied from bottles which could only be recharged from a ground supply source – so be careful when taxying and conserve your supply!

Jim Howie gives a pilot's perspective of the aircraft beginning with a colourful turn of phrase which results from many years of residence in Australia:

> It resembled an outback dunny with wings. It was simple, rugged, carried twelve passengers – and had its problems. Its tyres were prone to developing a sudden blister before rupturing. The centre engine tended to leak exhaust into the cockpit. A cold start in the cockpit was wondrous to behold. There was a wobble pump to build up fuel pressure, a ki-gas pump to prime the cylinders, a hand energiser for the starter, three lots of engine switches on a plate, and three throttles. One pilot pumped furiously and operated the ki-gas primer. The other wound the energiser and took care of switches and throttles. Several minutes of frantic activity were needed to produce a raucous roar from an engine. Taxying could be interesting too. The brakes were operated individually by the port and starboard throttle levers, and both together by the centre one. As the levers had to come back through the idle position to brake, an engine often died and had to be restarted. All good clean fun. In its favour, the Ju was strongly built and had a very low landing speed.

The Ju 52s remained in service for only a matter of months and had all been disposed of for scrapping within a year. Avro Ansons from Railway Air Services, classed as the Avro 19 in their civilian form, also made a brief appearance in Scotland around this time, but, on the Scottish

A happy landing on Lewis for passengers Shirley and Ruth Shepherd in 1968. (J. P. Shepherd)

A flavour of the early days of BEA in Scotland is indicated by the Flying Log of Radio Officer Archie Edmiston. G-AGIC, G-AGIF, G-AGLE, G-AGOJ, G-AHGI, G-AHLL and G-AIHN are de Havilland Rapides. G-AHBP, G-AHOD and G-AHOI are Junkers Ju-52 Jupiters. Airfields visited are CC - Campbeltown, IV – Inverness, IY – Islay, JW – Prestwick, LV – Liverpool, OY – Kirkwall, RW – Renfrew, SJ – Sumburgh, SV – Stornoway, and TG – Tiree. HEBS was often used to record the circle route through Tiree and Barra to Benbecula. (courtesy of Eva Edmiston)

Time carried forward :- 91·19

Date	Hour	Aircraft Type and No.	Pilot	Duty	REMARKS (including results of bombing, gunnery, exercises, etc.)	Flying Times Day	Night
14·2·47		GAIHN	CAPT. WOOD	IY		1·25	
17·2·47		"	" "	CC		1·12	
19·2·47		GAGIF	" W. McKENZIE	SJ up.	Overnight stop.	3·15	
20·2·47		"	" "	SJ down.		3·20	
24·2·47		GAHGI	F/O SIM	LOCAL.		1·30	
24·2·47		" Ju	" "	"		1·05	
25·2·47		GAHBP Ju	CAPT. W. McKENZIE	RW – LV.	Ju52 A/C delivery to Speke.	1·55	
"		GAHOI Ju	" "	LV – RW.	" " " – Renfrew.	1·35.	
27·2·47		GAGLE.	" FITTALL	SJ.	Refuelled IV. Returned direct RW from OY due to weather conditions at SJ.	4·25.	
4·3·47		GAHGI	CAPT. CLAYTON	RW-JW-RW.	Local flying and practice landings.	1·55	
5·3·47		GAGOJ Ju	" DAY.	SJ.	RW-OY-RW direct due weather at SJ.	4·10	
6·3·47		GAHOD	" W. McKENZIE	RW-JW-RW.	Ju52 local flying and landings.	1·45	
8·3·47		GAHLL Ju	" WOODWARD	HEBS-SV		3·55	
10·3·47		GAHOD	" W. McKENZIE	LOCAL	Ju Training flight.	1·30	
11·3·47		GAHLL	" WOOD.	HEBS-SV.		4·05	
13·3·47		GAGLE	" CLAYTON	" "	No landing at TG due weather.	4·10	
14·3·47		GAGIC	" McDERMOTT.	JW CHARTER		·40	
14·3·47		GAGOJ	" "	CIG. DROPPING & PHOTO CHARTER.		1·30	
15·3·47		GAGOJ	" "	FODDER DROPPING CHARTER.		1·35	

TOTAL TIME ...136·25

internal trunk routes, the place of the long-serving Rapides was taken up by Douglas DC-3 Dakotas, which were also refurbished and upgraded by Scottish Aviation, and were subsequently called the *Pionair* class by BEA.

With Pionairs providing much greater capacity than the Rapides, from 1948 mail was carried between Stornoway and both Inverness and Renfrew at unsurcharged rates, a facility also introduced at this time on the Renfrew-Islay service although that service continued to be operated by Rapides until 1952. Passengers, by the early 1950s, had a daily, except Sunday, Pionair service from Renfrew to Stornoway with a single stop at Benbecula, while the Inverness-Stornoway service operated three days a week, increasing to six during the peak summer months of July and August. Aircraft movements at Stornoway on Sundays were taboo in deference to religious sensitivities on Lewis, a practice which remains today. Between 1952 and 1954, services linking Stornoway with Renfrew again included Tiree as well as Benbecula as en route calls, with flights reduced to four times a week during winter. However, the overall trend was growth of the air service and Renfrew-bound passengers were also able to use connections through Inverness thus giving them a choice of two routes. Although the distance between Inverness and Stornoway made it, on paper, a relatively short sector, the intervening mountains could considerably lengthen the journey. Captain Jim Howie explains what it was like during Rapide operations:

> There are two valleys in the north of Scotland which offered a choice of route from Stornoway to Inverness. If these were considered risky, you went all the way round the north coast. If you had to do this it was a long, rough trip. As winter approached, we practised for the bad weather. We began map reading on the eighth inch to the mile topographical and progressed to the half inch Ordnance Survey. 500 feet is a good height for general sight-seeing and map reading but operations could take us down to 200 feet and sometimes less where things look quite different. If there wasn't a problem with the freezing level, there were let-down facilities at most of the island airports. These were 'teardrop' patterns, based on a string of QDMs, magnetic courses to steer to the ground unit, and they could be flown with surprising accuracy. As the QDM on the outbound leg had to be converted to its reciprocal for the course made good, the drift assessed and reversed for the start of the inbound leg, the rate of descent checked against the clock, and a maximum of six QDMs per minute in good conditions, there were five minutes of intense mental activity.

John Morton began his flying career with BEA with a posting to Scotland from 1956 to 1958 on the Heron. His routine was ambulance standby duty coupled with scheduled flights to the Hebrides and Wick. A typical day's roster consisted of six sectors – Glasgow to Barra via Tiree and return followed by a late lunch at Renfrew Airport, then Glasgow-Inverness-Stornoway:

> We would be the last aircraft of the day at Stornoway and the Air Traffic Controller, usually on a rest-cure posting from London, would close the airfield and follow us to the hotel. It served only a high tea at 6.00pm instead of dinner, so we usually had two high teas, one after the other. There was always some excellent salmon, fresh from a local stream, and a good choice of meat dishes.
>
> For entertainment we would often be invited to the hotel manageress's room to listen to her extensive collection of records. Helped by a dram or two, this usually turned into an opportunity for us all to perform our favourite party pieces. Alternatively, we could go to the cinema. Its programme usually finished at 10.00pm. The last bus to the outlying villages left at five past ten and Stornoway died, to be brought to life again at midnight when MacBrayne's steamer came in. A lot of the town's activity revolved around this event. We usually contrived to take with us, to the cinema, a couple of bottles of beer, not for our own consumption but to give to the foreman of the local kipper factory. This was only a few minutes' walk from the picture house and we would be expected. The foreman would have picked out one or two really plump herring from the day's catch and be smoking them over their own little pile of oak chips ready for our arrival. They were a real treat.
>
> Because the boat was scheduled in at midnight, the hotel staff would all work late and nobody would be available to make our breakfast when we rose at 6.00am to take out the early flight to

Inverness and Glasgow. We were each provided with an alarm clock and knocked on each other's doors to ensure we were both awake. The hotel provided the raw food in the kitchen and, as the Second Officer, it was my duty to cook the Captain's breakfast. As David Barclay and some of the other Captains were Scots, the porridge had to be good!

Stornoway may have gained a fully-fledged airport as a result of World War Two but this didn't deter informal activities both on the ground and in the air. As experienced by Bill Reid, it may even had aided them:

Approaching the runway at Stornoway one day, I was interested to see a motor car driving along beneath me on the same runway. After an unscheduled overshoot I found that it had been a local farmer taking his usual shortcut home. Indeed the Hebrides are a world apart.

In the 1950s I was asked by a zoologist sort of chap called J. Morton Boyd if I could help him with a study he was doing on the Atlantic grey seal. This required me to photograph the animals in the appropriate season when it was easy to identify the seal pups in their white coats on the Hebridean island of Taransay, thus monitoring the build up of the colony. Never loath to find an excuse for low flying I jumped at the chance. The Dakota passengers didn't seem to mind too much as I swooped low over Taransay with my camera stuck out of the cockpit window. It was worth while and an article by Boyd on the subject duly appeared in a prestigious geographical magazine.

The swinging sixties brought a new form of air travel to Stornoway with the displacement of the Pionair on the Renfrew service by the Vickers Viscount. Stornoway and Benbecula did not host the Handley Page Dart Herald as had occurred at Campbeltown and Islay. The Viscounts served Stornoway throughout the remainder of BEA service and well into the British Airways era. Between 1966 and 1974, Loganair made a small intrusion on the Stornoway-Benbecula-Glasgow route, but not the reverse, when it was authorised to carry a total of fifteen passengers each week. This was on the empty-leg of an early-morning newspaper service with aircraft used including Piper Aztecs, Britten-Norman Islanders, a Beech E18S and a Short Skyvan. Withdrawal of the Viscounts by British Airways coincided with the creation of its Highlands Division which involved staff reductions and new work practices. Robin Mackenzie, who had succeeded Jimmy Steen as station superintendent at Stornoway in 1954, found his diminished team moving from their long-established office at the Royal Hotel to Stornoway Airport. In addition to issuing tickets and handling reservations, their duties now included checking-in passengers, handling freight consignments, and being on the tarmac to greet the 'Budgie', the familiar name given to the Hawker Siddeley 748, and turn it around and send it on its way again. As with Benbecula, Loganair flew a competing service in 1991/92, which operated non-stop to Glasgow, but British Airways services were also non-stop by this time and here too the Loganair service was not sustained. British Airways had been operating BAe ATPs from 1989 and, since 1996, British Regional Airlines has continued the route with the same aircraft type under its franchise arrangement with its predecessor. BAe ATPs were also used on the Stornoway-Inverness service by British Regional from 1996 until 2000 when the route was taken over by Loganair. Loganair introduced Saab 340 aircraft to the twice-daily service but also extended one service to Edinburgh. The Loganair schedule also included a new non-stop service between Edinburgh and Stornoway on Saturdays, the being the first such service between Lewis and the capital.

The appearance of Stornoway Airport underwent major change in 2001 with the construction of a new terminal building three times the size of its predecessor which was catering for 90,000 travellers annually. A 'new' name appeared on Hebridean routes from September 2001 when Highland Airways, formerly known as Air Alba and a member of the Atlantic Airlines Group, began scheduled services from Inverness to Stornoway and became the contractor for Comhairle nan Eilean Siar supported route between Stornoway and Benbecula. The Prestwick built BAe Jetstream 31 is flown by Highland Airways on these services.

5

The Northern Isles

Inhabitants living on the islands off the west coast of Scotland talk about making a trip 'to the mainland' when they travel to Glasgow or Inverness. The islanders of Orkney and Shetland have a very different affinity which reflects their Nordic heritages. Each island group has its own 'mainland' and to a Shetlander travelling to Aberdeen, or an Orcadian flying to Wick or Inverness, the journey is to Scotland. While these might be islands apart, their air links with Scotland were established right at the beginning of sustained domestic air services in Scotland. This is not strange, because the sea crossings by boat could be daunting experiences, making the air alternative an extremely attractive proposition.

Orkney Odyssey

The name of Edmund Fresson has long been synonymous with air travel in the north of Scotland and with the islands beyond. While Fresson saw scope for air services between Scotland and Orkney and set out to create Highland Airways to bring this vision to reality, the idea itself emerged by accident. Fresson arrived in the north of Scotland in 1931, flying de Havilland Gypsy Moth G-AAWO and seeking suitable fields for a touring programme of aerial displays and joy rides for the North British Aerial Company Ltd of Chester. During the course of this survey, he crossed the Pentland Firth from Wick to Kirkwall. During the season's tour which followed, Fresson was paid by two passengers to fly them from Wick to Kirkwall. Similar requests from both sides of the Pentland Firth followed and Fresson realised that the twenty-minute flight was preferred by many as an alternative to the sea route which could entail a stomach-jerking voyage of as much as five hours in adverse conditions. Two years later, Highland Airways was established at Longman Aerodrome, Inverness, and on 8 May 1933 Fresson began scheduled services from Inverness via Wick to Wideford Farm, Kirkwall with General Aviation Monospar G-ACEW. This was less than a month after the beginning of the first sustained scheduled air service in Scotland, by Midland & Scottish Air Ferries from Renfrew to Campbeltown.

The Monospar was a stopgap aircraft and in July 1933, Highland Airways took delivery of de Havilland DH84 Dragon G-ACIT. It was the first of many Dragons to join the Highland Airways fleet, but the only one to continue in the service of BEA in 1947. On 7 May 1934, Fresson began a second Orkney service, this time from a landing site at Seaton, Aberdeen. Earlier that year, Eric Gandar Dower had registered Aberdeen Airways and secured an airfield at Dyce, the site of the present Aberdeen Airport. Gandar Dower initially endeavoured to launch a service to Glasgow, but this brought little success because of the long-established rail services which were both fast and reliable. Gandar Dower quickly realised that Fresson had the correct formula in focusing upon sea crossings, emphasised by the failure of another briefly operated land route in 1935, this time from Aberdeen to Edinburgh. Captain Eric Starling, Chief Pilot of Aberdeen Airways and later to become Flight Manager Scotland for BEA, inaugurated Aberdeen Airways' first service to Orkney. This occurred on 27 May 1935, with former Hillman's Airways de Havilland Dragon G-ACAN flying from Dyce to Stromness. A call at Thurso was included from 11 June and, from 29 June, additional flights operated on the Stromness-Thurso sector. Aberdeen Airways began calling on demand at St Margaret's Hope, South Ronaldsay, from 3 December 1935. On 15 January 1936, competition with Highland Airways intensified with Aberdeen Airways' opening of an airfield at Quanterness to serve Kirkwall. Aberdeen Airways acquired its first de Havilland

The Northern Isles

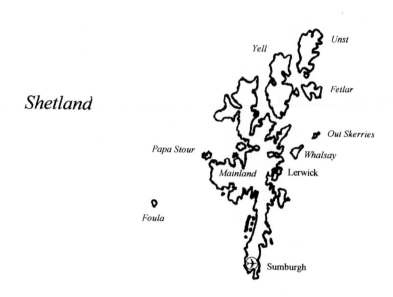

Unst

Yell

Fetlar

Shetland

Out Skerries

Papa Stour

Whalsay

Mainland

Lerwick

Foula

Sumburgh

Fair Isle

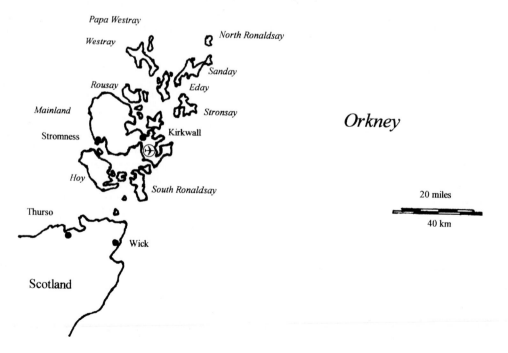

Papa Westray

Westray

North Ronaldsay

Sanday

Rousay

Eday

Mainland

Stronsay

Orkney

Stromness

Kirkwall

Hoy

South Ronaldsay

Thurso

20 miles

40 km

Wick

Scotland

DH89 Rapide in 1935, primarily for use on services to Shetland, but from 1938 other Rapides gradually joined the Dragons by which time Aberdeen Airways had been renamed, from 13 February 1937, as Allied Airways (Gandar Dower) Ltd. Highland Airways received its first Rapide in 1936, also with Shetland in mind and, following amalgamation with Northern & Scottish Airways, became Scottish Airways from 12 August 1937. From 3 May 1938, this link-up resulted in a through service from Renfrew to Kirkwall, and on to Sumburgh, with stops at Perth, Inverness and Wick. However the Air Travel Licensing Authority (ATLA), in designating route licences in February 1939, removed Scottish Airways' authority to fly from Aberdeen leaving it as Allied Airways' sphere of operations.

World War Two had differing effects on the two competing airlines. Both companies were barred from civil flying on 3 September 1939, but within a fortnight this order was withdrawn. At Aberdeen, Gandar Dower's airfield at Dyce was requisitioned, control passed to RAF Coastal Command, and concrete runways laid. His airfields at Thurso and Stromness were both disabled and made unsuitable for further use by the military. Fresson had continued use of his field at Longman, Inverness, despite requisition. His airfield at Wick had tarmac runways, constructed by RAF Fighter Command. At Kirkwall he was given access to the Naval Air Station at Hatston in 1941, but later transferred operations to Grimsetter which was built for RAF Fighter Command and remains in use as the civil airport for Kirkwall today. During the war, Scottish Airways joined the Associated Airways Joint Committee (AAJC), which provided an arrangement enabling civil airlines to pool resources. Gandar Dower, with his independent spirit, remained outwith the AAJC and made separate arrangements with the military authorities for the duration of wartime operations, but this was generally not to his advantage as he struggled to obtain sufficient aircraft for his needs.

Gandar Dower fought off the postwar plan for nationalisation of the independent airlines, while Fresson, and George Nicholson, his counterpart at Renfrew, had to resign themselves to the acceptance of events. Both airlines continued to operate their respective routes from Aberdeen and Inverness to Orkney after the war. Scottish Airways was taken over by BEA on schedule on 1 February 1947, but Gandar Dower put up a dogged resistance to remain an independent scheduled operator. He succeeded in doing this for two months, but BEA officials felt that Gandar Dower's failure to operate his schedules on 11 April, when his small pool of aircraft had all 'gone technical', gave them sufficient authority to curtail the rebellion by stepping in and taking over the Allied Airways operation. Tasked with this duty was Edmund Fresson who was spared the unpleasantness of a direct confrontation with his old rival, Gandar Dower being in Switzerland at the time. Gandar Dower was left with a couple of his aircraft and a hangar at Dyce where he remained for many years – down but not out. Throughout the existence of BEA, he fought a war of attrition to obtain compensation from the Ministry of Aviation, Board of Trade – and BEA. BEA was the last to settle, which it did with the writing of a cheque for £132,530 on 30 May 1973.

Fresson's tenure with BEA was not a happy one. Because of his belief in the need for autonomy of the Corporation in Scotland so as to respond best to the unique operating conditions of which he had nearly two decades of experience, he had argued for the creation of a separate Scottish Division within BEA. This was conceded, but as illustrated by the imposition of Junkers Ju 52 aircraft as Rapide replacements, in name only. The pretence was quickly given up with the merging of the Scottish and English Divisions within a matter of months. The Scottish Division was reinstated in 1949 but this was too late for Fresson. In the intervening period his services had been dispensed with. Fresson recalled an example of how he earned the displeasure of his London-based superiors, through use of his discretion and local knowledge. The incident which caused the provocation was an ambulance flight in February 1947, immediately after the BEA takeover, and the resulting disapproval was transmitted to him via Renfrew:

> The Press gave the flight some publicity and within a few days I received a short terse letter from the manager of British European Airways at Renfrew, saying it was understood I had carried out an ambulance flight to Stronsay on the 11th inst., and I was requested to inform them who had given me the authority to make the flight, and that in future, I was not to carry out any further flights of a like nature. I replied, saying that I had not received any instructions forbidding me to carry out mercy flights. In fact, I understood the reason for stationing G-ACIT at Inverness was for that very purpose, plus the carrying out of any charter flights which might occur. I concluded by adding, that if I had not been near at hand and had failed to carry out that mercy flight call, the surgeon at Balfour Hospital told me the boy would most certainly have died, for he was sorely injured.

Edmund Fresson, obviously a thorn in the sides of BEA's higher echelons, was sacked the following year and given compensation of £2,000. Upon receiving notice of the termination of his employment, he had expressed interest in purchasing G-ACIT to use on a private venture for air ambulance and charter flights serving the Northern Isles. His memoirs record that, 'I was brusquely refused, and to make sure that I did not keep the plane, it was removed (to Renfrew) in a stealthy manner out of my reach.' G-ACIT remained with BEA as a communications aircraft until January 1949 while the de Havilland Moth G-AAWO with which Fresson had surveyed Orkney in 1931 was given to him - but his destiny now lay with a new position in Kenya. BEA's treatment of Fresson and the other pioneers of the Scottish independent airlines created an inauspicious start for the new state corporation, although Fresson qualifies his own bitterness towards BEA:

> The Corporation which existed in 1947-48... was ruled by the personnel of the wartime A.T.A. organisation, who applied wartime 'know-how' to commercial operations which were doomed to disaster from the beginning. When Mr Peter Masefield became Chief Executive, BEA was reborn and became a businesslike organisation. Before long, under his management and leadership, the huge losses of previous years were turned into a profit. ... I bear no ill-will to the BEA of today.

These sentiments were penned by Fresson in 1963. By many accounts, Fresson was a proudly independent man who was unable to adjust to the constraints and hierarchical system that came with the creation of BEA, and his patience was pressed to the limit when he was witnessing decisions being made which were adversely affecting air services in the north of Scotland, and when his advice, resulting from long experience, was repeatedly shunned.

BEA had an initial presence at Hatston Aerodrome. Lena Esson took her first job upon leaving school there, where she was employed as a teleprinter operator at a wage of £2 6s a week. She recalls that, 'This job lasted only one year until BEA gave up the use of their teleprinters'. BEA also set up a booking office in Kirkwall and operated its own bus between it and the airport. Audrey Hercus recalls that the BEA bus was 'quite a novelty in Orkney'. Audrey joined BEA in September 1947 and spent the next decade with the airline. Family links with Orkney aviation had previously been established by her father, Gillies Hercus, who took Highland Airways bookings at the Orcadian newspaper office for Ted Fresson during the 1930s when Wideford Farm provided the airfield for Kirkwall.

Grimsetter was, however, to be BEA's Kirkwall terminal for almost the entirety of its 26 years of operation and in the winter of 1949/50 it was served by four flights on each weekday. Flight S229A left Inverness Dalcross Airport at 0830 to arrive at 1000, followed by Flight S229E at 1210, arriving at Kirkwall at 1335. Flight S208A departed from Aberdeen at 0940, arriving at Kirkwall at 1120. These services all called at Wick and were operated by Rapides. Additionally, Flight S205A left Glasgow at 0825, arriving at 1045 and then continuing to Sumburgh. This service called at Aberdeen but omitted Wick and was flown by a Dakota.

Although during postwar scarcity it was to the Hebrides that some flight crew often flew with empty egg boxes in order to make small transactions, it is Orkney which has long been famous for its egg industry. Tom Young had regular four-box consignments sent to him from Kirkwall: 'Every one was double yolked. I sold them on at no profit but purely for the sake of the boys.' Eggs frequently travelled from Orkney as legitimate cargo. Ian Scott describes one consignment:

> When we were returning to Renfrew from Orkney, tins of broken eggs for bakers in Glasgow were put in the front hold of the Pionair. Our flights took us via Wick and Inverness. After take off from Inverness, and having to climb over the Grampian mountains, we were alarmed by mighty bangs from the front hold positioned just behind the First Officer's seat. These were caused by the press-on lids blowing off the egg tins by the drop in the atmospheric pressure. The luggage in the hold was liberally covered in egg.

Aircrew acquired fresh produce for their personal use from Orkney but here, rather than eggs, meat and butter were in vogue.

Wick, situated at the north-easterly tip of the Scottish mainland, like Campbeltown could almost be likened to an island outstation because of its distance from other parts of Scotland. It was certainly heavily integrated with Northern Isles air operations for which Kirkwall developed as the hub, and was a popular landfall for Orcadian air travellers holding the short thirty-minute hop in preference to the longer and more expensive journey to more southerly destinations. Wick had been upgraded from the pre-war grass airfield for RAF Fighter Command between 1939 and 1941 and, upon return to civil use, it was endowed with tarmac runways and extensive hangarage. From the late 1950s, passenger traffic at Wick was increased by personnel associated with the siting of the United Kingdom Atomic Energy Authority's reactor at Dounreay.

Lyn Lovie, who joined Allied Airways at Aberdeen in 1946 and transferred to BEA in 1947, spent the winter of 1952/53 as Traffic Clerk at Wick:

> For the winter schedule, a *Pionair* (Dakota) service was operated Aberdeen-Wick-Kirkwall-Sumburgh and, since the traffic staff at Wick had little experience of completing a Dak loadsheet, I was posted there to help. All passenger handling was carried out in small offices which formed part of one of the two very large hangars. The staff at the aerodrome consisted of Station Engineer, Jim Smith; Senior Traffic Officer, Alasdair Leask; and two Traffic Clerks, Laurie Hendry and myself. We used to have one-engine turnarounds, average time five minutes. The Dakota's port engine would be shut down, the passengers, baggage, mail and cargo from Aberdeen would be offloaded and the passengers, etc., for Kirkwall boarded and loaded. The traffic 'bod' would then take the loadsheet up to the cockpit for the skipper's signature. One day, because of extremely poor weather, snow on the ground and high winds, it was decided to bring the aircraft round to the front of the hangar for the turnaround. The boarding passengers were assembled just within the hangar doors for embarkation. The Senior Traffic Officer marshalled the aircraft but, either he got it wrong, or the Dak slithered on the ice on the tarmac, for the starboard wing slammed into the hangar door. The effect, of course, was similar to that of striking a gigantic gong. The noise was deafening. The skipper shot out of the aeroplane to survey the damage. The navigation light had been written off and other damage sustained. The service had to be cancelled although, if memory serves, the aircraft was flown back to Aberdeen.

In the Summer of 1952, *Pionair* service S206C was a through flight from London Northolt via Manchester, Edinburgh and Aberdeen to Kirkwall where it terminated, while Renfrew originating service S204C called at Aberdeen and continued from Kirkwall onwards to Sumburgh. With the introduction of the 1952/53 schedule, Rapides, which had remained familiar over the Inverness-Wick-Kirkwall route, were removed from schedules to the Northern Isles. From this time, the Dakota operated all services to Kirkwall – from Aberdeen, Edinburgh, Glasgow, Inverness, London, Sumburgh and Wick. London services were phased out with the introduction of Vickers Viscounts on the London to Renfrew and Edinburgh routes, and the arrival of the de Havilland Heron resulted in a brief appearance of Heron services from Inverness to Wick until the reduction of the Heron fleet from three to two aircraft following the crash of G-AOFY on Islay in 1957. A fifteen year association between the Dakota and the Northern Isles came to a conclusion in 1962 with the introduction of the Handley Page Dart Herald, the one aircraft type committed to the area which was, in the words of Shetland's Jimmy Burgess, 'not a hand-me-down' – as were the Viscounts which operated these routes from 1966 until the end of BEA in 1973 and beyond, despite their sustained popularity.

Eric Pert travelled monthly to Orkney in his occupation as a surveyor. The Herald had a very large fin and rudder and, he notes, on takeoff, unless the wind was straight down the runway, when the weight came off the main undercarriage the aircraft would weathercock into the wind giving the impression of crabbing down the runway – disconcerting to the nervous traveller. Having a high wing with the undercarriage located below the engines, there was a very long undercarriage leg and even the best of landings could result in a bounce:

> I well recall 26 January 1966 returning from Orkney with my boss who came from Glasgow and had a rather dry sense of humour. It was a filthy afternoon, a gale blowing with rain and mist, and many of the passengers returning from Shetland and in a delicate condition. Over the Pentland Firth at 2,000 feet was like sitting on a big dipper with the stewards working overtime on sick bags. It was with some relief that I heard the rumble of the undercarriage and flaps going down. After an age, flying over the moors in the gathering gloom, the threshold lights flashed below us and we hit the runway very hard. The next minute we were thirty feet in the air at which point my boss remarked, 'For God's sake don't applaud. He might do an encore.'

Just as Fresson had operated his Monospar and Dragons as an aerial bus service, so the Viscount continued to serve Orkney. The short hop across the Pentland Firth from Wick to Kirkwall regularly flew at 1,000 feet. The service was basic. There was no inflight catering on these routes so the attendants in the cabin were not referred to as 'stewards' but were instead titled 'flight clerks'. Their duties could be diverse, including loading baggage and de-icing the aircraft. They sometimes also took on additional duties of a voluntary nature as Eric Pert illustrates:

> It was about Easter, on a Viscount from Aberdeen with some children on board, that one of the stewards decided to enter the pressurised hold at the back of the cabin and bring out some day old chicks to show the kids. Everything went fine until he went to put them back and the plane gave a lurch. Next thing, dozens of chicks were running below the seats!

Les Young did not consider among his flight clerk's duties the physical restraint of a passenger who was imbibing from a whisky bottle and becoming increasingly obstreperous. He sent for the captain who, fortuitously, was a big fellow with a black beard. The captain came aft, towered over the drinking passenger and said, 'Right. Give me that bottle. Not a word out of you until we get to Renfrew.' And that finished it. When they arrived at Renfrew, he ran off the plane and left his bottle of whisky!

Jimmy Steen was BEA's station superintendent at Kirkwall for many years. Jack Ridgway transferred from Islay at the beginning of 1973 to oversee the last months of BEA in Kirkwall. He also oversaw proceedings in 1982 when the great and the good in British Airways assembled in Kirkwall to celebrate the Viscount upon its withdrawal. Guests were flown to Kirkwall in a fleet of four Viscounts, G-AOYM, G-AOYO, G-AOYR and G-APIM. Several of BEA's Viscounts were about to be sold to British Air Ferries with whom they would continue to be regular visitors to the Northern Isles, especially Shetland, and the new owners were charged with the task of 'looking after them and giving them a good home in their latter years'. In service with BEA in Scotland, the Viscount had been extremely reliable but was involved in one tragic incident. During an engineering test flight over Perthshire on 19 January 1973, G-AOHI struck the summit of Ben More (3,852 feet/1,174 metres), resulting in the deaths of Captain Walter Durward, Second Officer Stanley Kemp, and two engineers, James More and John Quinn.

Under British Airways, the Viscount had already been operating beside the Hawker Siddeley

748 which was introduced on the Aberdeen-Kirkwall run in 1975. The first of these flights was inaugurated with Captain Viv Gunton in command. Gunton had been BEA's first pilot to graduate from Hamble, which he did in 1962, and he took to the left seat in 1970 on the Heron, primarily to the Western Isles. He remained with British Airways throughout his flying career and upon retirement he was a Captain on the Aerospatiale/BAC Concorde. With the 748 in service, British Airways began to diversify with charter work for oil personnel on the Isle of Flotta. Occasional special interest charter flights from Kirkwall to Bergen had been inaugurated with the Viscount and a seasonal scheduled service was introduced with the Hawker Siddeley 748 on 6 June 1987.

Loganair launched scheduled services from Edinburgh to Kirkwall in 1980, a move prompted by British Airways schedule changes in 1979 under which Edinburgh passengers who were required to change at Aberdeen found that they no longer had a connecting service. The direct Loganair service from Edinburgh to Kirkwall was operated by the Shorts 330, at that time the flagship of the Loganair fleet, but the DHC-6 Twin Otter gradually took over the route with occasional support from the Embraer Bandeirante and a stop at Wick was incorporated from 1981. From 1985 the route was shared between the Twin Otter and the Shorts 360 which operated the full schedule from 1989. The Shorts 360 was supplemented by a Twin Otter in 1991, and with a BAe ATP in 1993. In Loganair's penultimate pre-British Airways franchise timetable, all of the services were operated by ATP but, with the passage of these aircraft to Manx Airlines Europe following reorganisation within the Airlines of Britain Group, the service reverted to Shorts 360 operation in Summer 1994. This arrangement continued with the transfer of the route to British Regional Airlines following the Loganair management buyout in 1997 and the transfer back to Loganair in October 1998. Since 9 August 1999, Loganair has operated the Edinburgh Kirkwall service with Saab 340 aircraft.

From Glasgow, Loganair launched the first non-stop service to Kirkwall in October 1991 with the introduction of the BAe Jetstream 31, a journey of only one hour and ten minutes. With the transfer of Jetstream 31 and 41 aircraft to Manx Airlines Europe, the schedule was operated by Shorts 360 in 1994 and incumbency passed to British Regional Airlines in tandem with the Edinburgh route – and back again in October 1998. The Saab 340 was introduced to the service on 3 July 1999.

Unaffected by the arrival of British Regional in the Northern Isles has been the Kirkwall-Wick route which Loganair has operated since 1976, primarily using the Britten-Norman Islander, and with some services continuing to Inverness. An Inverness-Wick direct service is now flown with the Saab 340. It was a Loganair Britten-Norman Islander which was used for the launch of the controversial British Airways 'world images' identity with the unveiling of G-BLDV sporting the tartan tail design by Peter MacDonald dubbed 'Mountain of the Birds'. First serving in Orkney in 1967 when it launched inter-island services, Loganair is now entrenched as the Orcadians' airline. By December 2001, passengers were passing through a new terminal building at Kirkwall, double the capacity of the former structure, and a development which heralded a seven day operation from the summer of 2002.

Sumburgh – aerial toehold on Shetland

The Shetland Isles saw construction of an airfield at Scatsta in 1940 for use as an RAF Fighter Command base to complement the seaplane base at RAF Sullom Voe, and in the 1970s they witnessed the addition of Lerwick Airport at Tingwall along with several airstrips linking this with other islands in the group. Yet Sumburgh has always been the main gateway between the islands and the rest of the world. Situated at the southern end of the Shetland mainland, its approach remains 'interesting'. Lars-Axel Nilsson, a co-pilot on Boeing B-17 Flying Fortress aircraft operating the wartime ball-bearing run for AB Aerotransport of Sweden from Stockholm to Aberdeen, had an unscheduled visit to Sumburgh on 7 November 1944. Number four engine failed as the aircraft was crossing the mountains of occupied Norway. Captain Marshall Lindholm decided that continuation of the westward journey would be safer than a return to Sweden, but the aircraft was unable to maintain height on three engines, despite jettisoning a load of 250kg of ball-bearings, and a diversion to Sumburgh was quickly planned even although this carried its own risks:

> We had no maps over the Shetland Islands and we had not received any information from the Air Ministry. We could contact Sumburgh and got clearance to land. To assist us, light beacons were switched on and information about obstacles, landing direction, etc. was transmitted. The surrounding terrain was rather high and the runway only 1,350 yards with a 300-foot hill on finals close to the runway. As this field was unknown to me, I ordered, just in case, the radio operators and navigator to go back to the cabin before landing.

Lindholm, displaying heroic flying skills under difficult circumstances, wrestled the Flying Fortress on to the ground at Sumburgh with all seven crew and fourteen passengers none the worse for the experience, the latter being blissfully unaware of events occurring on the flight deck and beyond the masked windows. The extent of Lindholm's dexterity was only brought home to his young co-pilot many years later when Nilsson made a return visit to Shetland and occupied the jump seat of the BAe ATP of British Airways for the flight from Aberdeen to Sumburgh:

> We flew in towards the beacon and landed in daylight on the same runway as the last time – now lengthened. I could without any doubts see that it was not only Captain Lindholm's skill which had saved us that night almost 50 years ago. We also owe great thanks to Providence. Just a little bit further to the right on finals and we would have been stuck on the slope of the 420-foot hill close to the approach line.

As aircraft have become larger, the topography surrounding Sumburgh has placed limitations on the types which can be handled. But it was neither the landing run nor the hills which were the foremost problems impeding regular air services to Shetland when they were already well-established in Orkney. It was the relatively long stretch of water, weather conditions which could shroud the islands in mist when Scotland and Orkney were basking in sunshine, and the absence of navigational aids, which kept Shetland at arm's length.

Flights to Shetland had taken place, before navigational aids were installed, both by occasional flying boats and land planes. The first land plane to touch down was DH83 Fox Moth G-ACEB of SMT Aviation under the command of Captain Bill Caldwell on 19 April 1933, fulfilling a charter carrying officials of the Commercial Bank of Scotland in Edinburgh to the company's Lerwick office. The Fox Moth had routed via Longman Field, Inverness, and Kirkwall, before arriving on Sumburgh Links taking five hours and fifteen minutes of flying time and a total lapsed time of eight hours. During the final stage of the journey from Orkney, Caldwell, in the open cockpit, had endured snow showers and a strong northerly wind. However, had the same journey been undertaken by train and steamer, McCallum and Adams, the representatives of the bank, would not have stepped ashore in Lerwick Harbour until fifty-five hours following their departure from Edinburgh.

During the following weeks, further visits were made by SMT with DH84 Dragon aircraft undertaking photographic surveys and joyriding flights. Shetlanders were rapidly becoming used to the appearance of SMT's aircraft and had hopes that an air service would be a natural progression by the company. SMT were aware that the lack of navigational aids would make a scheduled service difficult to maintain – and were also of the view that Edmund Fresson's position in the north was already sufficiently well established to make such a development difficult for SMT. Indeed, Edmund Fresson also made the journey north later that year, landing not at Sumburgh, but on the Isle of Bressay opposite the town of Lerwick. He had set out for Sumburgh on 4 October 1933, but had turned back to Kirkwall when he encountered low rain cloud. During another attempt on the next day, he landed on the Isle of Bressay upon the suggestion of his charter passenger, Peter Angus, who had knowledge of the area. A return visit on 17 October convinced Fresson that Shetland must become a natural extension of the Highland Airways scheduled route network, bur he was acutely aware of the impediments at Sumburgh which militated against the provision of a safe and reliable service. Pilots trying to reach Shetland while flying to a predetermined timetable, a prerequisite for a regular scheduled service, ran the risk of being engulfed in fog and either coming to grief on the cliffs of Fair Isle or Sumburgh Head - or missing the islands altogether. The presence of a suitable landing area at Sumburgh was therefore not enough. The airfield would have to be equipped with the latest navigational aids.

Progress was therefore deferred for three years by which time the two competing airlines in the north of Scotland, Fresson's Highland Airways and Eric Gandar Dower's Aberdeen Airways, both had aspirations of serving Shetland. It was not until May 1936 that radio equipment for installation at the airfield arrived by sea at Lerwick, and Shetland could, in the words of its Member of Parliament, Major Neven-Spence, 'get better communication with the adjacent islands of Great Britain and Ireland'. The all-important direction finder was located in a shed at Sumburgh while the transmitting equipment was installed on a trolley which could be manoeuvred between two masts to home in on the best reception.

Because the radio equipment had been installed by the Air Ministry, Sumburgh airfield was available to all operators. This contrasted with, for example, Dyce which Gandar Dower owned and which did not have Air Ministry navigational aids. While this could be a handicap during bad weather, it nonetheless enabled Gandar Dower to have control over his airport and exclude access by Highland Airways which had to arrange its own field at Kintore. Fresson had been openly planning his Shetland service for some considerable time and anticipated having, quite literally, a clear field, when he began his Shetland services.

On 23 May 1936, Fresson announced in the press that his services to Shetland would be inaugurated on 3 June. It was with some surprise and consternation that an Aberdeen Airways advertisement on 1 June greeted him with the news that it planned to begin services to Shetland next day. On the same day as Fresson was being confronted by the Aberdeen Airways advertisement, his agent in Shetland, Laidlaw McDougall, was writing to advise him that Gandar Dower had arrived in Shetland on 30 May and inform him that, 'He duly turned up, but did not pay landing fees although Black logged him and asked his pilot for same.' (Jim Black was Fresson's Sumburgh agent.) As the plot thickened, McDougall again contacted Fresson, advising him that, 'G.D. is bringing some Lord and Viscount tomorrow. Is aerodrome yet opened as a public aerodrome? Direction Finding station not yet completely calibrated. It's dirty work but not unexpected.' Realising that Gandar Dower would upstage him in the publicity stakes, Fresson wrote to him to advise him that Sumburgh would not be open for business until 3 June.

Fresson later recorded that he did not appreciate the spirited competition which Gandar Dower was going to offer, and a de Havilland Rapide of Aberdeen Airways duly arrived at Sumburgh on 2 June 1936 to inaugurate the first scheduled air service to Shetland. On board were Eric Gandar Dower, his secretary and partner, Caroline Brunning, and guest from previous inaugural flights, Viscount Arbuthnott. At the controls of the aircraft, named *The Aberdonian*, was his chief pilot, Eric Starling. Fresson, lest it be considered that he was the gentleman throughout this affair, later recorded that he regretted lacking the foresight to instruct Black to place obstacles on the airfield to prevent the Aberdeen Airways aircraft from landing! Eric Starling who, after World War Two, was to fly for Fresson, described this first scheduled flight as being 'a bit naughty'.

Highland Airways began its Shetland services, as originally announced, on 3 June with ticket sales being handled by Mackay Brothers in Aberdeen and Ganson Brothers in Lerwick. While the direct service between Aberdeen and Sumburgh could now be flown in as little as ninety minutes, both airlines settled into a regular flying pattern with most flights operating via Caithness and Orkney in a flying time of two hours and forty-five minutes. Aberdeen Airways' return air fare, from Aberdeen to Lerwick, inclusive of transport between the town centres at both ends, was £8 10s.

Highland Airways had inaugurated the first internal air mail service for the Post Office in 1934 carrying standard-rate letters, between Inverness and Kirkwall, and in November 1937, the Post Office decided to extend the service to Shetland. Fresson did not submit a tender and he reputedly laughed his head off when he heard that Gandar Dower had taken it on, believing it would be discredited by cancellations during the winter months. Even Gandar Dower had confided to his chief pilot that he accepted that flights would frequently have to be cancelled, especially as his own airfield at Dyce did not have radio and navigational aids. To the surprise of everyone, the service ran without interruption until the following March.

When, in 1939, air routes became regulated by the Air Transport Licensing Authority, Aberdeen Airways, now renamed Allied Airways (Gandar Dower) Ltd, was awarded the non-stop route from Aberdeen to Sumburgh. From Kirkwall, Allied Airways and Highland Airways (now Scottish Airways), were authorised to operate on alternate days. Sumburgh Aerodrome underwent a major transformation for RAF use between 1939 and 1941 by which time the former grass field had tarmac runways and was a hive of military activity. Sumburgh, like Kirkwall, because of its strategic importance, continued to be served by scheduled services throughout World War Two, after a brief stoppage of just two weeks following the declaration of the conflict, and despite the constraints placed on the airlines in their access to pilots, aircraft, and passengers. Allied Airways' non-stop service from Aberdeen, inaugurated by Captain Harry Reed on 10 July 1939, was not resumed until the end of the War. Jimmy Burgess recalls Scottish Airways being at Sumburgh under the sufferance of the RAF. Flights were of course cancelled if German aircraft were in the vicinity and occasionally the airfield would be strafed. On one occasion, a Rapide was at the end of the runway when a Heinkel shot up the barracks. It made a hasty return to the ramp, and the passengers exited the aircraft and ran for cover but, by this time, the Heinkel had flown off. Perhaps a greater danger were the RAF's own Beaufighters which were a hazard on the ground because pilots had difficulty steering them and they had a tendency to cause damage, and injuries, if they ran into things!

It was a vastly changed airfield which was put at the disposal of BEA when, in 1947, it inherited the operations of Scottish Airways and Allied Airways. While the facilities were very different from those in 1939, following the withdrawal of the military in 1946, the airfield was deserted and the boom brought by the presence of armed forces was over.

Along with Kirkwall, Sumburgh saw the arrival of Junkers Ju 52 aircraft almost as soon as BEA had taken over from Scottish Airways and Allied Airways. Following his preview of the aircraft at Renfrew, Fresson remarked on the aircraft's 'tremendous amount of power for the carriage of fourteen passengers' which would be uneconomic to operate and for which there were inadequate mobile power units, needed for starting the engines, for each station. Fresson recommended that Rapides be retained until another option was available, but this was not taken up and the Junkers went into service. The Junker's engines, the product of wartime production intended for only 100 hours of service life, caused chaos because of their unreliability and, when

Renfrew Airport was departure point for most Hebridean services until Glasgow's airport was transferred to Abbotsinch in 1966. (John S. Groome)

Mail is loaded on Heron G-ANXB at Barra. (John S. Groome)

Aberdeen was the embarkation point for many Northern Isles services. Pionair G-ALYX outside the old terminal at Aberdeen. (British Airways Collection)

Edinburgh also featured in northern schedules. BEA staff at Turnhouse Airport in 1956. Jack Ridgway (back row, first left) became Station Superintendent firstly at Islay and then at Kirkwall. (courtesy of Janette Ridgway)

BEA's Kirkwall staff were very proud of 'their' bus. This 1947 line-up consists of Jim Scollay, Robin Bain (who drove the bus), Jean Philips, Lena Esson, David Rendall, Jack Watson and Sheila Dickens. (courtesy of Lena McFadyen)

Differing attire worn by Kirkwall staff demonstrates the varied roles which they performed at the base when they were photographed with Rapide G-AHXX some time between 1948 and 1952. The line up is as follows: Back row, left to right – Jim Robertson, Jean Philips, Ken Wards, Olaf Mooney, Bill Moncreiff, Jean Leslie, Robin Bain, Jack Wood, Audrey Hercus, Gifford Johnson and Ivy Cooper; Front row – Harry Fisher, Ian Brander, Hugh Marshall, Jack Watson and David Rendall. (J W Sinclair, courtesy of the Orkney Library Photographic Archive)

The Dakota was the mainstay on Scottish routes throughout the 1950s. This is G-AGYX, RMA George Holt Thomas.
(Brian Thorne)

Benbecula – no doubt about it. (John S. Groome)

The Kirkwall office in Broad Street, in 1948, is modest – and is dwarfed by the BEA bus, which Audrey Provan recalls as being 'quite a novelty in Orkney'. (courtesy of Lena McFadyen)

... and 'more modern' downtown Kirkwall premises during the 1960s. (courtesy of Janette Ridgway)

Junkers Ju-52, BEA's Jupiter class, G-AHOJ, at Kirkwall, August 1947. (Lena McFadyen)

BEA personnel with an early Dakota arrival at Kirkwall. The gathering includes Captain Bill Baillie (fourth left), Captain Edmund Fresson (fifth left) with his son, Richard, Captain Eric Starling (tenth left), and former Scottish Airways Company Secretary, Bill Cumming (centre, before aircraft steps). (courtesy of the Orkney Library Photographic Archive)

Viscount G-AOHJ on the apron at Benbecula while en route from Glasgow to Stornoway. (Phil Lo Bao)

BEA Scottish Airways Viscount 802 G-AOHI at the London Heathrow. (*Brian Thorne*)

Aircraft Fitter Gifford Johnson poses with two of 'his' Rapides at Kirkwall's Grimsetter Airport, c. 1950. (courtesy of Bill Cooper)

Loading baggage on to the Dakota at Kirkwall was a challenge to handlers. (courtesy of Bill Cooper)

116

The hold of the Viscount was also located high above the ground. (courtesy of Janette Ridgway)

The sun, low in the sky, catches new technology in the form of the Handley Page Herald at Kirkwall. (courtesy of Tony Naylor)

Heron 1B G-ANXB at Tiree on an afternoon rotation during September 1970. (Phil Lo Bao)

The Herons were succeeded by two Short Skyliners in 1973. G-AZYW at Abbotsinch. (J. Mitchell via Brian Thorne)

Jack Watson, Senior Traffic Officer at Kirkwall, welcomes
Gwen Fresson (centre), widow of pioneer Edmund Fresson,
to Kirkwall. A Loganair Britten-Norman Islander named in
Edmund Fresson's honour forms the backdrop. (courtesy of
Janette Ridgway)

BEA Station Engineer at Sumburgh, Arthur Dodds, and
Pionair G-AKJH RMA Edward Hillman, named after the
founder of Hillman's Airways. (courtesy of Jimmy Burgess)

A BEA Rapide salutes the longboat which will be set alight
at the culmination of the annual celebration of Up Helly Aa
in Lerwick. (courtesy of Tony Naylor)

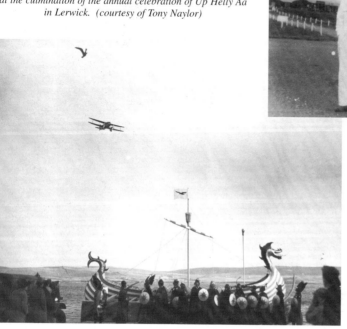

Captain Harry McDowell at Kirkwall wearing the 'old summer uniform' of BEA. (courtesy of Harry McDowell)

Sumburgh stalwarts, Jimmy Burgess (second left), and Jimmy Black (centre) with a Viscount crew at Sumburgh, late 1960s. (courtesy of Jimmy Burgess)

Wearing hybrid BEA/British Airways livery, G-AOHV starts up at Kirkwall prior to departure for Sumburgh in September 1975. (Phil Lo Bao)

they involuntarily stopped at stations such as Sumburgh, another aircraft had to fly from Renfrew with a starting unit causing delays of many hours. Fresson recommended their replacement by 16-passenger de Havilland DH86 Express airliners, but when the Junkers were speedily withdrawn in August 1947 they were replaced on the northern routes by Douglas Dakotas. This coincided with a programme of staff cuts by BEA in an effort to stem mounting losses at its Scottish stations. Jimmy Burgess, who began his airline career with Scottish Airways at Sumburgh in 1939, recalls that these cuts could be absorbed at Sumburgh because, while Rapide movements had extended across the full day from morning to evening, the Dakota was scheduled to call only once a day during winter.

The Dakotas were really too big for the job required of them at that time, especially as their capacity was increased from an initial eighteen passengers to an eventual thirty-two, but they resulted in a service from the Northern Isles which much more populous communities cannot aspire to today – a route to London's main airport – at that time Northolt. The Dakotas, to become BEA's Pionair class, initially operated the route pattern which had been given to the Junkers, namely Renfrew-Aberdeen-Kirkwall-Sumburgh, a single round trip circuit which operated on every weekday. While this was sustained, in 1950 it was joined by a service which left London Northolt at 0834 and arrived at Sumburgh at 1510 following intermediate stops at Edinburgh, Aberdeen and Kirkwall. The return service departed Sumburgh at 1545 and reached Northolt at 2145. This pattern continued until 1953. In 1954, non-stop services from Aberdeen to Sumburgh, launched briefly by Gandar Dower in 1939, were resumed by BEA albeit initially only three days a week. These flights also originated in London and called at Edinburgh. Through London services remained in place until 1957 when Vickers Viscounts replaced the Dakotas between London and Edinburgh.

Dakotas continued to serve Shetland from both Renfrew and Aberdeen until they were replaced by Handley Page Heralds in 1962. One of the last services, an inbound from Shetland with Stan Sickelmore in command of Pionair Leopard G-ALTT *RMA Charles Grey*, did not pass without event. Upon take-off from Inverness's Dalcross Airport on the final leg of its journey to Renfrew, rising temperature in the starboard engine was noted. Stan feathered the offending engine and, with the emergency services standing by, effected a perfect landing on the port engine back at Dalcross. The flight clerk was still working his way through the aircraft, advising the passengers to expect an emergency landing, when the aircraft touched down. However, as a precautionary measure, passengers were asked to quickly clear the aircraft by the rear exit. Stan was quite happy to accept credit for a faultless one-engine landing following the comments of 78-year-old Mrs Elizabeth Sinclair. 'Don't ask me what happened', she said. 'All I know is that the steward came and asked me to leave by the back door – and us just newly away. I thought of the height but he then said we were back on the ground again, so I came out with the rest of them.'

It was engine failure upon take-off from Inverness which persuaded Les Young to seek a transfer from his role as a flight clerk to that of traffic officer, and which subsequently provided him with relief postings around many of the Scottish islands. Eric Starling was in command of the Pionair which changed Les's career trajectory. The lost engine caused the tail of the aircraft to swing violently until Eric had taken corrective action to swing it back again and this, as Les reflects, 'was right where the flight clerk's seat was positioned.' Ian Scott rebelled when there was a move to relocate the flight clerk's position on the Dakota:

> I hadn't been a Captain for very long, whilst still at Renfrew, when BEA issued an instruction that, in certain loading circumstances, the Steward or Air Attendant had to sit on the jump seat in the cockpit for take-off and landing. This would allow 40kgs extra baggage and freight to be loaded in the rear hold. This worried me so much that I initially refused to do it. It was generally understood that the

two most likely times that an accident would occur were on the approach and landing, or on take-off. The only passenger door was behind the rearmost row of passenger seats and the two escape windows were halfway down the cabin. If one had an accident, there would be no crew member there to open the door.

Scott's concerns were eventually addressed, but only after the British Air Line Pilots Association (BALPA) had become involved and adjudication at an Airways Industrial Tribunal found in his favour. Extra carrying capacity was then achieved by fitting a rack, to hold four lead bars, in the floor of the cockpit. These enabled manipulation of the aircraft's centre of gravity when carrying extra baggage while still permitting the flight clerk to occupy his seat in the rear of the aircraft.

With the introduction of the Heralds, a morning service left Renfrew at 0940 to reach Sumburgh at 1155 with an intermediate stop at Aberdeen. An afternoon service began at Renfrew with calls at Inverness, Wick and Kirkwall. These two aircraft then 'swapped' routes for the southbound journeys so that the flying programme of one was Glasgow-Aberdeen-Sumburgh-Kirkwall-Wick-Inverness-Glasgow while the other flew the reverse of this and each crew had a total of six take-offs and six landings before returning to base. The first such service was flown on 16 April 1962 by G-APWB and this marked BEA's introduction of the Herald into scheduled service. The following year, the two routes became independent so that the round-trip route through Inverness, Wick and Kirkwall involved a total of eight take-offs and eight landings. This pattern was continued initially with the introduction of the Viscount in 1966. The capacity of the Viscount was restricted to a load of 46 passengers because of the runway length at Sumburgh. With the discovery of oil in the Scottish sector of the North Sea, BEA Helicopters stationed helicopters in Shetland for oil support work. It was to service a helicopter starting unit that Tom Young made his first visit to Sumburgh: 'I'd got my big parka, waterproof trousers, waterproof jacket; I'd got wellingtons, all interlinked, all ready for action on a wet blustery day. When I got there, the sun was beating down! I walked over to the unit and it would start up but it wouldn't hold in. I opened the small side door and a terminal fell out. I just lifted the terminal and screwed it in and that was it.'

When British Airways first began its flirtation with the Hawker Siddeley 748 in 1975, they were introduced on the Aberdeen to Sumburgh route and, with the creation of British Airways Highland Division in 1982, further 748s replaced the remaining Viscounts. In December 1984, British Airways began replacing leased 748s with the introduction of 'quieter and more fuel-efficient British Aerospace Super 748 aircraft' while two 748As, bought in 1975, were to be modified and upgraded to 748B specifications. By this time, British Airways' monopoly over the traditional island routes inherited by BEA from the independent airlines in 1947 and sustained by them throughout its 26-year tenure were now under attack in the north. While British Airways had passed some Hebridean services over to Loganair by mutual agreement from 1975, Aberdeen-based Air Ecosse adopted a more aggressive stance. In 1979, with Embraer Bandeirante aircraft seating up to eighteen passengers, Air Ecosse launched three daily flights from Aberdeen to Wick, one of which carried on to Sumburgh, and the Civil Aviation Authority withdrew British Airways' licence to serve Wick. The through Air Ecosse service to Sumburgh actually began in Dundee with Aberdeen and Wick both being intermediate stops. In 1982, a short-lived endeavour was made to extend the service further to the north-west, from Sumburgh to Vagar in the Faroe Islands, but by 1983 both Vagar and Sumburgh had disappeared from Air Ecosse timetables.

Loganair, which began Shetland internal services in 1970, also began services between Shetland and the Scottish mainland. These also commenced in 1979, but were not as confrontational as the Air Ecosse challenge, as they consisted of a non-stop DHC-6 Twin Otter service from Edinburgh, not to Sumburgh, but to Lerwick's Tingwall Airport. With upgrading to

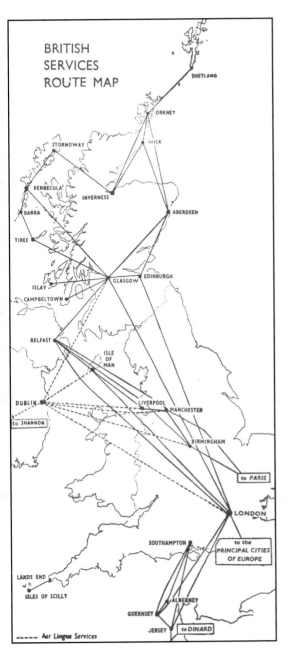

BRITISH
SERVICES
ROUTE MAP

SHETLAND

ORKNEY

STORNOWAY
WICK

BENBECULA
INVERNESS
BARRA
ABERDEEN
TIREE

ISLAY
GLASGOW   EDINBURGH
CAMPBELTOWN

BELFAST
ISLE
OF
MAN
DUBLIN
LIVERPOOL
to SHANNON
MANCHESTER

BIRMINGHAM

to PARIS

LONDON

SOUTHAMPTON
to the
PRINCIPAL CITIES
OF EUROPE
LANDS END
ISLES OF SCILLY

ALDERNEY
GUERNSEY
JERSEY   to DINARD

----- Aer Lingus Services

BEA British Isles network

1950

1967

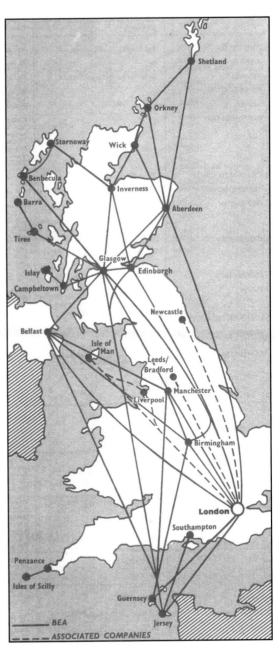

Shetland

Orkney

Stornoway   Wick
Benbecula   Inverness
Barra   Aberdeen
Tiree

Islay   Glasgow   Edinburgh
Campbeltown

Newcastle
Belfast
Isle of
Man   Leeds/
Bradford
Manchester
Liverpool

Birmingham

London
Southampton

Penzance

Isles of Scilly

Guernsey
Jersey

——— BEA
- - - ASSOCIATED COMPANIES

the faster BAe Jetstream in 1992, Loganair transferred operation of this service to Sumburgh. Loganair simultaneously introduced the Jetstream to a new non-stop Glasgow-Sumburgh route. Business Air later arrived on the Aberdeen-Sumburgh route, but in 1996 with British Airways' withdrawal from island routes and their passage on a franchise basis to British Regional Airlines, Business Air made a tactical withdrawal. Ironically, in 1997, Business Air became part of the Airlines of Britain Group, which also owned British Regional, and soon had a Saab 340 flying Aberdeen-Sumburgh, in British Airways colours, for British Regional Airlines to supplement its BAe ATPs. British Regional also employed Shorts 360 aircraft and used both these and ATPs for services to Glasgow and Shorts 360s to Edinburgh, Kirkwall, Wick and Inverness. However, in October 1998, as Loganair re-established its position in Scotland, it took over the services linking Sumburgh with Kirkwall, Wick, Inverness and Edinburgh and competed with British Regional to Glasgow with the Shorts 360s which it absorbed into its fleet. In 1999, Loganair began a phased replacement of the Shorts 360s on these services with the faster Saab 340s. The twentieth century closed with Newcastle-based Gill Air serving the Aberdeen-Wick route, but on 25 March 2001 Eastern Airways of Humberside, which had already established a significant presence at Aberdeen, became the latest incumbent on the Wick service, operating twice daily with Jetstream 32 aircraft. September 2001 saw Loganair replace British Regional Airlines on the Aberdeen-Kirkwall route.

As previously mentioned, a load penalty was stipulated when BEA introduced the Viscount to Sumburgh schedules. Although Runway 09/27 was extended by increasing the run-off areas by around 100 metres in 1975, the operational length remained unchanged. The 15/33 runway provided greater length, but runs towards Sumburgh Head and could not be used if wind speeds reached thirty knots and, in such conditions, pilots would often taxy to the end of the runway where they would await a drop in wind speed and then let their aircraft roll at the appropriate moment. The shorter Runway 15/33 remains the preferred option. Sumburgh can still supply some exhilarating flying as recounted by Dave Stephen, a private pilot, following his departure as a passenger in a British Regional Airlines ATP in the year 2000:

> The wind in the morning was twenty to twenty-five knots and my wife was concerned that it was so breezy to which I replied that it would be straight down Runway 15. On taxy out I was perplexed when the captain announced that the 'runway in use was not their favourite runway' only to find him turning off 15 and on to 09. Even after a turn round to line up, he was still in no hurry to stop until it was dead centred on the centreline. I have never experienced this before in an ATP but he then applied full reverse pitch and reversed this thing back at least 100 feet until I was behind the numbers and passengers in the last couple of rows must have been over the main road. Something must have been seriously up with Runway 15 that he chose 09 but he certainly waited at least thirty seconds with full power on before either plucking up the courage or convincing himself that the hurdy-gurdies were going to last long enough for the take-off!

Sumburgh has lost little of the thrill which the first intrepid air travellers experienced in 1933.

6

Flying the Scottish islands

BEA – new boy on the block

While many personnel who had served in Scotland with the independent airlines before World War Two were to be found working for BEA, and later with British Airways, the war did cause some disruption, especially to continuity of aircrew. This meant that, after 1945, many new faces appeared. Jim Howie explains:

> There was quite an influx of aircrew after the end of World War Two, from the RAF and the Royal Navy. We had to have the 'B' licence to be accepted, and seniority literally depended on which train you caught. Towards the end of 1946, when it became clear that BEA would swallow Scottish Airways, a number of old hands left. They were not about to work for a Government company. A few remained, but the atmosphere was very much as it had been in the services. It took a long time to shake off the war.

> We were automatically members of the Scottish Flying Club, whose premises were on a floor above the reception area at Renfrew Airport. Flying was daylight only, except for the Dakota from London, but even that was down by 8.00pm and it became a habit to drop in to the bar for a quiet pint on the way home. A happy camaraderie developed and a great deal of knowledge was traded.

> Flying in the RAF had been mostly daylight, except for night-fighters and heavy bombers. So my first trip with Scottish Airways was memorable. I turned up at Renfrew in my new uniform – my RAF one dyed navy blue with a thin gold ring on the sleeves – and introduced myself to the crew who were waiting in the crew room for the Dakota to finish refuelling. It was a typical winter day with low cloud, wind and driving rain. The lights were on in the offices and hangars emphasising the gloom. Clearly flying was off. 'When is this supposed to lift?', I asked the skipper. 'Some time this evening if you want to believe Met.', he replied without, I thought, a great deal of interest. 'What's the deadline for the scrub decision?', I asked. The skipper and F/O looked at me, astonished. 'You can't expect Group Captain's weather any more', said the skipper. 'This is comparatively good. You'll see.' At least nobody would be shooting at us but I was far from reassured. As we taxied out, I had the brief hope that the plugs would not stand up to the sheeting rain but the Pratt & Whitneys rumbled sweetly and ran up like silk. I watched in fascinated horror as the runway lights disappeared at less than two hundred feet and we saw nothing but grey rain as we turned for Aberdeen. We settled at about five thousand feet where the air temperature was just above freezing point. After some time, there was a break in the cloud and, looking over the F/O's shoulder, I saw a small clear area with a rocky coast and a grey surf breaking on grim dark rocks. 'Stonehaven,' said the F/O. The skipper nodded. The F/O took a cigarette packet out of his pocket, scribbled a couple of figures on it, and announced, 'Dyce at two four'. The skipper nodded again. At about ten past, the F/O twiddled a knob on the radio panel and an absorbed look appeared. Moments later, the skipper nodded to the F/O, eased the throttles back, and we began descending. The F/O picked up the mike and informed Dyce which responded with the runway direction and surface wind. My hair stood on end. I had a vision of a map of Scotland which seemed to be all Grampians from the Caledonian Canal to the East Coast. The F/O glanced round and grinned. 'It's broken at 1,500 feet,' he said, 'and bags of visibility. It does that with this wind.' It did too, to my enormous relief, and below cloud we could see for miles.

> I don't remember the rest of that trip except that we landed back at Renfrew in darkness and rain. 'A good trip that,' said the skipper, 'for this time of year. Did you enjoy it? Any questions?' 'How did you know it was Stonehaven?' I replied. This was the only thing I could ask without finding myself out on my ear as unsuitable material. 'Have a good look at it on a clear day. It's fairly distinctive and, in this weather, there is usually a hole in the cloud just over it. You'll see. Stay with it. You'll enjoy it.' And, in time, I did.

Captain James Mackreth joined BEA in April 1947 from Allied Airways (Gandar Dower) Ltd., when its owner, Eric Gandar Dower, who had resisted takeover by the new nationalised airline was dramatically brought to heel. Mackreth recalls that, because Gandar Dower had refused to talk to BEA, he was not at Dyce when the takeover occurred, and no record of service could be found, he lost his two years seniority and was taken on by BEA as a new pilot. He was glad to get the job: 'I was immediately sent to Renfrew for a couple of months to be indoctrinated into the almost RAF ways of BEA after my free and easy life with Allied where every pilot was a law unto himself.' However he savours the memory that 'In my two years with Allied Airways, I polished my own method of bad visibility approaches to airfields and used them in BEA. I managed to get away with a great deal in BEA because I used my RAF experience, kept quiet and few people knew!'

In June 1947, along with Phil Rushmore and Mac Old, Ian Scott was one of the first new recruits to join BEA at Renfrew. Scott recalls, 'We joined an amalgam of aircrew made up of the former private airlines with the result that we wore various uniforms. The three of us were all First Officers (F/Os), there being no Second Officers at that time, and so we were to fly as co-pilots.' Jim Howie has mentioned the gloom of the hangars. Scott expands on the role it played:

> The Operations Office was situated in a large hangar along with offices for the airport management and a restaurant. Quite often the Captains would come in early and have their breakfasts in the restaurant. The F/O, having picked up the meteorological report, would then take it across to the Captain in the restaurant for his decision on the flight. Due to lack of further office space, two wooden buildings had been erected in the hangar; one for traffic personnel to weigh and process passengers, baggage and cargo.

This reveals that, in the early postwar period, the hangars played a multi-faceted role including that of terminal building. The presence of the BEA airport office within the cavernous pre-war hangars meant that the airline's coach, which brought passengers from Glasgow's St Enoch Square, would swing straight through the large doors upon its arrival at Renfrew to disgorge its load. Passengers would check-in at the office and then emerge through equally large doors at the other side of the hangar where their aircraft was awaiting them.

Tom Young joined Lockheed Aircraft at Renfrew, which served as a receiving point for USA lend-lease aircraft for the Allies. The Lockheed hangar was next to the Scottish Airways hangar and, at the end of World War Two, it was a friend there who suggested to Tom, who had risen from electrician to head of the Inspection Department, that he 'was daft working for coppers' and should 'join the airlines'. Tom ended up with BEA for the remainder of his working career and into the infancy of British Airways. 'In the early days, everybody mucked in. If there was an aileron that was too high, I would give a hand. It wasn't a case of, 'That's not my job'.' Tom's son, Leslie, soon followed him, initially as a flight clerk and then as a traffic officer, putting in a total of thirty-seven years with BEA and British Airways. They were typical of many for whom BEA, with its predecessors and successors, was a career path which saw them through to their pensions.

A special kind of flying

Disruptions caused by weather could call for some innovative solutions. This was particularly true in the Northern Isles following the discovery of oil in the Scottish sector of the North Sea which increased BEA traffic and brought much additional oil-related charter traffic. Closure of Sumburgh Airport by fog for several days in 1973 resulted in many passengers being stranded in Kirkwall, representing a major logistical problem even when the fog dispersed. Jack Ridgway, BEA's man in Kirkwall, resolved the situation with the aid of Captain John Burgher, not a pilot of the airline but master of the Orkney Isles Shipping Company's ferry *Orcadia*, who sailed into the night to deliver 200 passengers to Lerwick Harbour at 1.00am. Ridgway expressed his gratitude, agreeing that 'the shipping company certainly got us out of a fix'.

Adam Thomson, a name which was to become famous in aviation as chief of Caledonian Airways and British Caledonian, cut his flying teeth in passenger air transport during a brief period in 1951 as a co-pilot with BEA. Assigned to the Dakota in Scotland upon completion of the appropriate training course, he describes a trick which became well known in the Western Isles. Thomson attributes this landing to Stornoway, where a mean wind is not an unknown occurrence, but his description of the location suggests Balivanich:

> It was a manoeuvre which I had never seen before and have never seen since. Stornoway, in the Hebrides, was prone to extremely strong westerly winds from the Atlantic and the runway headed out to the western shore. At times when heavy gales were blowing, the procedure was to land on the runway, stop, maintain the lock on the tail wheel, release the main brakes and select full flaps on the aircraft wings. The aircraft thus became a sailing ship and would be blown sedately backwards down to the beginning of the runway. A van would be waiting with passengers to the mainland and to take away those disembarking. As soon as the loading process was completed we would be in a perfect position to take off straight down the runway.

Captain Tony Angus recalls experiences of the Benbecula winds forcing his Rapide involuntarily into reverse while airborne. It was at Stornoway that Captain George Stone put the wind-powered pushback to the test for the first time, having landed in 70-80 knots, to discover that his scepticism that it could possibly work was quite misplaced.

Captain Kenneth McLean has memories of being almost stationary over the runway at Stornoway during gusting winds of around 60 knots and touching down at such a low ground speed that the Pionair stopped in about ten yards. There was no question of manoeuvring on the ground with a tail-wheel aircraft and with no steering facility. The wind would keep the propellers rotating quite rapidly even after the engines had been cut so the procedure was to use the airport fire tender and fuel bowser as windbreaks to enable the propellers to come to rest while staff, hats secured with chinstraps, serviced the bucking aircraft. 'On departure, the fire tender and fuel truck were driven away, the engines were restarted and we took off from where we were. We probably got airborne in about another ten yards already having about eighty per cent of flying speed before we let the brakes off.' Ricky Campbell recalls having to point out to a colleague, who had just advised a Birmingham-based pilot that the weather at Stornoway was 'good', that there were actually eight octas of cloud at Stornoway. In relaying this adjustment to the captain, the meteorologist added, 'For Stornoway, that's good!'

In addition to witnessing a Dakota being reversed at Benbecula by wind power alone, Coll Macdonald recalls a southerly gale turning a Dakota into the wind when it was taxying along the perimeter track – in spite of brake power on one side and engine power on the other side. The DH89 Rapide was much lighter than the Dakota and could be an even greater hostage to high winds:

> When the DH89 landed in very high winds it was standard procedure for the fire crew to hold the aircraft down when it was taxying. On one occasion a gust lifted the aircraft about thirty feet into the air, dropped it lightly again without any damage, but leaving four men sprawled on the runway. The DH89 was a sturdy little aircraft. I have seen one flying directly overhead in gale force wind. It appeared to be 'crabbing' along sideways, heading about forty-five degrees into the wind to maintain track. At the opposite end of the scale, flying from Barra to Benbecula on a beautiful summer's day in a DH89 at about 200 feet above the white sands on the west side of South Uist was a pleasure I shall never forget. I once flew from Stornoway to Benbecula in a DC-3 and it was seat belts on tightly all the way while we were tossed about like a cork in an ocean. On landing, Captain Harry Hirst asked if I enjoyed the flight. I asked, 'Is that rough?' He replied, 'That's as rough as you will ever get it.' I never experienced turbulence like that again.

Donald MacPhee, fireman at Balivanich for thirty-seven years until 1985, also remembers the effects of high winds on the Rapide:

The Rapide served the islands well for many years but it did have a fault. It was so light that, when on ambulance service with only the crew on board, it was very difficult for the pilot to taxy in strong to gale force winds – with the result that two members of the fire service had to apply weight. We did this by jumping on the lower wings and lying on our stomachs while holding on to one of the struts. It wasn't a very pleasant experience as the propeller was only inches from our bodies. The extra weight helped the pilot to taxy to the passenger terminal where he collected the patient. We had to repeat the exercise for the aircraft's departure.

One day the air ambulance arrived to collect a desperately ill patient who only had so many hours to live without hospital treatment. The air ambulance arrived in the circuit and the famous, daring Captain Barclay was the pilot. He requested two of us to be at the touchdown point to apply weight to the aircraft, otherwise he couldn't taxy all the way to the passenger terminal to collect the patient. Myself and a colleague were detailed to do this but, by the time Captain Barclay had his patient, the wind was getting stronger. With the patient safely on board, my colleague and I took up our positions on the wings as before. Captain Barclay started his engines up and we began to taxy down the east taxyway. After he passed the control tower and wind direction cone, the aircraft suddenly swung round facing the wind. We thought he had lost control when suddenly the cockpit window opened and Captain Barclay shouted, 'Jump off!' As he moved forward, we jumped off and ended up flat on our backs on the grass. By the time we got to our feet, the aircraft was airborne across the grass. I'm sure he was back in Renfrew by the time we got over the shock. We thought he was taking off with us still on the wings.

Another aspect of climatic conditions at Benbecula made an impact on Donald when he joined the Civil Aviation Authority's fire service at Balivanich in 1948:

In the first years of my employment at the airport, deep frost and heavy snowfall were very common during the winter months. On reporting for duty in the early morning, our first priority was to ensure that all fire vehicles were fully serviceable and that the airfield was safe for the landing of scheduled flights and the air ambulance. On frosty mornings, four members of the fire service had to head out to a sandpit on the north-west corner of the airfield, equipped with a three-ton lorry and four shovels. After loading the lorry, we had to spread the sand evenly on the runway – not only one runway, but three runways in case of a change in wind direction.

After a heavy snowfall, you couldn't tell the runway from the grass area. In such conditions, we had to put red or purple dye in the water tender and spray a straight line of dyed water on each side of the runway in use, also the touch-down point, plus the taxyway and parking area at the passenger building. After all this work was accomplished, air traffic control was advised and they passed the information to the inbound pilot. In the early days we had no sanding or snow-clearing machines.

Wild weather could manifest itself on any part of the network with a variety of consequences. This was highlighted at Wick where arrivals might be cancelled – or progress no further than the end of the runway. Lyn Lovie, a traffic officer at the Caithness station cites an instance of the former:

During the Great Storm of January 1953 when, amongst others, the passenger vessel *Princess Victoria* was lost in the Irish Sea, Laurie Hendry and myself went to the aerodrome as usual but Operations at Renfrew told us that there would be no movements at all that day. Being the end of the month, we took the opportunity to get our statistics up to date but, around 1100hrs we decided to close down and take our papers to the Station Superintendent at the Town Office. In those days, we had ex-RAF officers greatcoats as part of our uniform. Coming out of the hangar office, having stuffed the papers inside my greatcoat, we made the mistake of putting up the collars of our coats. These acted as sails and, as soon as we turned the corner of the hangar, we were both blown over and rolled some distance by the force of the gale. Our papers vanished in the storm and I never found my hat. We were badly shaken but limped into town. I had badly grazed my hip and ankle and for some years bore the marks. They've faded now. (1999)

The latter instance is highlighted by the experience of Captain Jack Leask when he landed a Dakota in a crosswind at Wick just as a snowstorm had begun. The engines gave insufficient power for him to turn the aircraft against the crosswind after touchdown and the Dakota became stuck at the end of the runway as snow built up. After a couple of hours, a farm tractor rescued the passengers on a hay sledge and, in the course of two or three journeys, took them to a hotel in Wick. A tale, which has probably been embellished with constant retelling to the point of being libellous, was that Jack had a couple of nips of whisky while trapped in his snowbound cockpit to keep himself warm - and then aroused the interest of the police following his 'rescue'. The *John O'Groats Journal* provided a vivid account which illustrates just how bad the conditions were:

> A BEA plane on its way from Orkney to Aberdeen via Wick caught the full force of the blizzard when it touched down on the runway at Wick. Its crew of three and 20 passengers, including a 10-year-old boy and a four-year-old girl, were stranded in the aircraft for hours. Snowploughs and every other vehicle at the airport which could be commanded were brought into use before a track could be made through the deep snow to the plane.
>
> The passengers, who had landed at the airport at 1.45pm, were conveyed into the waiting room at 6.30pm. But another problem faced them. After being provided with tea by the BEA staff, they had to wait on a few hours longer before they could get into the town because the road leading from the airport was blocked. Eventually a tractor from Westerseat Farm, driven by Mr. George Gunn, and a plough supplied by the County Roads Department cleared the route. The tractor took ten passengers to Wick and a police patrol car, driven by Sergt. R. Dunnet accompanied by Constable A. Gunn, ran in relays to transport the other passengers and crew, the BEA staff and members of the Ministry of Transport and Civil Aviation staff who had taken part in the operations at the airport.

Upon another occasion at Wick, it took Geoff Northmore and his Captain half an hour after their landing to locate the terminal through the snowstorm that accompanied their touchdown. By the time they had disembarked their passengers and joining passengers had boarded, there were six inches of snow on the ground and a very light northerly wind:

> We made our way to the threshold of Runway 01 which was fairly short and uphill. Due to the drag of the snow plus the runway condition, the poor old Dak could only get to about 50 knots with take-off power so, after a leisurely discussion, we abandoned the effort. After some further head scratching, we made our way to the far end of 01, turned the aircraft around, put our wheels in the tracks we had made on the way up, applied full power and sailed away like a bird, downwind and downhill. Today we would be hung, drawn and quartered for even thinking of a similar solution.

Iain Crosbie recalls one flight 'which was the first of the daily eight sectors from Renfrew to Tiree, Benbecula, Stornoway, Inverness and return'. When the aircraft landed at Tiree, the wind was blowing at 75 knots and Iain decided 'not to tempt providence any further that day'. Colin MacPhail, the station superintendent, and Mary Munn, his assistant, managed to arrange accommodation for everyone – except the two pilots, and James Shaw Grant, editor of the *Stornoway Gazette*. The threesome had to spend the night in the passenger waiting room.

The Isle of Rum and the Isle of Scarba represented points over which turbulence could be experienced during certain weather conditions. Iain Crosbie tells of an instance, upon entering cloud over Rum en route to Benbecula, when an air pocket was encountered. Coffee cups sitting on the floor between the two pilots shot up to the roof and returned. Both pilots were strapped into their seats but some passengers were not, and they followed the same route as the coffee cups, leaving marked depressions where their heads had penetrated the ceiling lining. Dr John Macleod, from Lochmaddy, encountered 'the Rum experience' during a similar Pionair flight to Benbecula:

> The aircraft hit an air pocket and fell a considerable altitude. The mails, which were not secured with netting, flew up in the air and came to rest against the cockpit door, blocking it. Seat belts were not worn and passengers were catapulted from the seats upwards. I left my seat and hit my head off the luggage rack but the passenger next to me remained in his seat. I was long enough up in the air to be aware of this passenger reaching up with both arms and pulling me back towards my seat. Items of luggage were also becoming airborne. However, quite a lot of passengers had carry outs, girls taking

Captain Dave Whittick surveys the Shetland landscape from Pionair G- AGHM RMA Edward Maitland *during the layover at Sumburgh. (courtesy of Jimmy Burgess)*

G-AGHP awaits the call of duty on a wet tarmac at Prestwick. (Aird Crooks)

a bottle of whisky home to father, etc., and the whisky didn't rise into the air! The aircraft fell vertically, an observation confirmed by the dent in the lining of the luggage rack directly above my head. Upon arrival at Benbecula, the aircraft was grounded for maintenance.

It would appear this is an aircraft which Donald MacPhee recalls arriving at Benbecula. 'Some passengers suffered head injuries caused by their heads hitting and smashing the roof lights. I remember that the pilot, once he had escaped the turbulence and had regained full control, called air traffic control and asked for a doctor to be available at the passenger building to attend the injured.'

Fortunately, First Officer Stanley Brown had no difficulty keeping a steady hand when he flew Rapide G-AHXX on an inbound ambulance flight from Tiree to Renfrew, over the Isle of Scarba on 28 February 1950. Also there was no need for a doctor as Tiree's district nurse was fully in control of the events occurring within the cabin upon this occasion. It was precisely as the aircraft passed over Scarba that Lachlan Macfarlane was born. He was reported by district nurse, Edith Reid, to be 'squawking lustily' by the time they landed at Renfrew.

We all know that pilots are unflappable characters and Jim Howie maintains that you cannot tell from the expression on a pilot's face whether he knows what he is doing, or not. He describes an approach to Barra in dirty weather:

> You leave Tiree on something like 310 degrees (Magnetic) and stay below cloud because there is no let-down facility. Visibility is poor and you are in and out of rain at two or three hundred feet. You pay close attention to the water, reading the direction and strength of the wind. With practice, your tracking is reasonably accurate but, as you near Barra, you get a bearing from Tiree to confirm it. As you enter what is virtually the approach channel, now down low over the water, you keep a small conical rock close on your right. Here you note the amount of seaweed showing, which is an indication of the tide and the amount of beach to expect. Because of wind, this is not always the tabled figure. Passing the rock, you turn three degrees to the right, on final, and look for the seagulls. When you see them walking, you are safe to touch down. I had a new Radio Officer with me on such a day. When I shut off the engines he rose hurriedly from his seat to find he was securely strapped to his seat cushion which rose with him. He was quite white and clearly shaken. 'You OK?' I asked. 'Christ!' he said. 'I couldn't tell whether you knew what you were doing. I thought we'd had it.' When I told him exactly why I knew what I was doing, he said I should bloody well tell my crew and, if it was a new crew, give a running commentary. Memory of my own first trip flooded back. I took the point.

The approach to Barra remains today an enthralling experience for the uninitiated while the touchdown has been aptly described as like landing on corrugated paper with water flying everywhere – yet Orcadian, Vivian Bird, compares his own arrival at Barra as 'more steady than I remember Westray or North Ronaldsay field landings.'

The Northern Isles are just as prone to winds as are the Hebrides to which the almost total absence of trees on the islands is testimony. In the late 1950s, the instrument approach to Kirkwall was a Standard Beam Approach (SBA), an audio precursor of the Instrument Landing System (ILS). As co-pilot, Kenneth McLean was flying an approach which impressed his captain:

> The captain commented that I was having to apply 23 degrees of drift on the approach to stay on the beam - that is to say I was heading that amount into the wind to maintain the requisite straight line to the runway. My much more experienced captain was quite taken by this. I can no longer remember the wind speed and direction which produced this requirement but, in the many crosswind approaches I have been involved in over many years since, none has required quite as much drift correction as that day in Kirkwall.

Stan Sickelmore arrived at Aberdeen, with Geoff Northmore as his co-pilot, having left Renfrew at 0840 followed by a call at Edinburgh:

> The weather was really foul all over the country – low cloud, heavy rain and high winds. We arrived at Aberdeen at 1100. We changed aircraft there, leaving DC3 G-AMNW for G-AMDB. We were

bound for Wick, Orkney and Shetland and back. When we got into the waiting room for a quick cuppa, we found it full of passengers. I had to tell them that I did not think there was much chance of success but, seeing the disappointed looks on their faces, I said that if they were game we would have a try. Shetland was definitely out, so our plan was to have a stab at Wick and Kirkwall.

We took off with a good load of fuel at 1140. It was a rough and wild trip and Wick was covered with patches of cloud scudding across the surface. We made two approaches to well below minimum. The visibility was not bad between cloud layers and I hoped that, with luck, we might find a clear patch as we approached the threshold. After the second overshoot, and with the weather worsening, we made for Kirkwall. By the time we got there, the wind was gusting gale force and the cloud was on the deck. I think we made one approach but with little hope of success. We went back to Wick for another try and contacted Aberdeen to say that we were diverting back. They asked us if we would please try Inverness. I replied that I would but that, if I was unsuccessful, I would then be committed to divert to Renfrew, the only airfield which had reasonable conditions. On the way to Inverness, I talked to Captain John Wells who was at that moment trying to land there. After two attempts he had to divert to Renfrew. After one try, without seeing the ground at all, we did the same. We switched off at 1525. So after three hours and forty-five minutes, in very rough weather, and with only dry sandwiches and a cup of coffee to sustain them, our poor passengers were further from their destinations than when they started the journey. Still, not one complained. They understood our problems and knew we had done our best.

Like other BEA pilots, James Mackreth had experience of high winds which called for unorthodox methods of handling the aircraft on the ground, especially the Dakota with its large wings which its tail-dragging undercarriage exposed to the wind. However, on 17 March 1949, the conditions at Kirkwall's Hatston airport gave him a special treat:

We departed Dyce at 0845 for Orkney. This started as a normal gale-lashed flight W/V NW 40 knots. About half way along, the R/O gave me the weather at Orkney. It was unbelievable – calm 8/8 200-300 feet, visibility 2,500 yards, drizzle. Wick was still 300°/45 knots and the sea was full of white-topped waves with the tops being blown off. We had our usual drift, crabbing along going sideways at a considerable rate.

Soon after passing Wick, a heavy sea running, I got the same Orkney weather report and ran into cloud. Descending on a radio bearing, the buffeting ceased and true enough I broke cloud at 250 feet and landed in a flat calm. It was eerie and I was not sorry to take off again. At about 600 feet, I ran into the turbulence and once more was in the gale, landing at Wick 300°/45 knots. The only time I have landed in the eye of a storm. Next landing at Orkney some four hours later, it was back to normal gales. I felt disappointed.

It was not only on aircraft that weather conditions could have adverse effects. On one occasion, following an overnight snow storm, Captain Keith Warburton set the Heron down on Glenegedale aerodrome, Islay, to find a still silence. Station Superintendent Andy Morrison had been delayed when he found the driving wind had filled his garage with snow. He had to dig out his car, *inside* his garage, before he could get to work.

The hazards of ice

It was in the aftermath of an ambulance flight on 18 November 1950 that David Barclay began lobbying for the introduction of more sophisticated aircraft for the Scottish island routes. On that occasion, the journey from Benbecula to Renfrew had taken three hours and six minutes during which icing had forced the aircraft dangerously low to a collision course with the mountain peaks of Argyll. On aircraft without de-icing equipment, pilots endeavoured to steer clear of cloud when conditions presented a risk of ice gathering on the aircraft. Harry McDowell recounts such a flight from Tiree to Renfrew:

Following take-off from Tiree, the whole way home had to be flown underneath the cloud – over the whirlpool at Corryvreckan, past Scarba, down the Crinan Canal, Loch Fyne to Ardlamont Point – a sharp left hand down and into the West Kyle past Tighnabruaich then to a very sharp right hand down and into the East Kyle to Toward Point lighthouse, left up the Clyde to the Cloch lighthouse and up the shipping channel to Renfrew Ferry and not once having been higher than 100 feet. Fortunately the weather at Renfrew was a bit better and we could climb to 300 feet in order to find the runway and land. It was before the Erskine Bridge was built otherwise we would have had to fly under it.

That was not quite the end of the story however. After landing and the passengers disembarked, one of them remained behind, obviously waiting to speak to me. My immediate thought was, 'Oh, oh, one frightened passenger who wishes to express his displeasure and fear during the flight.' To my astonishment, he announced that he had enjoyed the flight enormously, thanked me profusely for the best, the most interesting, and most memorable flight he had ever had. In his own words, he said, 'It wasn't so much like flying to Glasgow – more like coming in a fast boat!' Another satisfied customer. He really made my day.

The Dakota could be similarly prone to icing as Harry McDowell recalls of a flight from Shetland, Orkney and Inverness to Renfrew one winter's night. On leaving Inverness, he climbed to 8,000 to find his aircraft still in cloud and icing up badly. He continued to climb, just clearing the top of the cloud at 10,000 feet where he managed to get rid of the ice. The first officer monitored the aircraft's progress to find that the aircraft had taken ten minutes to travel five miles, giving it a ground speed of 30 mph while the airspeed indicator was registering 180 mph. Harry McDowell takes up the story:

Just then I got a radio call from the captain of the Dakota which was en route from Benbecula to Glasgow to ask how I was getting on. 'Not terribly well but making slow progress,' I replied, 'How about you?' He replied that he was at about 9,000 feet and icing up badly. I responded with, 'I am at 10,000 feet and just in the clear.' He said, 'I can't climb to 10,000 feet with so much ice on board and my speed over the ground is only 20 mph.'

He decided to turn back to Benbecula and spend the night there but, on calling them up on the radio, he found that the airfield had closed up shop and everyone had gone home for the night. His only option was to head for Tiree which was just about to close also. He called up 'Tiree Homer' to ask them for a course to Tiree. There was no reply from them. After landing there he found that the 'Homer' situated on top of the only hill on Tiree had totally vanished – blown completely away by the storm winds.

John Morton revealed that the crew who made the dash for Tiree 'before it all went quiet' consisted of Jimmie Scotland as Captain and Ian Slight as the Second Officer. Jimmie Scotland's son, Barry, confirms that his father remembers that flight well. 'How could he forget? He thought his number was up that night!'

Jimmie was once the centre of another drama when he touched down at Renfrew in a Dakota with 29 passengers, inbound from Stornoway. He was confronted by fire tenders, ambulances, police and press to discover that his aircraft was at the centre of a full alert. On this occasion it turned out to have been a false alarm, the result of misinterpretation of a message from Stornoway. However, as Jimmie came into Tiree on the night of 31 January 1957, it was the real thing. To his passengers, he passed the drama off with, 'The winds were a bit high. That's all.' But to the press he admitted, 'In all my fifteen years of flying, this is the worst weather I have ever encountered.' Options had run out when Jimmie made his approach to Tiree; he had no radio contact and only a light on the runway to guide him. Colin MacPhail, BEA's station superintendent on the island concurred with Jimmie's assessment of the conditions, 'They made the landing by the grace of God. The plane was struck by a 115 mph gust – and almost stopped in mid-air as it approached the island. I've never known winds like it.' Yet it was ice which had been the instigator of the Dakota's troubles. The gales were an added extra. Colin MacPhail fixed Jimmie's passengers up with hotel rooms and, when they ran out, he booked the overflow into the RAF mess.

The Junkers Ju 52 was no favourite of BEA crews. Bill Reid cites frequent mag. drops, and tyre bursts. The last straw was when a crew was overcome by fumes from a leaky gasket in the centre engine in front of the cockpit. He jests (I think) that they did have one advantage, 'When caught in freezing cloud conditions, the ice smoothed out the corrugations of the wing leading edge and the machine flew faster!'

Getting there

Negotiating the rugged terrain of Scotland through diverse climatic conditions presented challenges which honed the skills of crews to a special kind of perfection. Teamwork was integral to this process. Ian Scott, who flew the Scottish air routes for the first decade of BEA explains the procedures during that era:

> Whenever possible, navigation was done by map reading so we cut up and stuck together maps to cover our routes, drawing in, where necessary, bearings from the Adcock D.F. (Direction Finding) Station at Houston, a few miles to the west of Renfrew. For contact flying we used, I believe, four miles to one inch scale maps, and for the rest, smaller scale topographical maps.
>
> At the destination airports, when necessary, we made QDM (magnetic bearing to steer to reach the D.F. station) let downs. All communications in those days were made by W.T. (wireless telegraphy) and so a Radio Officer (R/O) was a necessity. On instruction, he would transmit ETAs (estimated time of arrival) and other details, but of major importance were the QDM transmissions for the let down. Each out-station had a Bellinitosi direction finding system. After giving our call sign, the R/O would hold down the key, whilst the ground operator took a bearing which he then passed to the aircraft.
>
> From the 'nil bearings', which meant 'overhead', the R/O would get a 'string' of QDMs on which the pilot would start his timing and carry out a let down. This was in the form of a tear-drop pattern, letting down at a pre-set speed and a rate of descent of 500 feet per minute - a rate-one turn would be carried out at the end of a two-minute leg and the correct QDM sought, still continuing the descent, with the hope of coming in visual contact with the sea or the ground. If not, an overshoot would have to be carried out. In the case of Islay, because of high ground to the east of the airfield, this meant a 90° climbing turn to port to avoid it. Out in the islands one would often get westerly gales of up to 60 mph and, as the speed of the Rapide was about 110 mph, the timing of the outer leg would have to be extended greatly.
>
> The Rapide had a drift-sight in the floor to the right of the pilot which was quite useful at times when over the sea, such as between Tiree and Barra where one used QDMs from Tiree to locate Barra and the flight was done in contact with the water. There was no D/F (Direction Finding) at Barra and one had to keep one's eyes skinned as Barra had a 1,262 ft hill, Heaval, to the south. Before leaving Tiree, one had to find out if the tide was out and, if not, a delay ensued.
>
> When I arrived at Renfrew, and for some time after, certain F/Os flew the Rapides in command. Stuart Black was one of these. The Rapide and the Dakota had trailing aerials which the R/O let down before he transmitted. These could prove to be an embarrassment if not wound in before landing. It happened! Another use it was apparently put to was for letting down over the sea in bad visibility so that the R/O could let the Captain know when the aerial touched the water!
>
> Eventually we got VHF installed after an extra generator had been put on the top wing - the generators were wind driven. Slowly the R/Os were phased out and many were trained by BEA as pilots.
>
> There is the story of the Captain who was carrying out a 'coffin charter'; taking an ex-islander's body back to the island for burial. It was a warm sunny day and at the time when some aircraft had VHF and some didn't. I suppose, at some time, all of us have been flying 'automatically' in these clear conditions. The Captain got the fright of his life as a hand came on his shoulder. It was the R/O. This aircraft had not been equipped with VHF.
>
> I had one nasty moment shortly after I had gained my command on the Dakota. After this we had to fly Daks for six months before being allowed to fly the Rapides as well. I was going from Renfrew to Islay. It was a nasty day with a westerly gale and rain. I was to do it 'contact'. I had passed the northern tip of Arran and was making for the Skipness pass, along which there is a road (B8001). I was at about 200 feet and had been told that, if you could see the top of a certain hill, you would get through alright. The hilltop was in view so I went in, following the road at about 100 feet, when I

started to run into wisps of stratus. I couldn't go up as it was winter and the fear of bad icing was on my mind. So I turned the aircraft almost on its side and pulled round in a tight port turn, the aircraft shaking like a leaf. The turn was so steep that I nearly overshot the road down which I had to return. We got back to the coast and went south in the lee of Kintyre peninsula, getting hammered by the turbulence. We turned and crossed Kintyre at Campbeltown and eventually landed on Islay. After disembarking, one of the passengers came up to me and said, 'That was a near thing!' I said, 'What do you mean?' 'Oh,' he said, 'I was a Flight Engineer on Lancasters!'

Radio Officers were essential crew members during the early years of BEA but, as Ian Scott mentions, developments in technology were quickly to change this. Alex Miller joined BEA as a Radio Officer from Scottish Airways upon their absorption and 'flew in DH89 Rapides, Dakotas, some horrendous hours in Ju 52 Jupiters, and occasionally on Vickers Vikings'. He decided that his career prospects were limited following a particular European trip:

My decision to leave BEA took place after the Communists invaded Czechoslovakia and on a routine flight from Prague we lost our generator after take off so that we made our way back to Northolt faster using Radio Telephony than Wireless Telegraphy. This, combined with the Comet taking off from Alexandria after we left Paris on one flight and giving an Estimated Time of Arrival in England before we could land at Northolt convinced me that R/T operated by pilots spelled the doom of Radio Officers.[1]

Archie Edmiston also transferred from Scottish Airways to BEA in 1947, working as a Radio Officer on both Scottish and European routes until 1962 when the role became surplus to requirements. Some Radio Officers transferred to Traffic and others took up the offer of an opportunity to train as pilots. Archie decided to leave BEA at this time but it was a way of life which he had always enjoyed. He met his wife Eva when she flew as an air ambulance volunteer nurse between 1951 and 1953 and Eric Starling performed the duties of best man when they married. And he didn't meet his maker, when he should have, on 28 September 1957. Archie was scheduled for air ambulance standby duties that night, but Hugh McGinlay's father was in hospital and Hugh wished to be free during the daytime. The two radio officers therefore agreed to exchange rosters and it was Hugh, in Archie's place, who was with Captain Paddy Calderwood and the volunteer nurse, Sister Jean Kennedy, on board Heron G-AOFY which crashed on Islay causing their deaths.

Not all First Officers were qualified to operate on the Heron and when they flew on ambulance flights they carried out the duties of the Radio Officer. Some First Officers were qualified to fly on both the Heron and the Dakota. Terry Lakin was one of these and he notes that when he later transferred to London, he continued to fly the Rolls-Royce company Heron while also serving on BEA Dakotas, Viscounts and Comets.

Dakotas and Herons

Two of the most familiar BEA aircraft operating island routes in Scotland were the Herons and Dakotas. Some captains were simultaneously rated on both types and these included Ken Browning, Paddy Calderwood, Don Hoare, Bill MacKenzie, Mike O'Brien, Flight Manager Eric Starling, Bill Reid and Benny Yorston.

The Dakota has proven itself, over six decades, to be one of the most reliable and forgiving of aircraft. But even the Dakota required occasional nursing. Bill Cooper was relief engineer at Stornoway when one landed which did not sound quite right:

During the run-down of the port engine, I heard such a pronounced clanking that I knew all was not well. Eric Starling, the Flight Manager, was in command. I hesitated for a moment, then followed him into the restaurant. I said, 'Pardon me, Captain, but could I run up the port engine? I suspect a

---

[1] In 1948, the Communist Party of Czechoslovakia (CPC), led by Klement Gottwald, staged a coup d'état following the resignation of the non-communist members of the democratically elected postwar government of Czechoslovakia.

problem.' Captain Starling responded with, 'I have an appointment in Glasgow tonight so I hope that you'll find that it's alright.'

I started the port engine and, at idling, there was some roughness. I cautiously increased rpm to 1,000 and the engine nearly jumped out of the airframe so I immediately shut it down. Quickly, I took down the oil pressure filter, oil all over my hands and found a lump of piston in the filter which, suitably cradled in rags, I proceeded to show to Captain Starling. 'Right', he said to the official in charge, 'get another aircraft up here straight away. I want to be in Glasgow tonight.' Sure enough, later that day, a DC-3 Freighter with a spare engine, an electrician and Charge Hand Engineer John Marshall arrived at Stornoway.

Tom Young was called to Stornoway when a captain had been unable to get a Dakota to start. On that occasion the 'fault' was quickly rectified but it proved prudent not to demonstrate this too quickly:

When these engines start there is a two-way switch. You put the switch down and that energises it. Then you put it up, and that engages it to start up the engine. Well, sometimes you had a wee bit bother with this. Well, I went up to Stornoway. The Dak I went up in took away the passengers that were waiting. So we were left with the other aircraft, tried it, and the engines started up. 'For God's sake stop it,' shouted the captain, 'The passengers are away.' Well, once we were finished, we had a wee while to wait. The captain said, 'Do you fancy going in the town to get some fish?' We didn't stand about. We went into the back door of the fishmonger's, not the front door. So the fishmonger says to me, 'Would you like a bit of salmon?' I knew the price of salmon and I hadn't a pennyworth of money in my pocket. He said, 'Here's a bit. Three and a half pounds. How would that do?' I said, 'How much is that?' 'Ten shillings', was his reply! The captain, he took a box of kippers and we brought it back down.

Lack of technology and high noise level in the Dakota resulted in a novel form of inflight entertainment in the absence of intercom announcements from the flight deck and onboard catering. This consisted of the Flight Bulletin, a sheet of paper at the bottom of which was a piece of cartoon humour, uncharacteristic of BEA, as passengers were urged to 'Please pass on quickly'. The Flight Bulletin gave the name of the captain, the name of the aircraft, and the name of the flight clerk. It included such gems as:

'abeam Lybster, height 2,000 feet, air speed 164 mph – we are now 7 miles from Wick Airport. At 1.44 p.m. we pass Banff 21 miles to our left.'

'Fraserburgh 5 miles, height 4,000 feet, air speed 140 mph – we are now 35 miles from Aberdeen. At 1010 hours we pass Lybster to our left.'

'Isle of Scarba, height 4,500 feet, air speed 160 mph – we are now 55 miles from Glasgow. At 9.33am we pass the Isle of Iona 2 miles to our left. We call next at Tiree.'

Scheduled services did not represent the sole nature of the work carried out by BEA around the islands. The Rapide was ideal for charter by small groups of passengers and by the media for aerial photography. The air ambulance work carried out both by the Rapide and its successor, the Heron, was also classified as charter work. In 1947, a Junkers Ju 52 was used to make a dramatic aerial drop to the keepers of Dubh Artach lighthouse, perched on a rocky outcrop of the Torran Reef south of the Ross of Mull and the Isle of Iona, and which had been besieged by storms for ten weeks. The Dakota has been characterised by its versatility and it was used for flights from Stornoway with passengers who were very different from the regular complement of islanders commuting between Lewis and the mainland. Captain Geoff Colley was in command of the first of these, assisted by Iain Crosbie as First Officer and Hugh McGinlay who was the Radio Officer. The date was 25 November 1949, the aircraft was G-AGYZ *Charles Kingsford Smith*, the destination was Ploujean, near Morlaix in Brittany – and the 'passengers' were lobsters. The crew had positioned from Renfrew to Stornoway the previous day. Iain Crosbie takes up the story:

We had a bad start as we were supposed to leave at some unearthly hour in the morning but Stan Muir of the County Hotel forgot to give us a shake and we were accordingly delayed, even though we had

BEA FLIGHT BULLETIN

From Captain *J. M. Calderwood* to all passengers

RMA *Pionair "Percy Pilcher"*

TIME

Local time is *1.29 pm* { the same as one hour ahead of one hour behind } Local time in _____

POSITION

Abeam Lybster

HEIGHT

2000 Feet

Metres

SPEED

AIR SPEED *164* m.p.h.

CORRECTED FOR WIND (SPEED OVER GROUND) *183* m.p.h.

k.p.h.   k.p.h.

INFORMATION

We are now *7* miles from *Wick Airport* At *1.44 pm*

hours we pass *Banff* *2* miles to our right/left. We call next at

Aberdeen (Dyce) arriving there at approximately *2 pm* LOCAL ~~GREENWICH~~ time.

NOTES

Fine weather all the way

The traffic officer who will meet you on landing will be glad to assist you in any way he can.

The name of your Steward/~~Stewardess~~ is *Malone*

PLEASE PASS ON QUICKLY

F.144 (4th)   B R I T I S H   E U R O P E A N   A I R W A Y S

'Abeam Lybster' with 'fine weather all the way'. (courtesy of Jack Budge)

no breakfast. We went into Speke for fuel, as we had about three tons of lobster aboard, and then went on our merry way. Arriving overhead Ploujean, fortunately in clear weather, Geoff did a low pass since we had no information beyond the conventional sign for an airfield on our quarter-inch, wartime type maps. We noted that the runway had several bomb craters in it which had been filled in with shingle through which grew the odd clump of gorse. However landing was accomplished without trouble. As I recall, there were absolutely no airport staff of any kind, nor Customs. We were met by the agent for the charter, and the actual purchaser, who dropped us at a hotel in the town and left us whilst they went off to check the quality of the lobsters. In a very short time they returned, full of the joys, and wheeled us in to lunch at a table which was nicely set and seemed covered with numerous glasses. The lunch was delightful and by this time we were ready to do it justice. As it was Friday, Hughie 'two draws and a spit' McGinlay was in a quandary since the main course was a great big steak. However, after some reflection, he decided that he could seek absolution that evening and he got stuck in with the rest of us. We also had a glass or two and thoroughly enjoyed ourselves. We were afterwards presented with stockings for our wives, by the wife of either the agent or the purchaser, and in due course were driven back to the airfield. Thinking to repay our hosts a little, I prevailed on the taxi driver to stop at a sweetie shop en route and the lady came in with me. Recalling that a two pound box of chocolates used to be thought quite a nice present, I asked for 'un kilo de chocolat pour Madame'. The place went into uproar and I can only assume that it was like asking for a stone of chocolate. I cannot recall now whether or not she got the chocolate but we resumed our journey to the field. We were supposed to go on to Jersey and pick up a Dak engine to be taken to Northolt but by now we were quite keen to stop over. Arriving at the aircraft, we got Hughie to get on the W/T for the Jersey weather which, unfortunately, was okay so we had to go.

Iain Crosbie's log entries confirm the flight details, including the 'late' departure from Stornoway, as:

24 November 1949	Renfrew	dep	1219
	Stornoway	arr	1331
25 November 1949	Stornoway	dep	0547
	Liverpool (Speke)	arr	0803
	Liverpool	dep	0847
	Ploujean	arr	1050
	Ploujean	dep	1508
	Jersey	arr	1559
26 November 1949	Jersey	dep	0945
	Northolt	arr	1110

While the Dakota was advanced technology compared with the Rapide, it was utilitarian by modern standards as Kenneth McLean illustrates:

We had to keep our overcoats and gloves on for the first sectors in the Pionair on winter mornings until the exhaust heat exchangers gave out a hint of warmth. Like many others, I have slithered my way along the wings during a turnaround, wielding a broom to get the snow off – or enough of it to say we'd made an effort. Low-speed aerofoils were mighty forgiving of such cavalier treatment. Rain leaking in through the Pionair's sliding side windows was soaked up by copious supplies of paper towels or loo paper, but it usually managed to drip, ice-cold, on your knees anyway.

Ian Scott recalls the moisturising tendencies of both the Dakota and the Ju 52:

One of the great advantages of pressurised aircraft was that, in precipitation, they were water tight. In the Jupiter and the Pionair the escape hatches in the roof of the cockpits used to leak and, on the latter aircraft, the clear vision panels too. Paper towels were wedged in to stem the flow and, on more than one occasion, the Captain and I donned our hats and raincoats.

'The Heron', as John Morton recalls, 'was a four-engined version of the de Havilland Dove and carried sixteen passengers.' It was on this aircraft that he gained his first posting when he joined BEA as a Cadet Pilot in 1956:

Legally it required only one pilot and had hitherto been operated with a Captain and a Radio Operator. There was also no legal requirement for a Cabin Attendant. No instruments were installed in front of the right-hand seat, the space being utilised for radio equipment. The aircraft was fitted with a Decca Navigator in the form of three dials indicating position lines. There was no moving map as was later fitted to the Viscount. BEA decided to change to two-pilot operation although there was some overlap with Radio Operators during the first few months. The aircraft was used on a small number of scheduled routes and the Air Ambulance service which answered an average of one call a day. The seats down one side of the cabin were replaced by a stretcher.

There was no autopilot on our Herons which added to the workload, and instrument flying by the second pilot had to take account of parallax as he had to look across the cockpit to the Captain's panel. It was at this time that BEA's chief pilot, Bill Baillie, introduced the concept of the monitored approach by which the second pilot flew the instrument approach, monitored by the Captain but leaving him free to be looking out of the office window at decision height and to make the critical choice of landing or overshooting. So, it was important that the second pilot flew an approach accurately. The approach and let-down aids were very basic indeed, some airfields only having a direction finder. Inverness and Tiree had a Standard Beam Approach where the pilot heard a steady note in his headset if he was on centre line, and either Morse Ns if he drifted to one side or As on the other. Only Renfrew had the newly introduced Instrument Landing System which gave a visual indication of centreline displacement, the degree of it, and a similar display of the glide slope.

My conversion course took place at the BEA Ground School, an estate of prefabricated huts near Hatton Cross on the south side of Heathrow. There I met two others who were to be second pilots; John Lester, later to become Flight Manager TriStar and Concorde, and John Olive, who retired many years later as a Senior Captain on Vanguards. In September 1956, BEA provided Rolls-Royce Ltd with aircrew for G-AOTI, a Heron 2 with retractable undercarriage, to carry Directors to and from meetings in London, Derby and Bradford. We were later to borrow this aircraft and, for a short time, another Mark 2, G-AMTS. I was amazed to find that after only two years with BEA my seniority was enough to secure me a position on the Viscount and I flew my last Heron on 8 February 1958.

Hebridean Hazards – Sundays and Sheep

In 1948, when the aircraft on which Alex Miller was flying as a Radio Officer became stranded in Stornoway, the problem was extended because Stornoway Airport did not open on a Sunday, a customary observance which endures today:

> We were scheduled to fly to Inverness via Stornoway and then to Renfrew. It was Saturday and, when we landed at Stornoway, we blew a tyre. As no tyre was available at Stornoway for a Dakota, Renfrew said they would fly a wheel up and we retired to the hotel in Stornoway. Our pilot then called Renfrew and was advised that the wheel would arrive next day – on Sunday. He was overheard by a retired army major who lived in the hotel. Within minutes, the major was on to the Prime Minister's office at 10 Downing Street and, shortly after, we heard that the wheel would arrive on Monday. Commercial activity was a 'no-no' in those days in the islands. We spent the weekend in Stornoway.

What were Miller and his colleagues to do? One of BEA's Stornoway staff had a proposal which he put to Alex:

> Jimmy McInnes suggested to me that there was a cèilidh on in the village of Back, a few miles to the north, that evening. The rest of the crew did not take him up on it but I did. I should mention that we had no overnight things so we were in uniform.
>
> We walked the few miles to the village but the 'all Gaelic' part was on and, since I could not understand, Jimmy suggested we enter by the 'committee' entrance. No sooner was I inside when I was grabbed and thrust against the wall, people jabbering in Gaelic at me. I could see Jimmy talking to a rather distinguished gentleman in the background. Moments later, I was released. They thought I was a Revenuer! After that, everything was fine and bottles were brought in. There were enough cases of whisky in the back room to last for months. Bear in mind that, in those days, whisky and all liquor was rationed. Needless to say, I had a wonderful time.

Tom Young was deprived of island hospitality during one visit to Benbecula. 'We finished the

Time off at Stornoway. First Officer Webber (top), Captain Alex Miller, and two Lewis lovelies, November 1947. (Alex G. W. Miller)

The 'egg lady' of Benbecula, Flora Macmillan.
(Alex G. W. Miller)

service of this plane and the villagers invited us to a cèilidh that night, before we came home.' I said, 'Oh lovely, that's ideal, we'll thoroughly enjoy that.' Then the blinking phone went: 'Send the electrician back with the next flight.' That was me. I missed my cèilidh.' Tom described Benbecula as 'a godforsaken hole' but that was for reasons which were probably nothing to do with the island but due to the trials of the job. 'I used to stand there at night looking away into the sea. And I would say, 'Oh, I wish I was home.' My wife hated it. She said it was the most unsociable life.' This was because of the shift system which allowed only one weekend off each month. When other workers were beginning their weekends off on a Saturday afternoon, Tom would be heading for the airport to begin the two-thirty shift.

Tom had also had a previous experience in Benbecula at the hands of a tight-fisted gaffer:

> There was a Dak grounded up there with engine trouble and it needed an engine change. There was no hangar space so it had to be done outside. And it was March, so you can appreciate that it wasn't exactly comfortable. It was grim. They shined a torch up and I said 'Are you still holding that?' They couldn't even feel it. It was horrendous. Well, the chap who was in charge of the squad was the most miserable character you ever met. Well, we came to the end of the first night. Lochboisdale was the nearest hotel. That was about 23 miles away. So the gaffer said, 'We'll just sleep in the terminal in the passenger lounge and that will save cash and you'll get all that money in your pocket.' But it was deep basket chairs and you couldn't sleep. There was a big log fire. Your front was warm but your back was frozen and where we dined was a wee Anderson shelter hut. On the second night he said 'Right. The same again?' 'Not me', I said, 'I'm hiring a taxi. I'm going in to Lochboisdale and I'm going into a hotel. I'm definitely not having another night like that. No way.' So that started the revolution. One of the boys said, 'Wait a minute. The rocket site. The rocket site is just about five or six hundred yards from us. Away down and see the major in charge.' The commanding officer said, 'What? That's ridiculous. Sleeping up there? Not at all. Come down here tonight.' We had a bedroom each, hot and cold running water, electric blanket on your bed, and a batman attended to us and all our requirements. What a vast change. The funny thing was, the next morning, I went to see the major. 'Right what do I owe you?' 'Oh. Just drop the batman something.' Well, the gaffer said, 'What about half a crown each?' So, I said, 'No way. That's farcical.' 'What do you suggest?' he replied. 'I would suggest thirty shillings each', I said. So, it was pared down to a pound each. I mean, that gaffer, he was... When the time went down to actually change the engine, we all went into a bar at night and it was brown ale. Well, I'm not a drinker. One bottle of brown ale would do me all night. But of course there was a round and it came to my turn and all the usual carry on. It came to the gaffer's turn. He says, 'We'll have a wee change boys. I'll buy the crisps.' And he did!

It was a Dakota landing at Stornoway, on which he was First Officer, which earned Kenneth McLean a reputation for low flying. At the time of the 1957 incident which instigated this allegation, it was the norm for landing aircraft to touch down 'on the button' of the runway as soon as possible after the aircraft was above the start of the paved surface. On this occasion the field adjoining the perimetre of the airport contained sheep:

> The sheep started to scatter as usual but one broke through the fence and ran towards the runway giving us no chance whatever of taking evasive action of any kind. The throttles were closed and we were flaring to land 'on the button'. We felt a slight impact and, on completion of the landing run, the captain turned the aircraft back to see what had happened. There, right on the end of the runway, with a distressed lamb in agitated attendance, was a dead sheep which we must have hit with one of the main wheels just before touchdown.
>
> It was such a sad sight that we were both a bit upset but the whole event took about two seconds and was totally unavoidable. We heard later that the farmer was in fear of prosecution for allowing sheep to be involved in an aircraft incident, but it appeared to be 'just one of those things' and no harm was done – although the sheep might have had a different point of view about that. The event has lived on down the years in the shape of a slightly sick story which I have retold many times at any time low flying has come up in conversation, 'I was flying so low over a field of sheep that, when one stood up, I hit it!'

From 1955 until 1959, Lionel Baston was Ministry of Transport airport manager at Islay, a role in which Air Traffic Control, Meteorological Service and Aerodrome Manager was amalgamated into one. As Aerodrome Manager he was trained to provide Aerodrome Flight Information Service (AFIS) to pilots but it was up to their discretion how they used this. Livestock was one aspect of airport operations over which neither Lionel nor pilots had control:

> Isla Shaw had grazing rights on the aerodrome so sheep had to be cleared for aircraft movements. Services were usually around midday and the sheep became used to being moved. However, if an aircraft was delayed in its departure, they did not take kindly to this and tended to move back and, with the help of an Airedale Terrier, had to be moved again. In the summer an additional Renfrew-Campbeltown-Islay-Tiree evening service operated and the sheep did not readily accept being moved outside the familiar schedule. If one of these flights was delayed in departing, they drifted back and strongly resisted being cleared again.

Off the beaten Track

BEA's routine of scheduled services in Scotland followed a pattern very similar to that developed by the pre-World War Two independent airlines and which is not dissimilar to that operated today. For the larger aircraft to occasionally stray on to longer distance forays was simple utilisation of the range capabilities for which they were built. For the smaller aircraft types such assignments represented more of an adventure. Some of these journeys were presented by air ambulance charters, such as one performed by David Barclay on 24 May 1948 with Rapide G-AGSH from Renfrew to Shannon via Dublin, total flying time five hours and fifty-nine minutes. His patient was 84-year-old Elizabeth Watson of Waterbury, Connecticut. Mrs Watson had arrived at Shannon a fortnight earlier in anticipation of six months holiday in Kilmarnock, her hometown in Scotland. Upon descending the aircraft steps for the transit stop at Shannon, she had lost her footing and fractured her hip as a result of the fall which followed and was rushed to hospital in Limerick. Acknowledging that the trans-Atlantic journey had been quite an undertaking for a lady of such advanced years, and that she nearly had not made it, her daughter-in-law revealed that it was important to the octogenarian. 'I knew we were taking a grave risk flying her to Scotland but, if she is to die, I know she would rather do so in her native land.'

Another epic was performed by Jim Howie when he flew to Land's End to collect a director of the Glasgow firm, Stenhouse, who had become ill while on holiday in Cornwall. Jim More, who was the radio officer for this journey, noted that the Land's End crews were also experienced at ambulance flights but Stenhouse had insisted that a Scottish Air Ambulance Service crew collect its executive.

Much has been made of BEA's failure to resume the pre-war Scottish Airways internal Orkney air services. However BEA aircraft were occasionally seen on islands surrounding the Orkney Mainland. BEA aircraft also occasionally landed outwith the chain of Hebridean airfields which formed the scheduled network. These had been the subject of surveys when the Air Ambulance Division had been set up following creation of the National Health Service. One of these set off using Ted Fresson's old DH84 Dragon, G-ACIT, with David Barclay up front. Sitting behind him was his radio officer, Jim More, who gives an account of the excursion:

> We flew from Renfrew to Prestwick on 31 May 1948 to pick up H. Johnston of the Ministry of Civil Aviation who was the authority to certify airfields. Then we landed in a field at Kilmartin to pick up Bob McIntyre, the surveyor for Argyll. We had intended to land at Salen, by Loch na Keal, on Mull, but this required a gap to be made in a dry stane dyke separating two fields. A gap had been made for our arrival, but only wide enough to accommodate the wheels of the Dragon, not the wings, so we had to do a touch-and-go. We continued to another site by the Sound of Mull but the wind was not right and the site was on a slope so we continued onwards to Tiree. At Tiree we encountered technical problems and Bert Farminer, the only engineer with the Dragon on his certificate, had to attend. We then returned McIntyre to Kilmartin before proceeding to Benbecula for an overnight stop.

Now, that's different. G-ALXN, seen landing at Renfrew, and appropriately named after Henry Royce, became a Dart DC-3 from 1951 until 1953. (Wilf White)

The interior of the de Havilland Heron with Captain David Barclay at the front end. (John S. Groome)

Next day we went to Sollas and Northton where David was unhappy about a 'damp patch' of sand on the beach and I had to photograph it from the Dragon as we flew over it. A horse and cart was used to tow the aircraft at Northton. From Northton, we went to Stornoway then on to Orkney.

Barclay's flying log records the journey continuing from Grimsetter Airport, Kirkwall to the Bay of Houseby, Stronsay, to Hammerbrake, Sanday, and then back to Grimsetter. On 2 June they flew from Grimsetter to Garbo Field on Sanday, to North Ronaldsay and then to Aikerness on Westray before return to Grimsetter. The homeward flight to Renfrew on 3 June was via Stornoway and Prestwick. Jim More remembers their arrival on one Orkney island resulting in the closure of the school following the declaration of a holiday, so that the children could come and see the aircraft and inspect the cockpit. 'About ten children came to see the plane and David said they could each have a turn at sitting in the pilot's seat as long as they didn't touch anything!' He also notes that, while at Northton on the Isle of Harris, they received a request from Skye to do a survey of the pre-war airfield at Glenbrittle but when they learned that it had been ploughed, they decided that such a diversion would be fruitless and they continued to Stornoway. The landings at Kilmartin on 31 May were sufficiently 'off the beaten track' to escape recording in Barclay's log, perhaps because of their unofficial nature.

Barclay's visit to Westray on 2 June 1948 was recorded by Jack Scott on that very day as he put pen to paper to his girlfriend, Nan Pottinger, who was boarding at the school in Kirkwall. He wrote:

> Guess what a lovely experience I had today, something I've never had before. No, I'm sure you'd be wrong every time if you had twenty tries. Dad and me were up for a flip in an aeroplane!! Captain Barclay, whom you've probably ready about in the Journal, was here looking for a field for ambulance work and he has chosen our field for east and west winds and the one at Cleat for north and south winds. Him and another man came up to the house and got some butter home with them. Dad said he would go down with them to see the plane. So, I thought I'd go down and take a photo of the plane and then Captain Barclay tore at Dad to come up for a trip. He wasn't too keen but he managed to get him persuaded in the long run if I'd come too. I jumped at the chance and took my wee camera with me. I fair enjoyed seeing the Aikerness holm and sea below us when we took off and I took a photo of the Holm, Vere and Skaith. We circled the village and then back around Skaill and Breck. As we came in to land, I saw Tommy and James W. and Mum and Jean and Ivy o' Westbreck waving to us at Skaill, and I waved back. It was great and I was sorry when it was over, only I was ever so pleased to have had the chance. The pilot said it was very simple but I don't know. I think it takes a cool head anyhow.

Nan Pottinger became Nan Scott and she comments that the field used by David Barclay is situated in the district of Aikerness and is now part of the airfield used for the Orkney inter-island air service. Nan also writes that, '2 June 1948 was a red letter day in Jack's life and David Barclay will always be his hero.'

The Orkney epic followed two one-day surveys on 21 and 22 May. Again calling at Prestwick to collect Johnston, the first of these had visited Islay, Colonsay and Oronsay while the second had routed through Tiree to Coll. Ambulance flights were subsequently operated to some of the islands outwith the BEA scheduled network during the early years of the Corporation. Archie Edmiston's log, for example, shows him in his capacity as radio officer accompanying David Barclay in 1951 to Coll on two occasions, and one visit to Oronsay with Jim Howie. It was the Isle of Coll on which Paddy Calderwood had a mishap with a de Havilland Heron G-ANXA on 20 February 1957 when he landed on the field in wet and windy conditions, slid sideways, hit a ditch, and wrote off the undercarriage. The aircraft had to be removed by sea and sent to Hatfield for repair. After this incident, BEA withdrew authority for pilots to land on Coll until a Pierced Steel Planking (PSP) strip consisting of metal matting, as used during World War Two for creating ad hoc landing sites, was laid. BEA was prepared to pay for the PSP strip but not for its installation. Captain Terry Lakin takes up the story and an immediate consequence which unfolded on 30 June 1958:

The local people refused to put down the PSP unless they were paid. BEA refused to pay them so there was a stalemate. As this occurred, the local doctor insisted on having an air ambulance to uplift seven-year-old Margaret Macdonald. The girl was suffering from appendicitis and, although we were prepared to go to the island, we were told that we must not and the girl should be brought over to Tiree in a small boat as the sea was quite calm. Eventually a helicopter, which had to come from Belfast Aldergrove, was used. Because it was a long, over-water crossing, the helicopter had to be escorted by an Avro Shackleton and ferried the girl to Tiree where Captain Ken Browning and myself were waiting to take her to Renfrew and hospital. The helicopter was low on fuel and an Avro Anson had to come from Stornoway to refuel the helicopter on Coll. Then all three RAF aircraft went back to Aldergrove. The total cost of this operation would easily have paid for a contractor to lay the PSP on Coll. With all the delay, the poor girl was in considerable pain but I am glad to say that she did survive this experience.

One airfield which received regular BEA visits despite not being a scheduled service station was Sollas on the Isle of North Uist. An airfield overlooking the machair had operated during the 1930s and was then the hub of Outer Hebridean air transport, equipped with a hangar for an aircraft based there, a resident pilot to fly it, and a fuel pump to keep it flying. The pre-war scheduled services of Northern & Scottish and Scottish Airways to Sollas were not taken up by BEA but it did continue to serve it with ambulance flights for many years. Some of BEA's flights landed not on the old airstrip but on Vallay Strand, a vast expanse almost enclosed from the sea by the islet of Vallay. Captain Kenneth McLean explained to me that the major landmark for reaching Sollas for the VFR segment over the final stage from Benbecula was a red postbox. It marked the point where the aircraft stopped following the main road along the west side of North Uist, and took a right turn to follow a track across the hills. This track was known as the Committee Road as it had been constructed in former times under the direction of the Committee of Poor Relief, in order to create work for the able-bodied unemployed to relieve them from the effects of destitution. The following extract from a 1957 article describes one writer's experience of the approach to Sollas from Benbecula. Captain Don Hoare was in command.

A Decca can be used for a let-down, but this has its hazards for in murky weather one bit of beach looks very like another, and only one at this point is capable of bearing the weight of an aeroplane. The less scientific approach, but perhaps the more foolproof, is to carry out a VDF let-down at Benbecula and then to head across the water to North Uist and pick up the Committee Road on the coast. On this occasion we followed the road, which turns inland and winds its way between hills nearly 800 feet high. The valley was narrow without room to turn round and I hardly liked the thought of an aircraft battling its way against an Atlantic gale, with lowering cloud and driving rain obscuring the winding cart-track of a road to which the pilot must cling, knowing that high ground lay on either side. But, sure enough, the Committee Road led us eventually to the northern shore and I am told that pilots, experienced with this sort of thing, have used the route for years as the only positive way of finding the landing area.

As we flew over the beach, which is in a semi-circular bay, the dark shapes of two vehicles and a small group of people could be seen on the edge of the sand waiting for us and we headed slightly out to sea before turning back and approaching into wind towards the land.

The speed was reduced below the 135-knot flap-lowering limit and the first 20° of flap was selected. The nose-up couple was trimmed out and the power adjusted to give 80 knots and a descent of about 400ft./min. On the approach I had the greatest difficulty in deciding where the sea ended and the shore began, for the sand had been left in characteristic ripples by the receding tide and these ripples were still filled with water. The drag associated with the landing flap setting being considerable, the flaps were not extended until quite late on the approach, then a little extra power was needed to maintain the speed at 70 knots.

During the flare-out I was having some difficulty in judging our height, when a seagull obligingly

Lining up at Sollas airfield are Radio Officer Archie Edmiston; an unnamed nurse, probably from the Southern General Hospital, Glasgow; Dr Alex J. Macleod of Lochmaddy; Nurse Macarthur; the Lochmaddy district nurse; and Captain David Barclay. (Iain Mackenzie via Dr John A. J. Macleod) got up in front of us, giving me some clue. The power was kept on for a slow nose-up touch-down and the sand, although being comparatively firm, had a smooth but marked braking effect on the machine and, after splashing through several large puddles of sea water, we slowed down to a comfortable turning speed in a very short distance. As a result of this type of operation, the engineers have to keep a particularly careful watch for corrosion on the airframe and nosewheel mudguards have been fitted to each aircraft as a form of protection.

At Sollas, the tide encroaches in the shape of a tongue and, as the water gets higher, the landing strip gets narrower and more curved. Tide tables are always consulted when a call comes through from one of these places, but often, under urgent conditions, pilots have been know to carry out semi-circular landing runs and take-offs rather than wait for the next tide.

Having turned the aircraft so that its door was beside the vehicle that served as an ambulance, the engines were cut and we climbed out to meet Dr Macleod – a solid imperturbable woman who, with her husband, also a doctor, covers this territory. A basket containing meat sandwiches, home-made cakes and hot, strong coffee was produced and we sheltered against the cold wind and chatted while the patients were being loaded into the aircraft. Ours was the first machine in for over five weeks and it made, no doubt, an interesting diversion in that lonely place.

All too soon we were ready to leave and, the people in these islands being most undemonstrative, quietly we said 'good-bye' and climbed aboard.

The doctor was Julia P. Macleod who, in partnership with her husband, Alex J. Macleod, were the medical practitioners for the Isles of North Uist and Berneray, based in Lochmaddy, from 1932 until 1974. Their son, John A. J. Macleod joined the practice in 1973 and served these islands in the same tradition until his retiral in 2000.

The Shiant Isles have no airstrip but there was a time when they became part of the day's work for BEA crews as recorded by Harry McDowell:

During the summers in the 1950s and 1960s, we had an extra little job to do six days a week between Benbecula and Stornoway when passing the Shiant Isles. Each year, parties of schoolboys from Westminster School in London spent camping holidays on the Shiants which were uninhabited. There was no way for them to communicate with the outside world, but they had a transceiver on one of the aircraft channels so every morning we flew low over the islands and called them up to ask them if they were okay. If not, we would call Stornoway Coastguard to tell them what help was required. They seemed to enjoy the daily chat and asked for a quick resumé of the news headlines.

Harry also recalls that about once a year, in summer, if the weather was fine and they were a little ahead of schedule, they would treat the passengers to a run up the west coast of Lewis as far as Gallan Head, where there was an RAF early warning radar station, before crossing the island to Stornoway. This area is extremely rugged with only isolated communities. 'When we flew low over the base, they all came out and waved, unable to believe their eyes that a scheduled airline flight would come over to say 'hello' to them.'

Air Ambulance

The traditions of the Scottish Air Ambulance Service were laid down in 1933 when the first flights were flown by Midland & Scottish Air Ferries. Its role was emulated by Highland Airways, Aberdeen Airways, Northern & Scottish Airways and, after some initial deliberation in 1947, BEA took over responsibility for continuing the service when it absorbed Scottish Airways. David Barclay became responsible for the Air Ambulance Service under BEA and the de Havilland Rapide was used to operate these flights until the de Havilland Heron replaced it in 1955. The initial BEA air ambulance team in 1948 consisted of Captains David Barclay and Jim Howie along with Radio Officers Jim More and Hugh Murdoch. The two teams were on duty for twelve-hour shifts and their daily association with air ambulance operations enabled them to exchange information on individual patients who were regular visitors to hospital and whose condition or habits might affect a particular flight.

The air ambulance service had to respond to a variety of eventualities. Jim More was radio officer on one flight from Kirkwall to Aberdeen carrying a payload of seven mentally ill patients clad in strait-jackets. On 27 December 1948, More took off in response to a call on a day during which regular flying had been severely disrupted by extreme weather conditions:

> The call came from Benbecula for the Air Ambulance to pick up a boy in danger of developing peritonitis. Captain Bill McKenzie said he knew how he would feel if it was one of his sons so he said he would give it a go. We picked up the boy but had difficulty on arrival at Renfrew. During our efforts to land, we struck the golf course writing off the Rapide, G-AHXY, and suffered cuts and bruises. Later, we received a report that the boy had been suffering from severe constipation!

Paddy Calderwood, who took on the mantle of Chief Pilot of the Air Ambulance Service around 1956/57, put the postwar service into context when he said, 'The service is issued free by the National Health Service, which puts the Heron in roughly the same category as false teeth and wigs!'

As has been mentioned earlier, Paddy Calderwood was killed, along with Radio Officer Hugh McGinlay and volunteer nurse Sister Jean Kennedy, when Heron G-AOFY crashed on Islay while trying to land to uplift a patient in 1957. Lionel Baston, Aerodrome Manager on Islay, recalls the deplorable weather conditions which inhibited contact with the inbound Heron although a radio signal from the aircraft was picked up by a BOAC airliner. 'Paddy just tried too hard to get in', was Lionel's philosophical summing up of the night's tragic outcome.

Following the Islay crash, Flight Manager Captain Eric Starling imposed new operating minima for ambulance pilots which were to be applied no matter how critical a patient was. In the aftermath, the air ambulance service continued to remain closely associated with David Barclay until his retirement in 1965. Eric Starling, another veteran of pre-war airline flying in Scotland, stood down as Flight Manager in 1968 and dedicated himself to the air ambulance service until his retirement followed in 1971. Needless to say, the service was also supported by numerous other aircrew, and by the nurses who offered their services on a voluntary basis until and beyond BEA's withdrawal from the air ambulance contract in 1973.

BEA's links with the air ambulance service were severed when its Herons were replaced with Short Skyliner aircraft. However, the short-lived autonomous BEA Scottish Airways had floated plans for helicopter services to serve Scottish communities – proposing the use of Bölkow 105 helicopters to take the air ambulance service to the scene of accidents and to locations remote from airfields. While this plan proved to be ahead of its time, it did materialise more than two decades later when the Scottish Ambulance Service contracted Bond Helicopters in 1993 to share the air ambulance role with Loganair, the bulk of Bond's contribution being two Bölkow 105Ds based at Prestwick and Inverness.

To the rescue

BEA's humanitarian role was not limited to carrying out its obligations to the Scottish Home and Health Department in fulfilling the terms of the Scottish Air Ambulance contract. Harry McDowell undertook one unusual mission while the rest of Scotland was preparing for the celebration of Hogmanay:

> It was 31 December 1956 and it was during our lunchtime stopover at Kirkwall Airport that I got a phone call from HM Coastguard asking if I would help them. Apparently they had received a 'Mayday' call from a fishing trawler saying they had had an explosion in the engine room, they had some injured crew on board, and they were drifting without power. The lifeboat had been looking for them for hours without success and would I help by flying off to the north and looking for them. I said, 'yes' and we abandoned lunch and set off with an empty Dakota (and empty stomachs).
>
> After carrying out a square search, we eventually found the trawler miles from where it was

supposed to be. We then had to find the lifeboat and give it a bearing and distance to run to the trawler. I'm glad to say that I was informed that the trawler was located and the lifeboat took it in tow to Kirkwall harbour. We eventually got back to Glasgow, very late, and with a few disgruntled passengers and an unusual explanation for our lateness for BEA in London.

> Around 3 January I was back in Kirkwall, on a night stop this time, so I walked down to the harbour and, lo and behold, there was the missing trawler moored alongside. I went over to talk to the crew to find out what had happened to cause their explosion. They said they were on their way home to Lowestoft from the Icelandic fishing grounds and, as it was the night before New Year's eve, they thought they could start celebrating a little early. They had too many drams and fell asleep. As it was an old steam driven boat, the unattended boilers ran dry, hence one large explosion. Two of the crew were badly burned and they hadn't much of a clue about their position. As I left them, they said, 'Sorry to have bothered you – and thanks for your help!'

Captain McDowell later received commendation from HM Coastguard for being one of the captains of two aircraft who unhesitatingly agreed to carry out the search in the interests of life-saving. The trawler was the *Neath Castle* and the involvement of the BEA aircraft had enabled the Stronsay lifeboat to take off a badly injured man, north of Papa Westray, before the onset of darkness. The other BEA captain involved was Johnny Welford.

Around this period, McDowell was involved in another search, this time after leaving Benbecula for Glasgow. A radio call informed him that an RAF Handley Page Halifax bomber had gone missing during a weather reconnaissance flight from Aldergrove in Northern Ireland, last known position 30 miles south-east of Barra Head. After half an hour of circling at 1000 feet, the BEA crew spotted wreckage and empty dinghies. Part of the bomber's routine was to descend to sea level to begin meteorological recordings, which it continued to do through a long steady climb. Harry McDowell, who had flown Halifax aircraft during the Berlin Airlift of 1948, remembers that a very calm sea could create conditions under which it is very difficult for a pilot to ascertain his height. 'We assumed that the pilot had gone down a little too close to the sea and pitched in. All were lost.'

Finishing on a light note

The creation of the state airlines has been depicted by many as representing the loss of individuality, the rise of bureaucracy, and the era of doing things 'by the book' to present an image of military precision and efficiency. The days of the buccaneer spirit had gone and humour in the course of professional duty was out of place. However, the air and ground crews who served BEA in Scotland were often the same people who had nurtured the predecessor independent airlines from infancy. Their ingenuity did not suddenly desert them on 1 February 1947. Nor, of course, did their efficiency and professionalism, which had accompanied more than a decade of operations of reliable and safe service. Their sense of humour and mischief remained intact too.

Chief court jester was undoubtedly the bearded Johnny Welford who, in the 1970s, had the grave misfortune of being killed in a car crash during the week that was to have marked his retirement as a captain in the Trident fleet. Johnny's antics however remain the source of mirth and fond memories among his former colleagues. Peter Morgan recalls Johnny as 'larger than life in all respects – not only very extrovert but six foot two inches, weighing about eighteen stone, with a huge red face, and a white beard:

> In the sixties, he was a Viscount captain based in Glasgow. One of the routes involved a very early start from a small hotel where the crews stayed in Aberdeen. The lady who ran the hotel was determined that no BEA crew would be 'late on parade' while she was in charge. To this end she would bang loudly on the door of each room at wake-up time until a response was heard. Five minutes later she would return, bang once, and walk in carrying a cup of tea. Johnny did not approve of this and

asked her many times not to enter as he did not need a second call. This request was ignored until, one morning, she entered his room on her second call to be confronted by Johnny, with his back to her, viewing her from between wide apart legs and wearing absolutely nothing. There was a shrill scream, a tinkle of breaking crockery, and she never bothered him again.

Jim More recalls that Johnny became aware of a nice looking woman who lived at Southend on Kintyre and adopted the habit of dipping a wing as he passed over when flying in and out of Campbeltown. She returned the acknowledgement by waving to him with her dishcloth. Donald Thomson, a regular traveller from Benbecula between 1950 and 1965, was a passenger on a Glasgow-bound flight on which there were a few high spirited young islanders:

> During the flight, one of them produced a mouth organ and started to play. Everyone joined in, singing and clapping. Next, the pilot came out of the cockpit and everyone went quiet, expecting a telling off. Instead, he took the mouth organ and started to play Scottish airs. One lady near to him asked, 'If you are out here, who is flying the plane?' 'Ach,' he replied, 'this old plane knows the way back by herself.'

The captain was undoubtedly Johnny Welford. Iain Crosbie remembers Welford as being accomplished on the tin whistle and he was known to play this on board after a BEA directive to crew instructed that they should make a greater effort to entertain their passengers! Bill Reid reams off a list of Johnny's pranks:

> Climbing into the Rapide cockpit in fishing gear; entertaining the passengers with a penny whistle on the Dak; the stewardess entering the Dak cockpit to find the clear vision panels fully open and no one there; Johnny in dark glasses tapping his way across the tarmac towards his fully laden aircraft with his white stick; and him retreating from the flight deck with a piece of string in each hand, giving them to a lady passenger telling her to hold them steady while he went to the toilet or the plane might go out of control.

'Aviation seems a bit dull now that he has gone,' concludes Bill.

Returning to the subject of night stops, Peter Morgan remarks that it was St Enoch Hotel, Glasgow, that was favoured by crews on the London service:

> It was a massive Victorian railway structure with corridors, the ends of which could only be seen on a clear day. It never developed to the stage of having a bathroom en suite with every room. Indeed the 'facilities' were spaced at quite infrequent intervals along those endless corridors. For the convenience of guests, large items of Staffordshire pottery were therefore placed under the beds in each room. One morning a crew on the early service, on their way to Renfrew, were regaled by the Captain's story of finding himself embarrassed at having to utilise this article. In the early morning darkness, he decided to dispose of the evidence by emptying the contents out of the window onto a glass roof below. Unfortunately, the handle was not as firmly attached as he had supposed and about four pounds of earthenware and half a gallon of second-hand McEwans descended four floors through the roof of St Enoch Station and exploded like a bomb on the platform beneath – fortunately without injury to anyone. He vacated the room rapidly! The rest of the crew laughed uproariously but failed to believe him until he produced, from his briefcase, the handle of the offending item which he had retained as a souvenir.

Peter Black explains why a Viscount under the command of Jock Sneddon zigzagged down the runway at Belfast Aldergrove upon conclusion of a flight from Renfrew. The cause was not the crosswinds but an uninvited passenger. At Renfrew, a sparrow had been found inside the aircraft but it disappeared when the crew tried to chase it out. Its reappearance coincided with the crosswind landing when it chose to fly up the leg of Sneddon's trousers – causing him some difficulty in his manipulation of the rudders!

In 1951, Donald Macdonald, station superintendent at Benbecula, wrote a spoof article for BEA Magazine, intended to illustrate routines at his Hebridean outstation. It was meant as a light-hearted dig at the several Englishmen working at the airport, and described an elderly lady bringing a crate of hens to the airport for dispatch to Glasgow. Donald's narration ran like this:

> Peggy McFee came to us with all her worldly luggage, consisting of a cardboard box with 'Beatties

bread is best' printed large upon its side. Inside rested, contentedly, four Hebridean hens – all that was left of her hen flock, the rest having been claimed by the wicked fowl pest which ravaged the islands from Shetland to Lewis and beyond. An ordinary human being would appreciate the old woman's difficulties, but not so an efficient BEA Station Clerk who had imbibed deeply five hundred odd Traffic Instructions and much explanatory memoranda. Hens were no bona-fide luggage, but cargo, and live cargo at that, liable to livestock surcharges. Explanatory memoranda said quite clearly that such surcharges were to be levied on the livestock – and not on the container. Peggy was instructed to undo the tarred, lobster-creel twine securing her charges. The hens were to be weighed separately, but they had other views. Disdaining the scales, they all made for the passenger waiting room. They flew and hopped onto chairs, over and under the tables, and finally, through the outer door to the airfield. Peggy McFee never said a word.

Now we really had a problem on our hands. Our Station Engineer from Falmouth got early into the chase and, from the course taken and the speed he travelled at, I thought he was going to take leave of us for good. I phoned our London-born Controller and he promptly told me that he could do nothing with unauthorised flights such as this. I was about to ring our Air Ministry Works Department Clerk of Works, who hails from Market Harborough, when I was disturbed by our panicking Irish Fire Officer suggesting that he could discharge six banks of CO_2 gas at the escaped hens to stop their headlong flight. This suggestion seemed promising and I was about to accept it in preference to requesting the Clerk of Works for the assistance of his forty-strong force, when Peggy came into action. She stood in the door a-crying, 'Took, Took, Took, Took', and then the hens ran towards her and into the open box with welcoming cackles. She silently closed the lid, re-knotted the already much knotted string and, still without speaking, placed her charges, secure in their container, on the weighing machine.

'That will be seven and sixpence', said the hot and bothered Clerk. Peggy delved deep in her bosom and extracted a much worn purse. She tendered an English 'greenback' and waited for her change, staring, more in sorrow than in anger, at the modern Station Clerk.

Peggy left us and, departing, gave us one sad, sad look – a look that seemed to go down through the ages to the days when Red Tape was not.

Publication ensured that, within BEA, Benbecula was now on the map and Donald's fame and reputation were assured. In real life, 'woolly' situations did sometimes have to be defused. Passenger Donald Thomson cites the arrival of a crofter at the Balivanich check-in desk and insisting that the huge ram, which he had at the end of a rope, should accompany him in the passenger cabin. The situation was resolved with an explanation that there wasn't a spare seat available for the ram.

David Barclay frequently enjoyed his own sense of humour while getting the better of someone who thought they knew best. Jim Howie recalls the London-based Chief Pilot's scepticism when damage to the rudder of a Dakota was reported as occurring when hit by a 90 mph gust while parked at Stornoway:

'That's a hurricane', the Chief Pilot snorted. 'You don't get them in these latitudes! Someone is fiddling the books.' David Barclay explained that the Scottish weather is different to that in the south of England. Why didn't he come up and see for himself. He did, and David took him for a tour of the Western Isles on a nice dirty day. They went into Barra using the 'pass the rock, turn three degrees and look for the seagulls' approach. The Chief Pilot was chewing on an empty pipe as they landed, a sure indication of perturbation. The perturbation increased as David discussed the adjacent contours. Between the landing beach and the ocean beach to the west there is a low ridge of dunes rising at either end into two hills. The lower portions of these were visible from time to time from the airport building, a small weather-beaten hut, but not when they taxied out to the take-off point. 'It's no bother,' explained David. 'We can just aim between them and hope the directional gyro doesn't precess overmuch.' They were almost immediately in cloud and rain. At 500 feet, the Chief Pilot realised he had bitten through the stem of his pipe. By the time they stopped at Stornoway for the night, he had surrendered. David had a gentle and courteous way of putting over his point.

Geoff Northmore requested a posting to Aberdeen, a small base with six pilots who built up a close camaraderie and worked extremely hard to ensure the continuity of the base. One night Geoff and his wife entertained David Jones and they made 'quite a night of it'. Geoff had the following day off duty while David, with Wally Durward as his co-pilot, was operating the 0630 departure to Edinburgh and Renfrew. Geoff rented a farmhouse near the airfield and, snug in bed, he heard the engines start, followed by the run-up and then the takeoff. 'It was pitch dark and, as I lay gazing up the road, I saw these green and red lights coming down the road towards me. The landing lights suddenly went on and, with an ear splitting roar, the Dak flew just above the roof. About an hour later the phone rang and a voice said, 'Did we wake you?''

Geoff was co-pilot to a nameless captain when, one day, they climbed aboard their aircraft to find the 'boots', the black rubber inflatable tubes on the leading edge of the wings, labelled as unserviceable but with no further information:

> This was no problem as it was a fine day. When we had the engines running, the Captain decided to give the boots a whirl anyway, so on they went. Looking out my side, they worked correctly. His side seemed okay when he suddenly said, 'Look at the engineer outside'. This chap's eyes were like organ stops as he gazed at something on the Captain's side. Then, over the top of the port engine, a big black balloon appeared. I made to turn off the boots. 'Leave them alone and let's see how big it will get', said the Captain. Eventually, above the engine noise and our laughter, we heard the bang as it exploded. I cannot remember what we cooked up to explain the shredded remains in the Technical Log.

It was from Aberdeen that James Mackreth, posted back following his 'indoctrination' at Renfrew following BEA's absorption of Allied Airways, was assigned a coffin charter to Shetland on 26 July 1947 in Rapide G-AGOP. Once airborne, he was reflecting upon the sombre nature of the journey until his radio officer drew his attention to the four mourners travelling with the deceased. They were using the coffin as a card table.

Passengers were not immune to a bit of fun either. The advance party of the film crew which descended upon Barra in 1948 for the filming of *Whisky Galore* decided to prepare a reception for the arrival of technicians whom Bill Reid flew to the island:

> Someone had asked, during Ealing Studios' briefing, if passports would be needed for the Hebrides. On a lovely June day, I was very surprised to see a trestle table standing by the arrival hut, upon which was a large notice bearing the legend 'CUSTOMS'. Behind the table stood a figure wearing a long BEA greatcoat, a hat pulled down over his ears and dark glasses. Shouting at my passengers, 'Anything to declare?' he required them to put their opened cases on the table whereupon he rummaged about inside them, flinging many of their belongings onto the sand!

Tom Young recalls a Viscount sitting ready for the passengers to board and watching the captain welcoming the passengers. 'He stood at the foot of the steps and as all the passengers were going aboard he said, 'Now, after we take off, I want you to come up into the cockpit. All come up individually and I'll explain all the controls. You'll be very interested.' After all the passengers were aboard, he went away to his own plane!'

Appendix 1

Chronology

1933	18 Apr	Midland & Scottish Air Ferries launches an experimental service from Renfrew to Campbeltown. By 26 April this is being publicised as a scheduled service.
	19 Apr	First landing at Sumburgh, Shetland, performed by Bill Caldwell in a Fox Moth of SMT Aviation.
	8 May	Highland Airways begins scheduled service Inverness-Wick-Kirkwall.
	14 May	Evacuation of John McDermid from Islay marks beginning of the Scottish Air Ambulance Service.
	16 May	Midland & Scottish Renfrew-Campbeltown service is extended to Islay.
	18 Dec	First flight of Jersey Airways, from the beach at St Aubin's Bay to Portsmouth.
1934	7 May	Highland Airways launches Aberdeen-Kirkwall service.
	July	John Sword begins closure of Midland & Scottish Air Ferries.
	29 Sep	Last Midland & Scottish scheduled service – on the Islay-Campbeltown-Renfrew route.
	1 Dec	Northern & Scottish Airways begins operations from Renfrew.
1935	23 May	Northern & Scottish Airways and Highland Airways acquired by Whitehall Securities Group.
	27 May	Aberdeen Airways launches Aberdeen-Stromness service.
	3 Dec	Aberdeen Airways launches Aberdeen-Kirkwall service in competition with Highland Airways.
1936		Alderney is the first of the Channel Islands to have an airfield.
	2 June	Aberdeen Airways launches first Aberdeen-Sumburgh service.
	3 June	Highland Airways launches Aberdeen-Sumburgh service.
1937	13 Feb	Aberdeen Airways renamed Allied Airways (Gandar Dower) Ltd.
	10 Mar	Airfield at St Peter's on Jersey opens.
	12 Aug	Northern & Scottish Airways and Highland Airways become Scottish Airways.
	15 Sep	Channel Air Ferries begins services between Land's End and St. Mary's.
	27 Sep	Isle of Man Air Services launches its first route, Isle of Man-Liverpool.
1938	Spring	Great Western and Southern Airlines takes over Olley Air Services and its subsidiary, Channel Air Ferries
	3 May	Scottish Airways provides through service from Renfrew to Kirkwall and Sumburgh.
1939	12 May	Airfield at La Villiaze, Guernsey, opens.
	10 Jul	Allied Airways opens regular non-stop Aberdeen-Sumburgh service.
	3 Sep	Scottish internal air routes suspended following British declaration of war with Germany.
1940	1 Jul	German occupation of the Channel Islands.
1941	3 Jun	Great Western and Southern DH84 Dragon, G-ACPY, shot down on Scillies route. Six fatalities.
1945	9 May	End to German occupation of the Channel Islands.
	7 Jun	Resumption of Channel Island air services following end of German occupation.

1946		Civil Aviation Act creates British European Airways, British Overseas Airways Corporation and British South American Airways.
	Aug	**British European Airways officially comes into being.**
1947	1 Feb	British European Airways takes over operation of services of Great Western and Southern Airlines, and Scottish Airways.
	11 Feb	Edmund Fresson undertakes air ambulance evacuation from Stronsay. He is subsequently reprimanded by BEA.
	1 Apr	**BEA takes over Channel Islands Airways, the post-war successor to Jersey Airways and Guernsey Airways.**
	11 Apr	**BEA takes over Allied Airways (Gandar Dower) Ltd.**
	15 Apr	De Havilland Rapide G-AHKR written off on the Isle of Man.
	21 Apr	London-Jersey services transferred from Croydon to Northolt and de Havilland Rapide displaced on the route by DC-3.
	Aug	BEA withdraws Junkers Ju 52 aircraft from service.
	6 Aug	De Havilland Rapide G-AGJF written off on Barra.
	1 Nov	Last service to Guernsey from Croydon Airport.
1949		Jersey Airlines begins operations on a charter basis.
1950	28 Apr	Rapide summer service opened between Alderney and Gatwick.
	May	Channel Islands services to Birmingham and Manchester launched.
1951	Summer	DC-3 used to launch direct Jersey-Glasgow service.
	Aug	BEA uses de Havilland's prototype Heron, G-ALZL on route trials to Channel Islands.
	6 Dec	De Havilland Rapide G-AGPH written off on Barra.
1952	April	Jersey Airlines begins a Jersey-Exeter route under a BEA Associate agreement.
	June	Hard runway opened at Jersey airport.
	Summer	Alderney-Gatwick service withdrawn at end of the summer season.
1953	Summer	Airspeed Ambassador, BEA's 'Elizabethan' class, introduced to London-Jersey route.
1954	July	BEA operates Viscount proving flight to the Isle of Man.
	Oct	Services to Channel Islands from London transferred from Northolt to Heathrow.
1955	Summer	Viscount supplements DC-3 on Isle of Man-Manchester route.
1956		Introduction of Viscount on some Heathrow-Jersey schedules.
	20 Apr	BEA withdraws from Alderney. Also from the Southampton-Guernsey route and services to Dinard from both Guernsey and Jersey. Last BEA Rapide service in the Channel Islands.
	Summer	Direct seasonal service launched between Jersey and Belfast.
1957	Summer	Seasonal weekend service opened on the Jersey-Edinburgh-Aberdeen route.
	28 Sep	De Havilland Heron G-AOFY crashes on Islay. Three fatalities.
1958	9 Jun	Gatwick formally opened as London's 'second airport'. BEA transfers most of its London to Guernsey and Jersey flights from Heathrow to Gatwick.
1959	21 May	De Havilland Rapide G-AHLL written off at Land's End.
	15 Dec	Handley Page Herald prototype G-APWA demonstrated at Scottish airfields.
1960		Civil Aviation Act enables Jersey Airlines to compete directly with BEA on Channel Islands routes.
	1 Aug	Opening of a hard runway at Guernsey Airport.
	31 Oct	Last day of Pionair services to the Isle of Man.

1961		Dedicated freighter service from London and Southampton to Jersey by Pionair Leopard aircraft introduced.
	20 Mar	BEA transfers services from Southampton upon withdrawal of Pionairs from Channel Island services.
	21 Mar	Channel Islands services launched from Bournemouth Hurn Airport using Viscounts.
	12 Dec	De Havilland Rapide G-AKZB written off at Land's End.
1962		Jersey Airlines absorbed by British United Airways as British United Airways (CI).
	10 Mar	Delivery of first Handley Page Herald to BEA.
	Apr	London-Jersey freight service upgraded from Pionair Leopard to Armstrong-Whitworth Argosy.
	16 Apr	Handley Page Herald G-APWB performs first revenue service – on Northern Isles route.
	19 May	G-ALTT operates last BEA Pionair service, Islay-Campbeltown-Renfrew.
	21 May	Handley Page Herald begins service on routes to Campbeltown and Islay.
	21 May	Vickers Viscount begins service on Scottish routes to Benbecula and Stornoway.
	June	Vickers Vanguard operates once weekly Isle of Man-London Heathrow.
1963	Apr	Most flights to Channels Islands from London transferred from Gatwick back to Heathrow.
	1 Apr	BEA services to Isle of Man are taken over by Cambrian Airways.
	May	Argosy launches London-Guernsey freighter service.
1964	1 May	Last day of BEA de Havilland Rapide services – on St Mary's-Land's End route.
	2 May	Introduction of Sikorsky S61, operated by BEA Helicopters, to St. Mary's-Land's End route.
	1 Jun	Vickers Vanguard introduced to London-Jersey route.
	1 Sep	Penzance Heliport replaces St. Mary's for BEA services to the Isles of Scilly.
	31 Oct	Last Handley Page Herald services for BEA in Scotland.
1965	Nov	Sikorsky S61 helicopter operates between Guernsey and Jersey until Feb 1966 during daytime runway resurfacing at Jersey Airport.
1966	1 Apr	Following laying of hard runway at Southampton, BEA resumes services to Jersey.
	2 May	Abbotsinch replaces Renfrew as Glasgow's airport.
1967	18 Jul	Vanguard makes a proving flight to Guernsey and thereafter makes occasional visits.
	Aug	Loganair launches Orkney inter-island air services.
	1 Oct	**By a renaming of the dormant pre-nationalisation company, Railway Air Services, British Air Services is formed as a holding company for BEA subsidiaries BKS Air Transport and Cambrian Airways.**
	1 Nov	**Scottish Division formed as a 'profit-centred unit' within BEA.**
1968	1 Mar	Aurigny Air Services begins services linking Guernsey and Alderney.
	31 Oct	British United Airways (CI) ceases following merger with BUA (Manx).
1969	18 Feb	Intra Airways is launched with a Dakota aircraft.
	31 Mar	BEA withdraws from inter-island service linking Guernsey and Jersey.
	6 May	Aurigny begins operations on the Guernsey-Jersey route abandoned by BEA.

1970	30 Apr	Armstrong Whitworth Argosy freighters, used on scheduled cargo services to Jersey and Guernsey, are withdrawn. BEA's Channel Islands freighter services continue with Vickers Merchantman aircraft.
	1 Nov	**BKS Air Transport, part of British Air Services, renamed as Northeast Airlines.**
1971	1 Apr	**In a further reorganisation of operating units within the BEA Group, Scottish Division became Scottish Airways Division, and a new Channel Islands Airways Division was created.**
1972	May	Weekly Jersey-Amsterdam service launched with Vickers Viscount.
	1 Sep	**BEA Helicopters renamed British Airways Helicopters under management of the British Airways Board.**
	1 Sep	**Scottish Airways Division and Channel Islands Airways Division become part of British Air Services along with Cambrian Airways and Northeast Airlines. British Air Services is a division under the management of the British Airways Board, as are BEA, British Airways Helicopters and BOAC.**
1973	19 Jan	Viscount G-AOHI crashes on Ben More, Perthshire, during an engineering test flight. Four fatalities.
	1 Apr	Loganair takes over Scottish Air Ambulance contract.
	2 Apr	Short Skyliner begins service between Glasgow, Tiree and Barra.
	30 May	BEA settles compensation claims with Allied Airways (Gandar Dower) Ltd following take over on 11 April 1947.
	1 Sep	**BEA is renamed British Airways European Division, British Air Services is renamed British Airways Regional Division, and BOAC is renamed British Airways Overseas Division.**
1974	31 Mar	**BEA, British Air Services, and BOAC cease to exist.**
	1 Apr	**British Airways formally replaces BEA, BAS and BOAC.**
	Oct	Loganair serves Glasgow-Tiree-Barra under contract to British Airways.
1979		Intra Airways becomes Jersey European Airways.
1980	31 Mar	British Airways withdraws from Guernsey and from Southampton.
	1 Apr	Last British Airways routes to Isle of Man are passed to British Midland Airways (from London) and Air UK (from Manchester).
1982		British Airways withdraws its Viscount fleet.
	1 Nov	Manx Airlines begins operations.
1983	Summer	British Airways Helicopters introduces Penzance-Tresco route.
	2 Dec	Loganair acquired by British Midland Airways, both of which come under the auspices of Airlines of Britain Holdings plc in 1987.
1986	Sep	British Airways Helicopters is privatised.
1994		Loganair enters a franchise agreement with British Airways.
1996	Oct	Airlines of Britain Group creates British Regional Airlines by merging Loganair and Manx Airlines (Europe). British Airways passes its Scottish internal routes to British Regional under a franchise agreement.
1997	Mar	Loganair regains independence from British Regional following management buy-out. British Airways franchise agreement continues.
2000	May	Jersey European Airways renamed 'British European'.
2001	Apr	British Regional Airlines and Manx Airlines acquired by British Airways and integrated with Brymon Airways to form British Airways CitiExpress.

Appendix 2

Air Ambulance to Barra

For a flavour of one of the more dramatic air ambulance call outs during the 'Heron era', we are indebted to Captain Pat Eadie for the following narrative. Pat describes this evacuation account as being 'fictional but based on factual experience'.

'GET OUT of your bed Donald, there's been an accident,' Morag shrieked. A snort came from the form huddled under the bedclothes. 'There's been an accident. I distinctly saw car lights along the coast road disappear when they came to Devil's Elbow.' She continued to harry Donald until he finally surfaced from his slumber.

'What do you want me to do about it, if you are right?' he blurted out while putting in his teeth. 'It's two o'clock in the morning! Nobody should be on the road at this hour.' He knew he would get no peace until he had investigated the cause of Morag's disturbance. 'Are you sure you saw lights and not just a reflection?' He paused as he gathered his trousers over his long johns. 'Are you sure woman?'

He doubted there ever being lights on this deserted road without having them disappear at the bend. Admittedly, this was a black spot on the Island's small network of roads. But no one ever admitted wrecking his car during the hours of darkness.

'I may be nudging seventy but I still have a good pair of eyes in my head and I tell you there were car headlights travelling up that road and they disappeared at Devil's Elbow and did not come up on the other side.' Surely she was mistaken. But to question her further would be risking the wrath of God being brought on his few remaining grey hairs.

'Alright, I'll go and see, if that will make you happy.' She watched from the same curtained window as Donald's car disappeared in the distance along their private road from the croft to the main road half a mile distant. From there it was but a stone's throw to Devil's Elbow, so called because it was a hell of a corner. When the old bridge over a small backwater inlet had been declared unsafe, a culvert was constructed a short distance inland. Cost cutting had the new approach roads replaced with an S-bend each side of the culvert. To ensure the vehicles travelled over the culvert and not the bridge, a barrier had been erected. It had been smashed so many times that the bridge superstructure was removed. Not that the drop to the creek-bed was very much, but it was watery when the tide was in.

Morag saw Donald's car lights stationary at the point where she had earlier seen the lights disappear. She quietly hoped he did have something to report although not a serious accident; perhaps the vehicle had hit a sheep thereby damaging its lights.

'Is anybody there?' Donald called when he peered into the darkness where recent tyre tracks had marked the grass verge. There was no reply. Then, just within the car light's range, Donald saw four wheels of an upturned vehicle on the far side of Devil's Elbow. He got back into his car and crossed to the other side of the inlet where a Land Rover had indeed come to rest upside down at right angles to the road. It had apparently failed to take the bend. No, it had not even attempted to follow the curve in the road, but had gone straight ahead, missed the bridge piles, bounced on the bed of the waterless inlet, overturned, and arrived on the opposite bank, upside down.

'Is there anybody there?' he again shouted. This time the reply was a series of moans and grunts. Morag was right again. At two o'clock on a winter's morning she had recognised the signs of an accident.

'Get a doctor,' a voice from inside the battered vehicle pleaded.

'I'll go for a doctor. I'll be back presently.' Donald turned his car to return home, knowing Morag would be watching his lights. Three times he flashed three short bursts before starting to drive. He knew Morag would interpret this signal as trouble and alert the ambulance and possibly the doctor. Donald returned to confirm Morag's fears.

'I contacted the ambulance and doctor when I saw you signal,' she told Donald. Even so, he rang both to reconfirm the nature of the accident. 'There could be four or five men in the vehicle. All appear badly hurt. It's the Power laddies from Glasgow in the works Land Rover. It's upside down at Devil's Elbow. I'll go back down and do whatever I can for them until you arrive.'

From the moment Donald had returned, Morag had bundled up spare blankets plus those off their bed; a flask of hot, sweet tea, a half bottle of whisky, and some old sheets for bandages. 'Get the axe and shovel when you're in the shed,' she yelled at Donald who was already gathering rope and shackles.

When they arrived at the scene there were many more groaning than Donald had originally heard. Morag ferreted on her hands and knees on the gravel to push a cup of tea through to the driver pinned beneath the steering wheel, yet with a hand free and more compos mentis than the others. A moan of thanks came as he accepted the top of the thermos flask.

'How many are in there?' Morag queried. The air from the drivers lungs mixed with the warm tea trickling down his throat gave vent to the garbled word 'five'. 'Don't talk,' Morag said, 'the doctor and ambulance are on their way.' With the hype of excitement Morag did not realise that a snow shower had enveloped them. It wasn't until Donald turned on his headlights to see if he could pull the Land Rover back on to its wheels, that the full extent of the weather was appreciated. A cold February morning in the Hebrides was no place to be found in not much more than a nightdress with a fisherman's pullover covering. 'Never mind,' she thought, 'this was an emergency.' Morag was well known on Barra to be one who could cope with emergencies.

From the torch beam she could see that bodies were trapped in the vehicle, but until the vehicle was upright she could do little except add sympathetic words. Meanwhile, as Donald had threaded the rope around the vehicle and connected it to his tow bar, the ambulance had arrived, and the doctor was close behind. A quick survey by the ambulance chief and the OK was given to pull the vehicle half way, on to its side. It didn't take much to roll it half a turn, from which position the occupants were taken through what was left of the canvas roof.

In coming to rest upside down on the road, all five members had been scalped. The loss of blood appeared more than Morag would have expected. Their distorted faces, minus their scalps, looked more like a horror movie than a slice of real life. As each man was extracted from the vehicle, the Doctor removed the gravel from inside his scalp and replaced it as though repositioning a toupee. The ambulance only had three stretchers so the back of Donald's car was the bed for number four and a similar place was found in the doctor's car for number five.

The groans diminished after the doctor made them comfortable. Morag, a retired district nurse was well acquainted with pain, blood and accidents. But never had she seen a case of five patients who had had so much anaesthetic several hours *before* having the doctor's attention. They were so inebriate that the doctor was hesitant about the amount of morphine to administer. Two of the patients, conscious, and with big cheesy grins on their faces, he chose to give no further painkillers. The whisky was already doing the job for them.

'We should move them to the airline's terminal at Tràigh Mhòr where I can tidy them up before the air ambulance arrives,' the doctor told Donald and the ambulance driver. It was a five-minute drive to the terminal office on the edge of the beach they use as an airfield. For the next three hours the waiting room would serve as his temporary clinic while waiting for a daylight arrival of the air ambulance from Glasgow.

'GOOD MORNING, Captain, Glasgow operations. We have a call for both ambulance aircraft to arrive at Barra at first light.'

'What is the time now?' I asked.

'0325, Captain. Daylight on the beach is at 0722. The tide will be starting to come in by then, so the beach might be half covered with water. The doctor says that he would appreciate you arriving earlier if it could be arranged - regulations and all that. I told him it would more depend on how light it is on the beach, bearing in mind that snow showers have been depositing snow on the low lying areas of Barra during the night. So the weather is not straightforward.'

'I'll be with you in thirty minutes.'

My departure to the airport more resembled the scramble of a fighter pilot. From a sound sleep to mobile within ten minutes. The critical phase would be breaking through the overcast over the Minch, the waterway separating the Hebrides and the Scottish mainland, and finding my way around the snow showers drifting from the northeast. The flight to Barra was above the cloud and the early morning twilight at altitude did not duplicate the ground conditions which I knew would be inky black. 0722 was theoretical morning twilight, the earliest legal landing time, but this could be as much as 30 minutes later due to winter and the heavy snow showers putting a further barrier to the breaking of dawn. Even so, both the other Captain and myself felt the urgency of the situation required us to use our experience and slide onto the beach between the water and the cloud base of three hundred feet above the sea.

At four thousand feet on the descent in cloud, the ice was forming on all the leading edges of the airframe. I could see the new nurse was pale with fright as the ice started breaking off the propellers, ricocheting off the side of the aircraft. Night enclosed the aircraft as we descended towards the sea. At six hundred feet, I reckoned our position as twenty miles to run to Barra. High ground was ahead and above us. If my position was in error, we could be swatted like a fly.

FOUR HUNDRED feet and the most urgent, of all the critical factors, is flying into the water at 160 knots. You only have to brush the water to have a fatality at this speed. Although it is forecast that the cloud base is three hundred feet, the height indicated must be treated with great caution as it is only correct if the pressure at sea level is exactly the same as the approximation I have set on the sub-scale of the altimeter. A touch of Russian roulette. I hesitate to recall how many fatal accidents have been caused by just this error.

Three hundred feet and there is still no sign of the opening between the base of the cloud and the water. The next most crucial aspect is that a snow shower and my descent profile meet lower than the cloud base. That's a no win position and must be determined between the moment I arrive at three hundred feet and a height based on the probability of guesswork. The landing light is extended and flashed on and off. If I left it on while in cloud, the reflection would be blinding. Without it, the white crests on the water will not appear.

Two hundred feet. With this flash of the landing light, the white caps of the waves appear. The descent continues with extreme caution while I estimate if the altimeter is giving me honest readings.

One hundred and fifty feet indicated, but not proven, and the light is left on, as we are under the cloud and have 'contact' with the water. This is relayed to the following aircraft which now proceeds to follow me at a five-minute interval. Skirting around the cloud to the west will conflict not with high ground – but with any ground. Turning to the right I will be on collision course with several small islands. But I have to deviate around the shower straight ahead as it presents a massive pillar of blinding snow right to the surface. I go to the right - only to find that I am running into another shower. I go between them. Now I am completely blind and only one hundred, give or take thirty feet, above the water.

Abort! Abort! The only way out is to abort the approach. Climb straight ahead in a direction estimated to keep me clear of the scattered islands. I nudge the nose around a few more degrees to the right to counter the possibly-higher-than-forecast north-east wind. If it were considerably higher than forecast, I could end up decorating the mountain top on Barra which should be six miles to my left in that black void.

As the altimeter needle indicates each hundred feet climbed, I mentally cancel which islands I can now clear. With the height passing 2,400 feet, I can breathe more easily. My co-pilot has now regained his composure and informs the other aircraft that I am going around for another try, passing information that may help his attempt.

After we re-establish under the cloud at one hundred feet, the other captain tells me the water has already covered half the landing area on the beach. The north-east wind is indeed stronger than we were given to believe and this has brought the incoming tide further up the beach than anticipated. Our landing light, slightly elevated, reflects a large patch of choppy sea flecked with snow-white peaks. Memories of the 'Dambusters' and their spotlight convergence to determine their exact height would not go amiss here. The rock at H8 co-ordinates on the Decca Radio Navigator slips surreptitiously underneath. Plus thirty seconds and we should see the beach or again abort.

The white tips of the waves suddenly are no longer reflected. Beyond is a non-reflective gun metal grey of the sandy beach. I have been waiting for this moment. A quick turn selecting landing flap, no, not into wind, but downwind, and the wheels are rolling on the hard sand; the strip between the incoming tide and the grassy undulations of the higher beach.

Brakes hard on. Salt-water spray showers the aircraft causing a liquid blackout, totally defeating the windscreen wipers. The speed reduces, allowing me to swing the aircraft towards the loading ramp. Patients are already being loaded into the first aircraft and, as we pull alongside, their door is closing. As our door opens and the nurse disembarks, the first of three stretcher cases arrives and is loaded.

'I haven't given them very much morphine,' the doctor tells the nurse. 'They are full of whisky, which may wear off on their way to hospital. Here is the morphine should you need to make them comfortable.'

The other aircraft takes off into the wind with the waves nibbling at the take-off path, intermittently deep enough to spray the aircraft completely. His landing light illumination gives warning that time is running out for getting my aircraft airborne. A more hurried departure than usual and we are mirroring the previous take-off. The drama increases when it is our turn. Extensive pools of salt water from the encroaching tide encase the aircraft as it tries desperately to achieve the take-off speed. Of more concern is the retardation when we transgress each pool of standing water. The airspeed needle has to increase a further twenty knots before a rotation is possible when I catch a glimpse of an extended pool across our path.

This could be the beginning of the tidal water stretching forty-five miles to the Scottish mainland! I push the take-off flap down a notch to the landing position, even though taking off, to break the wheels from the surface and avoid the deeper water ahead. If I went into it, I would be in serious trouble. If thigh deep, the aircraft would certainly cartwheel. If only knee deep, I would be lucky to get back onto dry land.

Airborne - just - with the four Gipsy Queens struggling against overwhelming odds, plus the extra drag from the landing flap selection. The airspeed needle reluctantly vibrates up to the critical take-off speed, even though I am airborne. Wheels skim, if not brush, the white crests over deeper water; well beyond a re-landing.

Only when I imperceptibly ease the landing flap back to the climb position do the four Gipsy Queens feel they have a fighting chance of climbing positively away from the watery grave.

Back into the blackness of the snowstorm clouds for the next eight thousand feet - but at least we are in the environment with which the aircraft is happy and is designed for.

POSTSCRIPT - All the patients survived. Most left hospital within a fortnight and, when I met them on the scheduled flight to Barra, all had a distinct black line of dried scar tissue circling their foreheads. Black stitches, joining top and bottom halves of the forehead, made them look like actors made up for a monster series film set.

Appendix 3

Summary of BEA passenger routes operated 1947-1973

Isles of Scilly

St Mary's to

Land's End   1.2.47 to 31.8.64
                          Rapide, Sikorsky S61

Penzance Heliport   1.9.64 to British Airways Helicopters
                          Sikorsky S61

Frequency of Services on the Land's End-Isles of Scilly Route
(flights per week in the summer peak)

1947	1959	1962	1967	1973
54	54	58	53	59

Isle of Man

Ronaldsway Airport to

Belfast   1.2.47 to 31.3.63
                          Rapide, DC-3, Pionair, Viscount

Blackpool   21.4.47 to 6.10.48
                          Rapide, DC-3

Carlisle   21.4.47 to 6.10.47
                          Rapide

Glasgow   21.4.47 to 6.10.48, and 1.4.51 to 31.10.54.
                          Rapide, DC-3, Pionair

Liverpool   1.2.47 to 31.3.63
                          Rapide, DC-3, Pionair, Viscount

London Heathrow   1.11.54 to 31.3.63
                          Pionair, Viscount, Vanguard

London Northolt   18.4.48 to 30.10.54
                          DC-3, Pionair

Manchester   1.2.47 to 6.10.48, and 1.4.51 to 31.3.63
                          Rapide, DC-3, Pionair, Viscount

Newcastle   21.2.47 to 6.10.47
                          Rapide

Frequencies of services from the Isle of Man
(flights per week in the summer peak)

	1947	1959	1962
Belfast	14	21	14
Blackpool	27		
Carlisle and Newcastle	21		
Glasgow	19		
Liverpool	82	30	22
London		6	7
Manchester	27	41	32

Channel Islands

Alderney to

Guernsey	1.4.47 to 20.4.56 Rapide
Jersey (usually via Guernsey)	1.4.47 to 20.4.56 Rapide
Southampton	1.4.47 to 20.4.56 Rapide
London Gatwick (seasonal)	28.4.50 to 20.10.52 Rapide

Guernsey to

Alderney	1.4.47 to 20.4.56 Rapide
Amsterdam (seasonal)	3.5.73 to British Airways Viscount
Birmingham	13.5.50 to British Airways DC-3, Pionair, Viscount
Dinard (some via Jersey)	11.6.49 to 20.4.56 Rapide
Glasgow (seasonal)	4.6.55 to British Airways Pionair, Viscount
Jersey	1.4.47 to 31.3.69 Rapide, DC-3, Pionair, Viscount, Sikorsky S61
London Croydon	1.4.47 to 1.11.47 Rapide
London Gatwick	9.6.58 to British Airways Pionair, Viscount
London Heathrow	1.11.54 to British Airways Pionair, Viscount, Vanguard
London Northolt	2.11.47 to 30.10.54 Rapide, DC-3, Pionair

Manchester	13.5.50 to British Airways
	DC-3, Pionair, Viscount
Southampton (some via Jersey)	1.4.47 to 20.4.56
	Rapide, DC-3, Pionair, Viscount

Jersey to

Aberdeen (seasonal, via Edinburgh)	9.6.57 to 30.9.60
	Pionair
Alderney (usually via Guernsey)	1.4.47 to 20.4.56
	Rapide
Amsterdam (seasonal, some via Guernsey)	7.5.72 to British Airways
	Viscount
Birmingham (some via Guernsey)	13.5.50 to British Airways
	DC-3, Pionair, Viscount, Vanguard
Belfast (seasonal)	1.6.56 to 29.9.68
	Pionair, Viscount
Bournemouth	20.3.61 to 31.3.66
	Pionair, Viscount
Dinard	11.6.49 to 20.4.56
	Rapide
Edinburgh (seasonal)	9.6.57 to British Airways
	Pionair, Viscount
Glasgow (seasonal)	1.4.51 to 30.9.52 & 1.6.55 to British Airways
	DC-3, Pionair, Herald, Viscount
Guernsey	1.4.47 to 31.3.69
	Rapide, DC-3, Pionair, Viscount, Sikorsky S61
Liverpool (seasonal)	1.4.52 to 4.9.55
	Pionair
London Croydon	1.4.47 to 20.4.47
	Rapide
London Gatwick (some via Guernsey)	9.6.58 to British Airways
	Pionair, Viscount, Vanguard
London Heathrow	1.6.53 to British Airways
	Pionair, Elizabethan, Viscount, Vanguard
London Northolt	21.4.47 to 30.10.54
	DC-3
Manchester (some via Guernsey)	13.5.50 to British Airways
	DC-3, Pionair, Viscount, Vanguard
Paris Le Bourget	1.4.47 to 6.10.47 (and briefly, Summer 1951)
	DC-3
Rennes	1.4.47 to 10.6.49
	Rapide
Southampton (some via Guernsey)	1.4.47 to 20.3.61, and 1.4.66 to British Airways
	Rapide, DC-3, Pionair, Viscount

Frequency of Principle Services from the Channel Islands
(flights per week in the summer peak)

	1947	1959	1962	1967	1973
Jersey to					
Aberdeen		1			
Belfast		1	1	2	
Birmingham		22	19	17	14
Edinburgh		2	5	3	3
Gatwick		61	56	14	3
Glasgow		11	11	9	8
London	42	18	19	35	55
Manchester		27	24	13	13
Southampton	42	39	23	13	15
Guernsey to					
Birmingham		10	7	8	7
Gatwick		45	33	7	7
Glasgow		1	1	1	
London	21			31	28
Manchester		14	7	8	7
Southampton	33				

Highlands and Islands

Services to Kintyre and the Hebrides were served from Glasgow, with Stornoway, and briefly Benbecula, also having links with Inverness. Services to Wick and the Northern Isles were served in various permutations from Glasgow, Edinburgh, Aberdeen and Inverness.

Barra	1.2.47 to British Airways
	Rapide, Heron, Skyliner
Benbecula	1.2.47 to British Airways
	Rapide, DC-3, Pionair, Viscount
Campbeltown	1.2.47 to British Airways
	Rapide, DC-3, Pionair, Heron, Herald, Viscount, Skyliner
Islay	1.2.47 to British Airways
	Rapide, DC-3, Pionair, Heron, Herald, Viscount, Skyliner
Kirkwall	1.2.47 to British Airways
	Rapide, Ju 52, DC-3, Pionair, Herald, Viscount
Stornoway	1.2.47 to British Airways
	Rapide, Ju 52, Heron, DC-3, Pionair, Viscount
Sumburgh	1.2.47 to British Airways
	Rapide, Ju 52, DC-3, Pionair, Herald, Viscount

Tiree	1.2.47 to British Airways				
	Rapide, DC-3, Heron, Skyliner				
Wick	1.2.47 to British Airways				
	Rapide, Ju 52, DC-3, Pionair, Herald, Viscount				

Frequencies of principal Highlands and Islands services

Flights per week in the summer peak. Because many routes consisted of two or more sectors it is difficult to present this table by individual destinations. Services are therefore shown by routes operated.

	1947	1959	1962	1967	1973
Islay and Kintyre					
Glasgow-Campbeltown	15				12
Glasgow-Islay	10				14
Glasgow-Campbeltown-Islay		10	9	6	6
Hebrides					
Glasgow-Tiree-Barra-Benbecula-Stornoway	5				
Glasgow-Stornoway-Inverness	5				
Glasgow-Benbecula-Stornoway-Inverness		6	6	6	6
Glasgow-Stornoway					4
Glasgow-Barra					7
Glasgow-Tiree	5	5	6	6	8
Glasgow-Tiree-Barra		4	6	6	
Glasgow-Inverness-Benbecula		3			
Northern Isles					
Inverness-Kirkwall	10				
Aberdeen-Inverness-Kirkwall	5				
London-Edinburgh-Aberdeen-Sumburgh	5				
Aberdeen-Kirkwall	10	6		3	4
Glasgow-Inverness-Wick-Kirkwall		6			
Glasgow-Edinburgh-Inverness-Wick-Kirkwall		6			
Aberdeen-Sumburgh	5	6			12
Glasgow-Edinburgh-Aberdeen-Wick-Kirkwall			6	6	6
Glasgow-Inverness-Wick-Kirkwall-Sumburgh	5		6	6	6
Glasgow-Aberdeen-Sumburgh	5		6	4	

Bibliography

Bird, Vivian, 'Vicarious Travel', *The Orkney View*, 93, December 2000/January 2001.

Behrend, G., *Jersey Airlines International*, Jersey: Jersey Artists, 1968.

British European Airways, *Annual Reports and Accounts*.

British European Airways Magazine, 1947 to 1973.

Calderwood, Roy, *Times subject to Tides*, Erskine: Kea Publishing, 1999.

Clegg, Peter V., *A Flying Start to the Day*, Godalming: Peter Clegg, 1986.

Clegg, Peter V., *Flying Against the Elements*, Godalming: Peter Clegg, 1987.

Clegg, Peter V., *Rivals in the North*, Godalming: Peter Clegg, 1988.

Clegg, Peter V., *Sword in the Sky*, Godalming: Peter Clegg, 1990.

Clegg, Peter V., *Wings over the Glens*, Peterborough: GMS Enterprises, 1995.

Cramp E., 'Scilly', *Airways*, August 1998.

Doyle, N., *From Sea Eagle to Flamingo, Channel Islands Airways 1923-1939*, Dudley: Self Publishing Association, 1991.

Foy, Dudley, 'Highlands and Islands', *BEA Magazine*, May/June, July and November 1958.

Foy, Dudley, 'By Heron to the Hebrides', *BEA Magazine*, October 1959.

Foy, Dudley, 'Farewell to a Veteran', *BEA Magazine*, May 1965.

Fresson, Captain E. E., *Air Road to the Isles*, London: David Rendal, 1967.

Gaskell, Keith, *British Airways*, Shrewsbury: Airlife, 1999.

Gillies, J.D. and J. L. Wood, *Aviation in Scotland*, Glasgow: Royal Aeronautical Society, 1966.

Gunston, Bill, *Diamond Flight*, London: Henry Melland, 1988.

Handley Page Ltd., 'Herald on Scottish routes', London: Handley Page Ltd, 1960.

Hughes, Mike, *The Hebrides at War*, Edinburgh: Canongate, 1998.

Hutchison, Iain, *The story of Loganair*, Stornoway: Western Isles Publishing, 1987.

Hutchison, Iain, *The Flight of the Starling*, Erskine: Kea Publishing, 1992.

Hutchison, Iain, *Air Ambulance*, Erskine: Kea Publishing, 1996.

Ingham, Mike J, *To the Sunset Bound, 50th Anniversary of scheduled services to the Isles of Scilly*, Tonbridge: Air Britain, 1987.

Ingham, Mike J, *Atlantic Helicopter*, Nettleham: Beckside Design, 1989.

Kniveton, Gordon, *Manx Aviation in War and Peace*, Douglas: The Manx Experience, 1985.

Kniveton, Gordon, *Wings of Mann*, Douglas: The Manx Experience, 1997.

Lake, Chris, *Flight in Jersey: The Story of Jersey Airport*, Jersey: Jersey Airport, 1997.

Lo Bao, Phil, *A History of British Airways Helicopters and its Predecessors since 1947*, Tonbridge: Air Britain, 1987.

Lo Bao, Phil, *An Illustrated History of British European Airways*, Feltham: Browcom Group, 1989.

Lo Bao, Phil, 'Highland Heralds', *Propliner*, 39, Summer 1989.

May, Garry, *The Challenge of BEA*, London: Wolfe Publishing, 1971.

Mayes, Terry, *A history of Scatsta Airfield Shetland*, (Second edition) Brae: Terry Mayes, 2001.

Ministry of Civil Aviation and the Central Office of Information, *Renfrew Airport for Glasgow*, London: His Majesty's Stationery Office, 1949.

Nilsson, Lars-Axel and Leif A. Sandberg, *Blockade Runners*, Stockholm: Lars-Axel Nilsson and Leif A. Sandberg, 1996.

Robertson, Alan, *Lion Rampant and Winged*, Barassie: Alan Robertson, 1986.

Scott, Jack, *Wings over Westray*, Finstown: InformationPLUS, 1997.

Scott-Hill, Ian and G. Behrend, *Channel Silver Wings*, Jersey: Jersey Artists, 1972.

Staddon, T. G., *History of Cambrian Airways*, Hounslow: Airline Publications & Sales, 1979.

Stroud, John, *Railway Air Services*, London: Ian Allan, 1987.

Thomson, Adam, *High Risk*, London: Sidgwick & Jackson, 1990.

Wiggins, Paul R. & Alan J. R. Reid (eds.), *Scotland Scanned*, 5th Edition, Edinburgh: Central Scottish Aviation Group, 1982.

Acknowledgements

A project of this nature is dependent upon the enthusiasm and support of a large number of people and organisations. The authors would like to extend their thanks to Alderney Museum; Captain Tony Angus; Lionel Baston; Captain Peter Black; Dave Bougourd; British Airways Archives; Jack Budge; Jimmy Burgess; Catherine Cameron; Ricky Campbell; John Christal; E. Clapham; William E. Cooper; Anne and Alastair Cormack; John Corrigan; Ernie Cromie; Aird Crooks; Captain Iain Crosbie; D. Haentjens Dekker; Irene Dunster; Clive Dyball; Captain Pat J. Eadie; Eva Edmiston; Barry Edwards; Terry Faragher; Dougie Garnham; R. E. Gibson; John S. Groome; Sheila Harper; Eric Hartwell; Keith Hayward; Laurie Hendry; John Hinde Studios; Captain John Hobbs; Captain James C. Howie; Fred Huntley; Dick Jansen; Captain Terry Lakin; C. Lever; Lyn Lovie; Catherine Macdonald; Coll Macdonald; Ian Maclean; Doctor John A. J. Macleod; Donald MacPhee; Gordon E. Maddiss; Captain Harry McDowell; Lena McFadyen (nèe Esson); T. R. McIlroy; Captain Kenneth McLean; Alex G. W. Miller; Grant and May Montgomery; Jim More; Captain Peter Morgan; Captain John L. Morton; Captain George Northmore; Orkney Library Photographic Archive; Phil Pain; Eric J. M. Pert; Audrey Provan; Captain Bill Reid; David Rendall; Ron Roberts; Boyd Robertson; Ron Rogers; Barry Scotland; Captain Jimmie Scotland; Captain Ian B. Scott; Nan and Jack Scott; Lance Secretan; J. P. Shepherd; Captain Stan Sickelmore; Dave Stephen; Willa Stewart; Captain George Stone; John Stroud; Donald A. Thomson; Brian Thorne; Harry van der Meer; Captain Alan Voak; Wim van Westerop; Captain Keith Warburton; John Wegg; Wilf White; J. Young; Les Young; Tom Young.

We would particularly like to thank Janette Ridgway, and Tony and Marjory Naylor for the extensive archival material which they made available, and Captain James MacKreth and Captain Ian Scott for the many pages of hand-written memoirs which they painstakingly provided. Many of our respondents are advanced in years and their personal recollections and experiences are invaluable for the recreation of what island air travel was like during the third quarter of the twentieth century. We especially appreciate the willingness of a large number of people to share their experiences, memories, personal papers and photographs. Every effort has been made to trace the originators of all photographs in the book – our apologies to anyone whose copyright has been infringed or who may not have been afforded the appropriate credits.

To Rod Eddington, Chief Executive of British Airways, we express a special gratitude for his contribution of the Foreword to this book. He undertook this task during the aftermath of the bombing of the World Trade Center in New York, one of the consequences of which was unprecedented turmoil for the airline industry. British Airways was not immune from these effects and the pressure on its Chief Executive must have been immense. We therefore feel particularly honoured that Rod Eddington found time to write his most complimentary remarks as a prelude to our narrative at this time.

Finally, our thanks are extended to Douglas Nicolson and Chris Weir for reading the draft manuscript and for their many helpful suggestions. The authors accept full responsibility for any errors which have subsequently appeared.

Compiling a book is a rewarding experience. It also requires periodic bouts of recluseness. Both authors would therefore like to thank their families for their support and forbearance during the researching and writing of this volume. We hope you have enjoyed reading it as much as we have enjoyed creating it.

Index